WHO HE?

Who He?

*Goodman's Dictionary
of the Unknown Famous*

JONATHAN GOODMAN

Buchan & Enright, Publishers
London

First published in 1984 by
Buchan & Enright, Publishers, Limited
53 Fleet Street, London EC4Y 1BE

British Library Cataloguing in Publication Data
Goodman, Jonathan
  Who he?
  1. Biography
  I. Title
  920'.02   CT104

ISBN 0-907675-30-1

Set in Bembo by Centracet
Printed in Great Britain by Richard Clay
(The Chaucer Press) Ltd, Bungay, Suffolk

For Richard Boyd-Carpenter—
and to the memory of
James Keddie, Junior

Introduction

I know when I got the idea for this book, but I cannot say when its contents started gathering, higgledy-piggledy, in my mind. Certainly a long while ago: perhaps when I first smiled at the thought that if an Earl of Sandwich had publicised a kind of riding-boots, and the Duke of Wellington had popularised a kind of snack, we should now be chewing wellingtons and slopping about in sandwiches.

With exceptions, three types of person, domestic pet, or fictional character are referred to:

> those better known as things,
> those widely known by names they were not christened with,
> and those whose fame is shadowed by that of associates.

Until I had written a dozen or so entries, I was unaware of the smallness of the world; which accounts for a peppering of cross-references. Nor had I had an inkling of how often there would be the need for an aside; which has caused a flowering of footnotes. Recalling John Barrymore's grumble—that having to read a footnote was akin to having to go downstairs to answer the door just when he was coming—I have asked that the notes be tagged to the entries rather than make an untidy dado. As nearly all of them are semi-detached—not inhabited by main entrants—it is for the individual reader to decide whether to pop away from an entry to look at a note or notes, or to leave it or them till afterwards. Both the finding and the retracing of entries should be simple as, along with the main entries, aliases, and the names of persons both closely associated with and loosely connected to those entries, are listed in the index beginning on page 267.

There are errors, I know. The trouble is, I don't know where—though when they are pointed out to me, I shall insist they are deliberate mistakes. And yes, of course this is a comparatively small selection of worthies. I have picked and chosen from a list that, even now, with hundreds of names crossed off, is long. Perhaps I can use some of those denied entry—and presently unlisted candidates proposed by readers of this book—in a sequel.

A few of the entries, or parts of entries, resemble passages in articles that I have contributed to *Encounter*, the *Manchester Evening News*, and *Medicine, Science and the Law*.

I have had help from all sorts of people, several of whom are mentioned in the entries. All have been thanked, but I should like to repeat my thanks to friends: Jacques Barzun, Richard Boyd-Carpenter, Philip Chadwick, Baroness Diana Corsi, Peter Cotes, John Foster White, J. H. H. Gaute, Elliot Greenfield, Mary Groff, John Steward, Thomas M. McDade, the Hon. Ewen Montagu, Peter Murphy, Robert Scoales, Richard Whittington-Egan. And to my editors, Toby Buchan and Dominique Enright.

Ross, Harold Wallace

Born in 1892 at Aspen, Colorado, the son of an immigrant Ulsterman whose ambitions were in excess of his abilities, Ross was botchily put together. In her book *Ross, The New Yorker and Me* (published 1968), Jane Grant, who insisted on keeping that name after her marriage to him, recalls that when she first met him, in France in 1917,

> His hair flopped like an ill-bred chrysanthemum . . .
> There was certainly a mismating of his head, his hands and his feet to his gaunt, angular body; his hands, though he learned to use them gracefully, were too large; so were his feet, and his ears and his mouth were also oversized; his tongue was a real problem and he was really more comfortable when he let it hang over his loose lower lip . . . A chronic restlessness so plagued him that he seemed to be suffering from growing pains—perpetual growing pains—with such symptoms as fidgeting, scratching his head, jumping up suddenly, and walking nervously about as he jingled coins in his pockets. . . . His whole bearing was so provocative that [Alexander] Woollcott dubbed him 'a dishonest Lincoln'.

Ross was in France as a member of the American Expeditionary Force. He was probably the only private in any of the armies, on either side, to carry visiting cards: these announced that he was managing editor of the doughboys' magazine *Stars and Stripes*. Returned home, he was, during its short existence, editor of *The Home Sector*, which was a sort of civilian equivalent of *Stars and Stripes*; then, for a longer period and better pay, he edited the *American Legion Weekly*; early in 1924, completely fed up with ex-service matters, he resigned and, just as a stop-gap, joined the staff of the humorous magazine *Judge*. Almost exactly a year later, in February 1925, this most unsophisticated of men

founded, and subsequently made to flourish, that most sophisticated of magazines, *The New Yorker*.

He was obsessed with technical perfection, both in the
printing of the magazine and in what was printed. His marginalia
on scripts and proofs reveal much about Ross of *The New Yorker*,
and go some way towards explaining not only how the magazine
survived, then prospered, but why it became more influential
than even he could have thought likely. Many of his comments
were considered and considerate, written with the utmost polite-
ness, but it is the caustic or cryptic ones that are most often
recalled: 'Not certain I understand this exactly, but it seems like
the same old point again' . . . 'Hogwash' . . . 'Take it easy' . . .
'Transcends credulence' . . . 'Bushwah' . . . 'Mean Turck just
has to do with domestic business, or what? Indirection her
anyway' . . . 'Tinker' . . .

. . . *and 'Who he?'*

Accles, George

An ingenious engineer (before emigrating from America to Great Britain, he perfected the Gatling gun[1]), but a poor businessman, in 1899 he rented a steel-tube mill at Perry Barr, Birmingham, intending to cash in on the boom in bicycle production, and was declared bankrupt within eighteen months. His secretary, a young man named Charles Barlow, did not let the failure of the enterprise diminish his conviction that Accles's notion was sound; he scraped together sufficient money to start again in the mill and, calling the new company Accles Tube Syndicate (although George Accles had gone elsewhere), managed to survive until 1901, when financial backing was provided by a machinery broker called Thomas Pollock, who insisted that his name be coupled with that of Accles, thus giving the firm the fresh identity of Accles & Pollock.

Almost at once, Barlow was given notice to quit the mill at Perry Barr. In February 1902, he and his twenty-strong workforce transported the firm's materials and equipment—most valuable, the two drawbenches, twenty and thirty feet long—to a dilapidated shed at Oldbury, another suburb of Birmingham; the building was so small that the operator of the longer bench had to go outside to withdraw the plug from a tube. One of the relocated workers was the foreman, Walter Hackett, a man of creative mind as far as steel tubes were concerned; in the early days, bicycle frames were the firm's main, almost only, product, but Hackett was all the time thinking up new sizes of tube for new uses: in the manufacture of tools, furniture, and, as early as 1910 (by which time Accles & Pollock was in much larger premises, still at Oldbury), aircraft. In 1913—the year before the world war, which blew Accles & Pollock a lot of good—the firm created the world's first tubular-steel golf shaft; it remained a prototype for sixteen years before the Royal and Ancient Golf Club, St Andrews, sanctified its use. Walter Hackett was soon made a managing director, with Barlow, and his reputation as an ideas man spread throughout industry, nudged along by a catchphrase based on his name: 'you can't WHack it,' meaning that he was, in his way, a non-pareil. By the time he retired, his son, who shared his name and inherited some of his novative knacks, was himself progressing towards the managing directorship.

Accles & Pollock had a long rivalry, eventually almost cordial, with the Superior Tube Company of Pennsylvania. An anecdote concerning their competition has been recounted in the house-journal of the Tube Investments group (of which Accles & Pollock became a founder-member in 1919):

> In 1928, Superior sent over a small-diameter tube [intended for a hypodermic syringe] with the challenge: 'Beat this if you can.' Accles & Pollock's answer was a tube with an outside diameter of 0.02 inches, sent back *inside* their American rival's tube. The competition lasted 35 years and was finally settled with a tube, invisible to the human eye, which could only be identified as a tube by placing one end in water, passing a gas through it and looking for the resulting stream of bubbles. The pure nickel tube had an outside diameter of only half a thou and a bore of 0.00013 inches—one-fifth the diameter of an average human hair and so small that a bundle of 1,250,000 could go inside a wedding ring, seven ounces would stretch from Birmingham to London, and one ton would reach to the moon and back, with a few thousand miles to spare. Fred Boyce [the man who made the invisible tube and who was still working at the Oldbury complex of plants in 1976] recalls that 'it was a fiddly job'.

As far as one can tell, Accles & Pollock was the first British industrial concern to launch a general advertising campaign; that is, temporarily forsaking the *Tube Twisters Times*, the *Steel Drum*, and suchlike trade journals. The campaign's motif may have been an offshoot from W. Hackett = Whack It, but it seems more likely that the idea arose from the company's postbag, which on most days contained missives with variations on the addressee's name—itself an indication that the company's fame did not extend at all extensively beyond its circle of suppliers and regular customers. The first shot in the general campaign was aimed at readers of the issue of *Punch* dated 15 May 1935: the masthead of the advertisement, 'I'VE NEVER EVEN HEARD OF THEM', surmounted brief copy and was surrounded by apt examples of spoonerisms (◊ Reverend William Archibald Spooner) and malapropisms:[2] the best of a pretty uninspired lot was Apples & Scollop. But as the campaign got into its stride, eventually branching out into newspapers like the *Observer* and the *Sunday Times* and, appropriately, on to tube-cards on the London Underground, the inventiveness was unaccled (or rather, unshackled: Shackles & Wedlock was an early deliberate mistake), earning the applause of an American advertising specialist, who wrote of 'the lunatic charm' of specimens such as Pickles & Wallop, Raffles & Sherlock, Baffles & Padlock, Tackles & Dollop, Cockles & Polyp, and Hackles & Rowlock. The long-running campaign (it continued for more than a quarter of a century) was an advertiser's dream come true: members of the public sent thousands of suggestions, many on letterless envelopes, to Oldbury—but, sad to say, most of these, using a genitalial sound-alike for Pollock, were considered too naughty to be displayed. Of course, it is impossible to assess the financial returns from the advertisements; certainly, they paid for themselves many times over. When the first Russian trade delegation came to Great Britain after the war, they spotted one of the tube-cards, and as they had steel tubing on their shopping list, insisted on visiting Accles & Pollock; this resulted in a £2-million order.

1 Patented in 1862, in time to be used during the American Civil War, this revolving machine-gun was the invention of Richard Jordon Gatling, an American doctor who never practised medicine, and who was already wealthy as a deviser of gadgets for farmers.

The US criminal slang-word 'gat', a shortening of 'Gatling', is (or was; it seems to be archaic) applied to most types of fire-arm, *excluding* the machine-gun.

2 The nineteenth-century novelist George Eliot (real name, Mary Ann, or Marian, Evans) wrote in a letter: 'Mr Lewis is sending what a malaproprian friend once described as a missile to Sara.' The word comes from Mrs Malaprop, the dictional blunderer in the comedy *The Rivals*, first produced at Covent Garden Theatre on 17 January 1775, when its author Richard Brinsley Sheridan—later also a theatre manager and politician—was twenty-three. He formed the name from the French *mal à propos*, meaning inappropriate.

Acton, Lord

Dicta compressed between a capital letter and a full stop sometimes give unwarrantedly wide fame to their terse composers. Relatively few people would have known of the existence of C(yril) Northcote Parkinson[1] if he had not come up with the one law, among several of his devising, that 'work expands so as to fill the time available for its completion'; and hardly anyone but a few other American management consultants and the managers to whom he had tried to teach their job would have heard of Dr Laurence Peter if he had not thought up, and energetically publicised, the principle that 'an employee in a hierarchy tends to rise to the level of his incompetence'.

Among dicta-framing persons whose names are not attached to their most-quoted sayings, the greatest, I'm sure, was Lord Acton (1834–1902), who before his elevation was Sir John Emerich Edward Dalberg, Bt. A Roman Catholic who argued against tenets of that faith, a friend of and adviser to William Ewart Gladstone, a brilliant historian who in 1895 became regius professor of modern history at Cambridge, he it was who said:

Power tends to corrupt and absolute power corrupts absolutely.

In the early 1960s, Adlai Stevenson, who, according to some, was the best President America never had, amended Acton's dictum to:

Power corrupts, but lack of power corrupts absolutely.

1 Another Parkinson, Dr James, gave his name to the paralysis agitans, or shaking palsy, that he described in 1817.

Alice Grey:

Alice-Sit-by-the-Fire in the play of that title by J(ames) M(at-thew) Barrie, which was first presented at the Duke of York's Theatre on 5 April 1905, with Ellen Terry as Alice. She was still appearing in the play when, on 13 October, Sir Henry Irving,[1] whom she had known since 1867 and with whom she had starred at the Lyceum for many years, died after performing the title-role in *Becket* at Bradford. Though distraught, she refused to let her understudy take her place at the next performance of *Alice-Sit-by-the-Fire*. She showed no sign of her grief until she came to the final scene, and the line, 'I had a beautiful husband once, black as a raven was his hair.' Then she broke down and wept.

1 The first actor to be knighted. The announcement was made in the Birthday Honours of 24 May 1895, when Irving was playing Don Quixote at the Lyceum. The audience that night tittered when he uttered the line, 'Knighthood sits like a halo round my head', and cheered and clapped at the Housekeeper's reply: 'But Master, you have never been knighted.'
   Irving was devoted to a fox-terrier called Fussy. Originally Ellen Terry's pet (she had acquired him from the champion jockey

Fred Archer, who had told her, 'He's got a very good head, a first-rate tail, stuck in splendidly, but his legs are too long'), Fussy went over to Irving after—according to Ellen Terry—'he had his affections alienated by a course of chops, tomatoes, strawberries, 'ladies' fingers' soaked in champagne, and a beautiful fur rug of his very own presented by the Baroness Burdett-Coutts [◊ Thomas Coutts]'. Fussy loved the limelight, and often wandered onstage to become a distracting extra to duologues between Irving and Ellen Terry. And during a tour of the United States by his past and present owners, he encroached on a scene being played by John Drew and Maude Adams, who came closest to being an American equivalent of the Irving-Terry partnership: Miss Adams, sitting looking into a fire, did not notice the intrusion, and so was nonplussed when Drew departed from the text with the lines:

> Is this a dog I see before me,
> His tail towards my hand?
> Come, let me clutch thee.

Archer-Shee, George

In 1941, shortly before the Japanese sneak attack on the US fleet at Pearl Harbor—which caused America to declare war on Japan, this in turn causing Germany and Italy to declare war on America—and five years before Terence Rattigan (◊ Aunt Edna) turned ex-Naval Cadet George Archer-Shee into The Winslow Boy, the determinedly Anglophile American journalist Alexander Woollcott[1] published an essay, 'The Archer-Shee Case', in which he told the story truly and by which he augmented the Support-the-British campaign that he and some other American writers had been waging since the autumn of 1939. Woollcott ended his essay:

So that is the story of Archer-Shee, whose years in the land, all told, were nineteen. To me his has always been a deeply moving story, and more and more, as the years have gone by, a significant one. Indeed, I should like to go up and down our land telling it to young people not yet born when Archer-Shee kept his rendezvous with death. You see, I know no easier way of saying something that is much on my mind. For this can be said about the Archer-Shee case: that it could not happen in any totalitarian state. It is so peculiarly English, this story of a whole people getting worked up about a little matter of principle; above all, the story of the foremost men of the land taking up the cudgels—taking up the cudgels against the state, mind you—because a youngster had been unfairly treated. It would have been difficult to imagine it in the Germany of Bismarck and the Wilhelms. It is impossible to imagine it in the Germany of Adolf Hitler.

The basic question in the case, which began on 7 October 1908, was whether George Archer-Shee, the thirteen-year-old son of a bank official, stole, forged and cashed a postal-order for five shillings belonging to a fellow-cadet at the Royal Naval College at Osborne House (once a country seat of Queen Victoria), on the Isle of Wight—a crime that, having been proved to the satisfaction of the college authorities (who relied on the evidence of, among others, the charlatan graphologist who, four years earlier, had assisted in convicting [◊] George Edalji), resulted in the boy's dismissal. Despite ill health, and though he was not particularly well off, George's father, Martin Archer-Shee, decided to fight the Admiralty. And he enlisted the expensive aid of the Dublin-born but Ulster-supporting politician Sir Edward Carson, who had made his name as a barrister, most specifically as the defender of the Marquess of Queensberry in the libel action brought by Oscar Wilde (◊ Charles Thomas Wooldridge); Carson agreed to accept the Archer-Shee brief only after he had grilled the boy (an out-of-court cross-examination that Rattigan transmuted to great dramatic effect in his play) and concluded that he was innocent. The Archer-Shees' action went on for nearly three years, occupying the High Court twice and the Court of Appeal once, before the Admiralty surrendered, offering their apology for the wrong done to George and giving full compensation of the costs incurred by his father.

To quote Alexander Woollcott again:

If you will remember that the boy was thirteen when they threw him out of Osborne and fifteen when his good name was re-established, you will realise that when the great war began he was old enough to die for King and Country. And did he? Of course.

As a soldier, mind you. The lost years had rather discouraged his ambition with regard to the Navy. August 1914 found him in America, working in the Wall Street firm of Fisk & Robinson. Somehow he managed to get back to England, join up with the Second Battalion of the South Staffordshire Regiment, win a commission as second lieutenant, and get over to France in time to be killed—at Ypres—in the first October of the war.

At the start of his essay,[2] Woollcott spoke of the 'Notable British Trials' (◊ George Edalji), saying that he was 'an avid subscriber to the series', but expressing exasperation and puzzlement at the fact that the Archer-Shee case was not covered in it. His stated intention of remedying the omission was not fulfilled by the time he suffered a fatal heart attack while broadcasting on the radio in January 1943; but thirty years later, Ewen Montagu (◊ Mr X) accepted my invitation to introduce and edit the transcripts of the case as a volume in the 'Celebrated Trials' series.

1 He was the model for Sheridan Whiteside, *The Man Who Came to Dinner*. The stage-comedy by Moss Hart and George S. Kaufman (who, having no middle name, added the S. so as to give rhythm and balance to his byline) seems to have been inspired by a visit Woollcott made to Hart's country home, at the end of which he wrote in the guest-book, 'This is to certify that on my first visit to Moss Hart's house, I had one of the most unpleasant times I ever spent.' Monty Woolley, formerly a Yale professor under his real name of Edgar Montillion Woolley, played Whiteside in the first, long-running Broadway production (1939); also in the film (1941). The Chicago company was headed by Clifton Webb (really Webb Parmelee Hollenbeck), who in 1955 represented Ewen Montagu (◊ Mr X) in the film of *The Man Who Never Was*. (The death of his mother Mabelle in 1960 made Webb a severe trial to his friends, one of whom was Noël Coward, who wrote: 'Poor Clifton . . . is still, after two months, wailing and sobbing over Mabelle's death. As she was well over ninety, gaga, and had driven him mad for years, this seems excessive and over-indulgent. He arrives here on Monday and I'm dreaming of a wet Christmas.' Coward also remarked, 'It must be tough to be orphaned at seventy-one.')
During 1940, Woollcott played himself in touring productions of *The Man Who Came to Dinner*. While one of these

productions was in Washington, he stayed at the White House; he later recommended that place to Ethel Barrymore, saying that 'Mrs Roosevelt runs the best theatrical boarding-house in Washington'.

2 Which has been reprinted in, for instance, *Long, Long Ago*, a collection of Woollcott's essays published in 1943, and *The Portable Woollcott*, published 1946.

Aunt Edna

Named, delineated, and to some extent biographised by Terence Rattigan, prefacing the second volume of his *Collected Plays*[1] (published 1953), Aunt Edna is a miracle of longevity:

> She is universal and immortal, and she has lived for over two thousand years. . . . I believe that Aunt Edna sat on those hard seats at Athens, clutched her neighbour's arms in her excitement, and whispered: 'My dear, do look at that blood on the actor's mask. He's supposed to have blinded himself. How thrilling. I'm so glad it didn't happen on the stage, though. I always say you can rely on Sophocles.' I believe she was shocked and intrigued by Euripides, impressed, if a little bewildered, by Aeschylus, and dissolved into gales of laughter by her favourite, Aristophanes. At the Elizabethan Globe Theatre, too, her sway was absolute, though here perhaps she takes on the more formidable aspect of the great queen herself. A bolder genius than Sophocles was as bound as he by her tastes and prejudices, and when he contemptuously labelled the romantic goings-on in the Forest of Arden, *As You Like It*, it was surely Aunt Edna that he was addressing. He was right. It was indeed exactly as she liked it. It is as she likes it now, and I am sure that it will continue to be as she likes it for the rest of her limitless life.

Rattigan, whose instinct for what makes enjoyable theatre was more refined even than Coward's, went on to say, among other things about Aunt Edna, that:

. . . although she must never be made mock of, or bored, or befuddled, she must equally not be wooed, or pandered to, or cosseted. I even made a rather startling discovery; that the old dear rather enjoys a little teasing and even, at times, some bullying.

It is as well that she has this slight masochistic strain in her, for if she had not there would be no such thing as good drama, but only good theatre.

1 Rattigan borrowed from reality for several of his plays. *Adventure Story*—which, though it flopped, was his favourite— examined the character of Alexander the Great. Rattigan wrote: 'At least it was consistent with the artistic development of an author who was trying to subdue the Aunt Edna in his soul. Aunt Edna, in fact, proved this conclusively herself. She refused to come.'

The Winslow Boy was based on the case of (◊) George Archer-Shee.

And *Cause Célèbre*, an amplification of a play he had written for radio, was clearly (but carefully, for fear of libel) constructed from the most publicised components of the Villa Madeira murder case of 1935:

Mrs Alma Rattenbury, an attractive Canadian, mistress of a house called the Villa Madeira, in Bournemouth, used the pseudonym of Lozanne as a song-composer; she often played the piano accompaniment when her sentimental ballads were record- ed. George Stoner, a young servant at the house, was so smitten with his mistress that he murdered his master. When both he and Mrs Rattenbury were tried for the crime, he was found guilty but she was acquitted. Four days later, convinced that Stoner would be hanged, Mrs Rattenbury travelled to Christchurch, Kent; there, beside a quiet tributary of the Avon, she committed suicide by plunging a knife six times into her chest. Some letters were found in her handbag. They read, in part:

. . . If I only thought it would help Stoner I would stay on but it has been pointed out to me all too vividly I cannot help him. That is my death sentence . . . Eight o'clock. After so much walking I have got here. Oh to see the swans and spring flowers and just smell them. And how singular I should have chosen the spot Stoner said he nearly jumped out of the train once at. It was not intentional my coming here. I tossed a coin, like Stoner always did, and it came down Christchurch.

It is beautiful here. What a lovely world we are in! It must be easier to be hanged than to have to do the job oneself. . . . One must be bold to do a thing like this. It is beautiful here and I am alone. Thank God for peace at last.

Stoner was reprieved. A model prisoner, he was released in 1942, when he was still only twenty-six.

Bacon, Francis

Apart from William Shakespeare of Stratford (1564–1616), Francis Bacon (1561–1626), Lord Chancellor, is most favoured as being the author of the works of Shakespeare. Supporters of this notion, called Baconians, are sufficiently numerous to ensure the thrivingness of Bacon societies in Great Britain, America, and other places.

But authorship of the plays and poems has been ascribed to others, including:

Robert Burton (1577–1640), the author—or so it is said—of *The Anatomy of Melancholy*;

Robert Cecil, Earl of Salisbury (1563?–1612);

Sir Edward Dyer (d. 1607), a poet and courtier;

Michele Agnolo Florio (?), a Florentine gadabout, translator of Montaigne, tutor to the Countess of Pembroke, secretary to the Earl of Southampton ('Shakespeare's' patron), and acquaintance of just about everyone who was worth knowing in Elizabethan times;

Ben Jonson (1573?–1637);

Roger Manners, Earl of Rutland (1576–1612);

Christopher Marlowe (1564–1593);

Sir Walter Raleigh (1552?–1618);

William Stanley, Earl of Derby (1575–1627);

Edward de Vere, Earl of Oxford (1550–1604),

and syndicates of ghost-writers, ranging in size of membership from mere trios to crowds of seventy or so, but always including Bacon as main contributor, chief editor, Great Architect, 'polisher and reconstructor', or Secretary-General.

A great many of the anti-Stratfordian theories are based on hidden 'clues' winkled out of the text: anagrams, acrostics, and the like. For instance, in Act V, Scene 1 of *Love's Labour's Lost*, the clown Costard remarks: 'I marvel thy master hath not eaten thee for a word; for thou art not so long by the head as *honorificabilitudinitatibus*: thou art easier swallowed than a flap-dragon.' The long word was rearranged by a Baconian into a Latin sentence, 'Hi ludi F. Baconis nati tuiti orbi' = 'These plays, F. Bacon's offspring, are preserved for the world.' But in 1957, William and Elizebeth Friedman, an American husband-and-wife team of specialist cryptographers, published *The Shakespearean Ciphers Examined*, in which, always politely, they demonstrated that any message could be found if one knew what one wanted to find and looked hard enough for it; in passing, they noted Shakespearean anagrams that showed that the plays and poems were the work of Lewis Carroll, President Theodore Roosevelt, and Gertrude Stein ('Gertrude Stein writ this great work of literature—Bob Riplie [Robert Ripley—*Believe It or Not*]'), and cited an anagram in a poem by Matthew Arnold (1822–88) that proved that 'Matthew Arnold' was a pen-name of Francis Bacon.

It seems to me that there is good reason to accept that, if the plays and poems of William Shakespeare were not the work of William Shakespeare, they were written by someone of the same name.

Baddeley, Robert

Each year, on Twelfth Night, the actors playing at Drury Lane gather in the Grand Regency Saloon to drink wine and share a Baddeley cake—part of the bequest of Robert Baddeley, who was first a pastrycook, then a gentleman's gentleman, before he became an actor at Drury Lane in 1761. He died at the theatre thirty-three years later, while dressing for his most famous part, Moses in Sheridan's *The School for Scandal*, which he had created in 1777.

Baker, Frankie

The origin and history of 'Frankie and Johnny (or Albert)' songs, of which there are more than a hundred versions, is subject to debate. It may be that the original song referred to the shooting of Allen Britt, an eighteen-year-old Negro, by Frankie Baker, a mulatto woman with whom he was living, which happened in St Louis, Missouri, on 15 October 1899; Britt died four days later. Frankie Baker testified that he threatened her with a knife and that she fired at him in self-defence. In 1939, Miss Baker, 'the proprietor of a shoe-shine place', brought an action for $200,000 damages against Republic Pictures for defaming her character and invading her privacy with a film based on the song. During the case, which was eventually dismissed in 1942, she claimed that there were no 'Frankie and Johnny' songs until after she killed Britt.

But there appears to be evidence that the song has a longer history: one authority claims that it originated with Mammy Lou, 'a blues singer at Babe Connors' high-brown bawdy-house in St Louis', in the early '90s, and that Mammy Lou sang it for Paderewski; another theory is that the song was inspired by Frankie Silver, a white woman who murdered her husband at Toe River, North Carolina, in 1831. There seems to be little, if any, argument that Albert was rechristened Johnny by the Leighton Brothers, a vaudeville act, in 1911. An earlier version runs as follows:

> Frankie was a good girl,
> Everybody knows,
> She paid half a hundred
> For Albert a suit of clothes,
> He is my man, but he won't come home.
>
> Way down in some dark alley,
> I heard a bulldog bark,
> I believe to my soul my honey
> Is lost out in the dark,
> He is my man, but he won't come home.
>
> Frankie went uptown this morning,
> She did not go for fun,
> Under her apron she carried
> Albert's forty-one,
> He is my man, but he won't come home.
>
> Frankie went to the bartender,
> Called for a bottle of beer,
> Asked him, my loving Albert,
> Has he been here?
> He is my man, but he won't come home.
>
> Bartender said to Frankie,
> I can't tell you a lie,
> He left here about an hour ago
> With a girl called Alice Bly,
> He is your man, but he's doing you wrong.
>
> Frankie went up Fourth Street,
> Come back down on Main,
> Looking up on the second floor,
> Saw Albert in another girl's arms,
> Saying he's my man, but he's doing me wrong.

Frankie says to Albert,
Baby, don't you run!
If you don't come to the one you love,
I'll shoot you with your own gun,
You are my man, but you're doing me wrong.

Frankie, she shot Albert,
He fell upon the floor,
Says, turn me over easy,
And turn me over slow,
I'm your man, but you shot me down.

Early the next morning,
Just about half-past four,
Eighteen inches of black crêpe
Was hanging on Frankie's door,
Saying he was my man, but he wouldn't come home.

Frankie went over to Mis' Moodie's,
Fell upon her knees,
Says, forgive me, Mis' Moodie,
Forgive me, oh do, please.
How can I when he's my only son?

Frankie went down to the graveyard,
Police by her side,
When she saw the one she loved,
She hollered and she cried:
He was my man, but he wouldn't come home.

Police said to Frankie,
No use to holler and cry,
When you shot the one you loved,
You meant for him to die,
He's your man, but he's dead and gone.

Rubber-tyred buggy,
Silver-mounted hack,
Took Albert to the graveyard
But couldn't bring him back,
He was my man, but he wouldn't come home.

Balfe, Michael William

In the Rotunda of the Theatre Royal, Drury Lane (one door of which is marked King's Side, the other, Prince's Side,[1] recalling the uncordiality that existed between George III and his son, the Prince of Wales and Earl of Chester, after the former had boxed the latter's ears in full view of the assembled nobility, to say nothing of the gentry), is a quartet of statues: of Shakespeare, of the two great actors David Garrick (1717–79) and Edmund Kean (1787–1833) . . . and of the Dublin-born composer Michael William Balfe (1808–70), many of whose operas—'farragoes of balderdash', according to one musicologist—were immensely successful during his lifetime; 'I Dreamt That I Dwelt in Marble Halls', a song from *The Bohemian Girl*, is still rendered, usually as a tenor/pianist duet, at masonic concerts. James Agate, the most influential drama critic of this century, who 'exposed his clean linen in public' by publishing his diaries as nine volumes, all entitled *Ego* and each, apart from the first, with a differentiating number, felt that Balfe was so out of place in the company of the effiginised others that a verb, *to balfe*, meaning to exalt someone above his station, was called for. Agate seems not to have been aware that Balfe had been given stony immortality in a quite different setting: eight years after his death, a tablet was erected to his memory in Westminster Abbey, the English equivalent of the American Hall of Fame.

1 A box facing the stage from the left of the auditorium is the Royal Box, marked as such by a replica of the sovereign's coat-of-arms. When Queen Victoria's son Edward was Prince of Wales, he gave permission for his coat-of-arms to be displayed on a box on the other side of the auditorium; it remained there during his reign as Edward VII and afterwards—until in 1921 the

auditorium was rebuilt. On 24 September 1974, the new Prince of Wales came to the theatre, with a party, to see the musical *Billy*, and George Hoare, the general manager of Drury Lane, asked his permission to display his coat-of-arms on the Prince's Box. After consulting his uncle Lord Louis Mountbatten, the Prince said, 'I have no objection—as long as it doesn't cost me anything!' The three-feathers insignia, copied from a painting in the Prince of Wales pub in the village of Sandringham, was placed on the box in September 1977.

Baline, Israel

'Strange how potent cheap music is,' Elyot Chase remarks to Amanda Prynne during the balcony scene of Noël Coward's *Private Lives* (first produced in 1930), which, despite its last act, is, it seems to me, the finest comedy written by an Englishman (◊ Jack Worthing for the finest one by an Irishman). The truth of the remark is exemplified by early compositions of Irving Berlin— born Israel Baline in Russia in 1888—who had to sweat a lot before he earned the right to perspire. The titles of songs he published before and soon after the First World War evoke those eras more efficiently than whole shelves of social history books: 'My Wife's Gone to the Country', 'I Want to Go Back to Michigan', 'When the Midnight Choo-Choo Leaves for Alabam', 'Ragtime Violin', 'Everybody's Doin' It'. Jerome Kern, no mean song-writer himself, told Alexander Woollcott: 'Irving Berlin has no *place* in American music; he *is* American music.'[1] Kern was speaking in 1924, when Berlin was still to write the songs for many Hollywood musicals;[2] for *Annie Get Your Gun* (◊ Phoebe Anne Oakley Mozee); for the subsequent stage-musical *Call Me Madam*, inspired by Mrs Pearl Mesta, the Washington hostess ('with the mostest on the ball') who was US minister to Luxembourg during part of Harry S.[3] Truman's presidency; and, between times, countless songs that were not produced to order.

1 Berlin might have agreed with that statement when it was made. However, in 1953, on the day after he saw the Broadway production of Cole Porter's musical *Can-Can*, he wrote to Porter: 'It's a swell show and I still say, to paraphrase an old bar-room ballad, "anything I can do, you can do better".'

2 Including three starring Fred Astaire (real name, Frederick Austerlitz) and Ginger Rogers (real name, Virginia McMath) that were released between 1935 and 1938: *Top Hat* (featuring the numbers 'Cheek to Cheek' and 'Isn't It a Lovely Day?'), *Follow the Fleet* ('Let's Face the Music and Dance'), and *Carefree* ('Change Partners').

3 The initial didn't stand for anything. It was, so the story goes, a compromise by his parents, anxious not to offend either of his grandfathers, one called Shippe, the other Solomon. (◊ George S. Kaufman in George Archer-Shee's note 2.)

Balsam, Martin

The actor who played Juror No. 1 in the film *Twelve Angry Men* (1957), written by Reginald Rose. The other jurors were played by Ed Begley, Edward Binns, Lee J. Cobb, John Fiedler, Henry Fonda, Jack Klugman, E. G. Marshall, Joseph Sweeney, George Voskovec, Jack Warden, and Robert Webber.

Bazna, Elyesa

Once a professional singer, during the Second World War he was engaged as a personal servant to the British ambassador in his native Turkey. Taking advantage of lax security arrangements, he made copies of secret documents and sold them to the Germans, who gave him the code-name of Cicero. However, some of the information he supplied was so important that the Germans began to suspect that it was *intended* to be leaked, and that Cicero was a double-agent; therefore, many of the top secrets were either treated with caution or completely ignored. Eventually, American counter-espionage agents discovered the existence of Cicero—but before the British could be alerted, the Germans learned what the Americans had discovered, and warned Cicero to make his escape. He then found out that the Germans had paid him in counterfeit notes.

Beach, Sylvia

The daughter of a Presbyterian minister at Princeton, New Jersey, in 1919 she opened a bookshop and lending library on the Left Bank in Paris; at first, but for only a short time, she conducted her business, called Shakespeare and Company, at 8 rue Dupuytren, but then found permanent premises at 12 rue de l'Odéon. The customers and browsers included native authors, American writers living and working in Paris, and the expatriate

Irishman James Joyce, who in 1920 completed *Ulysses*, in which he looked back at the Dublin of his youth, the chosen date being 16 June 1904, the day on which he first walked out with his wife. As the book was banned in English-speaking countries, Sylvia Beach agreed to publish it under the imprint of Shakespeare and Company, and it appeared on 2 February 1922, Joyce's fortieth birthday, bound in the 'Greek blue' he had requested.

Ulysses was eventually published in America in 1934 and in England two years later. Long before, the book had influenced other writers, some of whom had actually read it; the most influential aspect was Joyce's use of the *monologue intérieur* or stream-of-consciousness means of narration.

James Thurber was one of the several open parodists of Joyce's style. In 1927, *The New Yorker* published his idea of how Joyce would report the case of Ruth Snyder and Henry Judd Gray, who, having been accused of the murder of Mrs Snyder's husband, beaten to death with a sash-weight, had changed from lovers to foes:

JOYCE FINDS SOCKSOCKING
IS BIG ELEMENT
IN MURDER CASE!

Trial regen by trialholden Queenscountycourthouse with tumpetty taptap mid socksocking with sashweights by jackals. In socksocking, the sashwiring goes: guggengaggleoggogg-snukkk. . . . To corsetsale is to alibi is to meetinlovenkillenlove. *Rehab des arbah sed drahab!* Not a quart of papa's booze had poison booze vor the killparty for the snugglesnuggle. . . .

Beau

A spaniel—'prettiest of his race'—belonging to the short-sighted, at times suicidal, at times delusional poet William Cowper, whose 'On a Spaniel Called Beau Killing a Young Bird' was a rebuke to a pampered pet who had no need to kill for food:

> My dog! What remedy remains,
> Since, teach you all I can,
> I see you, after all my pains,
> So much resemble man!

But Beau had the last word:

> If killing birds be such a crime,
> (Which I can hardly see)
> What think you, Sir, of killing Time
> With verse address'd to me?

When a friend's spaniel died, Cowper (who pronounced his name as Cooper) composed 'Epitaph on Fop', which ends:

> Ye squirrels, rabbits, leverets, rejoice,
> Your haunts no longer echo to his voice. . . .
> He died worn out in vain pursuit of you.
> 'Yes!' the indignant shade of Fop replies,
> 'And worn with vain pursuit, man also dies.'

As there is argument as to whether or not Cowper's best-known work, 'History of John Gilpin'—which was written in a single day in the summer of 1783, when Cowper was fifty-two—was based on a real citizen of famous London town, I shall say nothing about it.

Belaney, Archibald Stansfeld

Known to conservationists, escapists, supporters of ethnic minorities, and, perhaps, one or two members of those minorities as Grey Owl—the name he used when writing about his fellow-braves of the Red Indian Ojibway tribe of Bear Island,

Canada, and the antics of a couple of orphaned beaver-cubs that he had fostered and trained and, presumably without their knowledge, christened McGinnis and McGinty—his big day arrived early in 1938, when, during a goodwill tour of Great Britain, he told tales about Indians and beavers to the Royal family at Buckingham Palace. A trifle incongruous-looking in such surroundings—come to think of it, in just about any surroundings other than those reserved for Indians (he was wearing fringed buckskins, strings of beads and teeth, and moccasins, and had a feather sticking out of his braided black hair)—he particularly appealed to the eleven-year-old Princess Elizabeth, who, at the end of his recital, pleaded, Oliver-Twist-like,[1] for more; when, at last, he was allowed to leave, he touched King George VI on the shoulder (an instance of role-reversal) and said, with what newspaper reporters subsequently termed 'simple dignity': 'Goodbye, brother. I'll be seeing you.'

But that was not to be. Four months later, on 13 October, by then back in Canada, he departed this life for the Happy Hunting Ground. It was only then that people, chiefly members of the press, began to ask questions about Grey Owl. Cables flashed from Fleet Street, or thereabouts, to centres of population on the prairies; one, addressed to an undertaker in Saskatchewan, carried the cryptic instruction, COUNT GREY OWLS TOES. Doing as he was told, the undertaker reached a grand total of nine. More than anything else, this reckoning helped to establish the true identity of Grey Owl.

Archibald Stansfeld Belaney was the product of a bigamous marriage between a ne'er-do-well member of an otherwise respected English family and a girl of thirteen. During his childhood years in the seaside resort of Hastings, Sussex, where he was born in the late summer of 1888, he was much in demand for games of cowboys-and-Indians, for, going against the grain, he insisted on being an Indian; his hero was not Buffalo Bill (◊ Edward Zane Carroll Judson) but the Apache leader Geronimo. When he was seventeen, he sailed for Canada, ostensibly to learn farming but in fact to hide his true colour and become a surrogate Redskin. After shopping around among various tribes, he was taken on by the Ojibways, who came to know him as Wa-sha-quonasin (which is Ojibwayan for Grey Owl). It appears that he was not entirely sequestered from white men: in 1914, hearing of the outbreak of the World War, patriotism for his native land outweighed attachment to his adopted or adopting tribe: he enlisted in the army, served in France, some of the time as a sniper, was gassed, and was invalided out when a toe of his right foot was shot off. Returning to the wilds of Canada, though not to the Ojibways, he encountered, fell in love with, and was converted to the cause of animal conservation by, an Iroquois maid called Anahareo. The several books by and about him appeared subsequently.

1 Dickens's novel, written and published 1837–9, has formed the basis of at least seven films and a stage musical *Oliver!*, itself filmed in 1968, when it won six Oscars. I cannot vouch for the truth of this, but I have been told that the front cover of an American paperback edition of the novel carried a picture of a wild-eyed, barely-clothed Oliver being whipped by a noticeably female beadle, and a caption more prominently displayed than the title and author's name put together: '"More! MORE!!" he cried. He was Insatiable!!!'

Bell, Joseph . . .

. . . (1837–1911), M.D., F.R.C.S. Consulting Surgeon to Edinburgh Royal Infirmary and the Royal Hospital for Sick Children; editor of the *Edinburgh Medical Journal*, 1873–96; towards the end of his life, a member of the Court of Edinburgh University, Deputy Lieutenant of Edinburgh, and a Justice of the Peace for Midlothian.

There is little doubt (oh, come—none at all, surely) that he was the model for Sherlock Holmes. He was thirty-nine in 1876, when Arthur Ignatius Conan Doyle entered Edinburgh University to read for the degree of Bachelor of Medicine; Conan Doyle became his 'out-patient clerk', stationed in his waiting-room to make notes of cases and to act as usher. In *Memories and*

Adventures (published 1924), Conan Doyle recalled an interview
between Bell and a patient:

> 'Well, my man, you've served in the army.'
> 'Aye, sir.'
> 'Not long discharged?'
> 'No, sir.'
> 'A Highland regiment?'
> 'Aye, sir.'
> 'A non-com. officer?'
> 'Aye, sir.'
> 'Stationed at Barbados?'
> 'Aye, sir.'
> 'You see, gentlemen,' he would explain, 'the man was a
> respectful man but did not remove his hat. They do not in the
> army, but he would have learned civilian ways had he been long
> discharged. He has an air of authority and he is obviously Scottish.
> As to Barbados, his complaint is elephantiasis, which is West
> Indian and not British.' To his audience of Watsons it all seemed
> very miraculous until it was explained, and then it became simple
> enough. It is no wonder that after the study of such a character I
> used and amplified his methods when in later life I tried to build up
> a scientific detective who solved cases on his own merits and not
> through the folly of the criminal.

Conan Doyle had dedicated *The Adventures of Sherlock Holmes*:

> To my old teacher Joseph Bell, MD, &c.
> of 2, Melville Crescent, Edinburgh,

and in the year of that collection's publication, 1892, had written
to Bell:

> It is most certainly to you that I owe Sherlock Holmes, and
> though in the stories I have the advantage of being able to place
> [Holmes] in all sorts of dramatic positions, I do not think that his
> analytical work is in the least an exaggeration of some effects
> which I have seen you produce in the out-patient ward. Round the
> centre of deduction and inference and observation which I have
> heard you inculcate, I have tried to build up a man who pushed the
> thing as far as it would go—further occasionally—and I am so
> glad that the result satisfied you, who are the critic with the most
> right to be severe.

One is on less sure ground—some Sherlockians would say no ground at all—when it comes to suggesting how the master detective and the narrator of his exploits acquired their respective names.

The American journalist Vincent Starrett came upon, and reproduced in *The Private Life of Sherlock Holmes* (published 1934), a page from a notebook on which Conan Doyle had jotted down notes for *A Study in Scarlet*, the first of the Holmes tales, originally published in *Beeton's Christmas Annual*, 1887: the address, 221B Upper Baker Street, is there, but the detective is called Sherrinford Holmes, the chronicler Ormond Sacker. Starrett also found a newspaper report in which Conan Doyle was quoted as saying that 'years ago I made thirty runs against a bowler by the name of Sherlock, and I always had a kindly feeling for the name'. But other Sherlockians have different ideas, ranging from esoterically etymic to disappointingly down-to-earth—the latter represented by John Dickson Carr's[1] assertion, in his biography of Conan Doyle, published 1949, that the Irish name of Sherlock was chosen 'entirely at random'.

William Baring-Gould may be correct when he says—in *The Annotated Sherlock Holmes*, published 1968—that Ormond Sacker was

> a name that Conan Doyle speedily, and rightly, dropped as sounding much too dandified. 'John H. Watson, MD, late of the Army Medical Department' owes his surname to Conan Doyle's friend and fellow-member of the Southsea Literary and Scientific Society, *James* Elmwood Watson, MD, Edinburgh, 1863. House physician at the Edinburgh Royal, then a physician to the British Consulate at Newchwung, Manchuria, Dr James Watson had come to practise in Southsea in 1883.

1 His pen-names of Carr Dickson and Carter Dickson, which he used in addition to his own when he published crime tales, are so slight in their variation on each other and on his real name that it is perplexing to try to understand why he bothered with them.

Bentley, Edmund Clerihew

In 1891, when he was sixteen, doodling away a science lesson at St Paul's School, London, he jotted down,

> Sir Humphry Davy[1]
> Abominated gravy,
> He lived in the odium
> Of having discovered sodium.

Having discovered a new form of verse—a rhyming quatrain that intentionally doesn't scan—Bentley concocted examples over the next several years, and in 1905 included some in his book *Biography for Beginners*, using his middle name as a generic term for them.

Even if he had not invented clerihews, Bentley would be remembered, for he was the author of *Trent's Last Case* (1912), the classic novel of detection that was the model for the renaissance of the genre in the 1920s.

Later, perhaps influenced in some way by clerihewism, the American Ogden Nash turned unscanned verse into comic art; for instance, with 'If He Scholars, Let Him Go', a discussion of the nineteenth-century critic and historian Hippolyte Adolphe Taine, which ends:

> He did much to establish positivism in France,
> And his famous *History of English Literature* was written on purpose and not by chance.
> Yes, Hippolyte Adolphe Taine may have been only five foot three, but he was a scholar of the most discerning;
> Whereas his oafish brother Casimir, although he stood six foot seven in his bobby-socks, couldn't spell C-H-A-T, cat, and was pointed at as the long Taine that had no learning.

Nash himself seems to have invented a verse form: a four-line limerick, called a limick, exemplified by

> Two nudists of Dover,
> Being purple all over,
> Were munched by a cow
> When mistaken for clover.

1 After whom the Davy-lamp, safe in mines, is named—although in 1815, when it was introduced, two other scientists, George Stephenson and the Irish Dr William Reid Clanny, claimed to have had much the same idea.

Bessie, Alvah

Alphabetically, the first of the group of Hollywood directors and writers who became known for a short time as 'The Unfriendly Ten', then as 'The Hollywood Ten'. The others were Herbert Biberman, Lester Cole, Edward Dmytryk, Ring Lardner Jr, John Howard Lawson, Albert Maltz, Samuel Ornitz, Adrian Scott, and Dalton Trumbo.

In 1947, when the House Committee on Un-American Activities investigated Communism in Hollywood, 'friendly' witnesses included Gary Cooper, Adolphe Menjou, and Ronald Reagan. Of nineteen 'unfriendly' witnesses who were subpoenaed, ten refused to testify on the ground that they considered the Committee to be unconstitutional, and were imprisoned for contempt of Congress.

Betty Martin

When prefixed by 'all my eye and', she is a comment indicating scepticism. According to a naval explanation (one of many), a Jewish sailor landing with a church party somehow got into the wrong place of worship, and, try as he might to understand the Latin service, could only make out 'all my eye and Betty Martin,' which didn't make sense. The actual words were 'Ah, mihi, beati Martine'.

Betty, William Henry West

During the theatrical season of 1804–5, thirteen-year-old 'Master Betty', or the Young Roscius, took London by storm, playing many of the great tragic roles at Drury Lane and Covent Garden. William Pitt the Younger adjourned the House of Commons so that he and other members of parliament could see Betty as Hamlet; the boy was presented to the royal family, and James Northcote, RA, painted him as Norval in *Douglas*.[1] But in the following season, he was hissed off the stage when he essayed the part of Richard III. The bubble had burst: the Young Roscius was now 'the nine-days' wonder'.[2] That was so in London at any rate. From then on, he toured the provinces, drawing large audiences—and enormous fees. By the time he was thirty-three, he had amassed a sufficient fortune to retire; the remaining fifty years of his life were passed in lavish obscurity.

Several other infant prodigies of the stage have been dubbed, or have dubbed themselves, Roscius (after Quintus Roscius, the most famous Roman comic actor of his day, not long BC, who, according to Pliny, had annual takings of fifty million sesterces—something like three quarters of a million pounds in our money). To give just two instances: Henry Erskine Johnston, though English, was called the Scottish Roscius after first playing Hamlet, then Norval, at the Theatre Royal, Edinburgh, in 1791, when he was seventeen; unfortunately for him, he suffered from 'an excess of complacency' which prevented him from taking acting seriously, so his early promise was not fulfilled. Then there was Gustavus Vaughan Brooke, also English, but known as the Hibernian Roscius because his first stage appearances, as a boy of fourteen in 1832, were in Dublin. His life—which was cut short in 1866 when the SS *London*, on which he was travelling to Australia, sank in the Bay of Biscay—was full of ups and downs; among the latter was a period in prison as a debtor, partly attributable to a disastrously unsuccessful tenure of the Astor Place Opera House, Manhattan, in 1852—three years after the riot sparked off by comparisons between Edwin Forrest and (◊) William Charles Macready.

1 When this play by the Reverend John Home, a Scottish minister, was first performed, in Edinburgh in 1756, the audience went wild; a nationalist in the pit screamed, 'Where's ycr Wully Shakespeare noo?' But now it is rarely produced; not even in Scotland. Norval's main speech is used as an exercise at drama schools—chiefly to stress the importance of punctuation, for if the second full-stop is not given its due, a flock of sheep becomes carnivorous:

My name is Norval.
On the Grampian hills, my father feeds his flock.
A frugal swain . . .

2 Chaucer's 'A wonder last but nyne night never in toune' appears to have been borrowed from the Latin of Livy: 'Romanis quoque ab eodem prodigio novendiale sacrum publice susceptum est' = 'Also on account of that wonderful event, a nine days' solemn feast was celebrated by the Romans.'

Blair, Eric Arthur

He always had trouble with the titles of his books. The first, published in 1933, did not get its title of *Down and Out in Paris and London* until it was being set in type. At the same time, the publisher, Victor Gollancz, chose a pseudonym from four submitted by the apparently self-effacing author. The choice was 'George Orwell'. One's mind lurches at the thought that the world of literature could have been enriched by the works of Kenneth Miles, or P. S. Burton, or even H. Lewis Allways. That last suggestion seems as Pythonesquely ludicrous as 'G. Bernard Schwartz', yet it might, just might, have taken Gollancz's fancy, and thus we would have been deprived of the adjective, 'Orwellian'.

Born in India in 1903, the son of a member of the Bengal Civil Service, Eric Blair was educated at Eton, after which he spent five years as a police officer in Burma. Then—quite suddenly, it seems—he decided to opt out of the middle class, and spent the next five years learning 'the facts of poverty' by experience, as a dish-washer in Paris and (calling himself P. S. Burton) as a tramp in England.

While roughing it, he must often have felt confused, not knowing whether he had truly changed or was just playing a role; and it is understandable that when he came to publish his account of life as a down-and-out, he should have wanted to mask his real identity. From then on, George Orwell took over—or *seemed* to take over—from Eric Blair. Some ten years later, his friend Anthony Powell asked him if he had ever thought of legally adopting his pseudonym. 'Well, I have,' he said slowly, 'but then, of course, I'd have to *write* under another name if I did.'

To revert to his difficulty in inventing titles, when he completed the book that turned out to be the last he wrote, he toyed with various ideas before deciding simply to transpose the last two digits of the current year-date, 1948, so that the book was called *Nineteen Eighty-Four*.

Bounce

A Great Dane belonging to Alexander Pope, who in 1728, having made many enemies with his *Dunciad*, a mock epic lampooning other poets, took the precautions of carrying a brace of pistols and having the dog—'my only friend'—with him when he went on walks.

John Gay, the author of *The Beggar's Opera* (which made 'Rich [the theatre manager] gay, and Gay rich') extolled the value of Bounce's progeny in the poem, 'Bounce to Fop, an Epistle from a Dog at Twickenham to a Dog at Court':

> None but a peer of wit and grace
> Can hope a puppy of my race.

When the Prince of Wales received one of Bounce's pups, Polyphemus, the animal was wearing a collar on which was inscribed a couplet by Pope:

> I am his Highness' dog at Kew.
> Pray tell me, Sir, whose dog are you?

Brasher, Christopher

On 6 May 1954, he and Christopher Chataway were the pace-makers when Roger Bannister ran the first four-minute mile. The three were members of an Amateur Athletics Association team competing with a team representing Oxford University. Bannister's time was 3:59.4, Chataway's 4:07.2, and Brasher's unrecorded since, by the time he reached the finishing line, the track was crowded with revellers.

Brodie, Deacon William

Deacon Brodie's Tavern in the Lawnmarket, Edinburgh, is named after the man whose double life—respectable by day, criminal by night—inspired Robert Louis Stevenson to write *The Strange Case of Dr Jekyll and Mr Hyde*. Brodie was hanged for theft in 1788 on gallows that he himself had designed.

Of the several screen adaptations of Stevenson's novel, the most notable is the 1932 version, directed by Rouben Mamoulian and starring Fredric March (real name, Frederick McIntyre Bickel), who was awarded an Oscar for his performances in the dual roles.

At the opening of the film the camera took the place of the leading character, driving up to the club in a carriage, from which it descended and entered the building, then swinging to look at itself

in a mirror, at which point Fredric March, as Dr Jekyll, is first seen
. . . In the transformation scenes the camera for the first time
revolved 360° on its axis to give an effect of vertigo, recorded
heartbeats (Mamoulian's own) were synchronised with gong-
strokes to build up tension, and successive layers of specially
coloured make-up were revealed by the use of colour filters to
avoid the necessity for cuts and optical dissolves.

The Oxford Companion to Film
(edited by Liz-Anne Bawden, 1976)

Going back in time, it appears that the story was the basis of
the first horror film, a one-reel production released in the spring
of 1908 by the Selig Polyscope Co. of Chicago; the star was
Richard Mansfield, and the supporting cast was composed of
members of his company, at that time touring with a Jekyll-and-
Hyde play. The first British horror movie, made by Lucius
Henderson in 1912, was also based on the story.

Brooks, Henry Sands

The son of a Connecticut doctor, he was forty-six in 1818, when
he opened a clothing store on the south-east corner of Catherine
and Cherry Streets, in lower Manhattan, having acquired the
building and ground at an auction sale with a bid of $15,250.
After his death in 1833, the store was enlarged and refurbished by
his sons—Henry, Daniel, John, Elisha and Edward—but they
waited seventeen years before changing its name to Brooks
Brothers. The store was sacked, chiefly by Irish-Americans,
during the riots against conscription to the Union Army in July
1863. That was not the reason, though, why the Brothers
subsequently moved uptown: the city's business and commerce
was moving northwards, and it made sense for them to follow
suit. After brief stops at locations on Broadway, they came to

rest in 1915 at a bespoke building on Madison Avenue; still the firm's 'flagship premises'.

Brooks Brothers' advertising has always been only slightly less discreet than its wares. The comparatively low budget and the usually reticent copy are equally understandable, for the firm's customers—unintentional placards or droppers of the name—make both a heavy outlay on space and a spieler's style in the space acquired superfluous. The most famous article of clothing bought at the store was the frock-coat worn by Abraham Lincoln at his second inauguration and when he was assassinated (◊ Lord Dundreary). Other presidents who took the oath of office in Brooks attire include Ulysses S(impson) Grant (who had fought his major Civil War battles in gear from the military-tailoring department), Theodore Roosevelt, and Thomas Woodrow Wilson. Franklin Roosevelt's naval capes came from the store, and Richard Nixon shopped there both before and after his curtailed tenure of the White House. F. Scott Fitzgerald was a customer; and so were several of his heroes (◊ Max Gerlach)—all of them, no doubt, though he doesn't invariably say so. The male characters John O'Hara approved of wore Brooks suits; they were, to him, as strong a symbol of urban correctness as a white stetson (named after the hatter who had the idea) was of goodguyness in cowboy films. And although Brooks Brothers did not open a women's department until 1976, an authoress, Mary McCarthy, had, several years before, freely advertised the firm with her short story 'The Man in the Brooks Brothers Shirt'. When Charles Augustus Lindbergh came to New York in 1927, after making the first solo flight across the Atlantic, in a Ryan monoplane christened Spirit of St Louis, the mayor, 'Gentleman' Jimmy Walker, himself a Brooks customer, insisted that the firm's tailors stay up all night, making a suit for Lindbergh to wear in what turned out to be the city's most littering ticker-tape parade; afterwards, the mayor contended that the publicity was sufficient payment for the suit—only to be told that 'publicity is not in our area of interest, and the matter of the bill remains'.[1]

1 When 'Lucky Lindy' touched down in Paris on 21 May 1927, there had already been half a dozen transatlantic flights, the first of them almost exactly eight years before:

Between 16 and 27 May 1919, the US Lieutenant-Commander Albert 'Putty' Read and a crew of five flew—or, almost as much, floated—from Trepassey Bay, Newfoundland, Canada,to Plymouth, England, in a flying boat called the *Lame Duck*.

In the following month, two former RAF officers, John William Alcock and Arthur Whitten Brown, took off from St John's, Newfoundland, in a Vickers Vimy bomber fitted with extra fuel tanks, and the next day, the 15th, landed nose-down in a bog near the village of Clifden on the western hem of Ireland. Their flight, the first to be accomplished in one hop (taking, coast to coast, 15 hours and 57 minutes, at an average speed of 118.5 m.p.h.), earned them a prize of £10,000 from the *Daily Mail* and knighthoods from King George V. Six months later, Alcock flew to France in a Vickers Viking amphibious aircraft, which he intended to exhibit in Paris; forced to come down near Rouen, he fractured his skull on landing and died without regaining consciousness. Brown became a senior representative for Metropolitan-Vickers, but returned to the RAF during the Second World War to train pilots in navigation and engineering; he died in 1948, at the age of sixty-two, from an overdose of veronal, deemed by the coroner's jury to have been taken accidentally. There are two memorials to Alcock and Brown, one close to the field in Newfoundland from which they took off, the other at London Heathrow airport.

A fortnight or so after the Alcock-Brown flight, between 2 and 6 July, the British airship R-34 became the first dirigible to make the crossing, from East Fortune, Scotland, to Mineola, Long Island; on board were Major George Scott, a motley collection of helpers and passengers—and the first transatlantic airborne stowaway, William Ballantine, who had been supposed to stay behind so as to lighten the load.

More than five years passed before the next flight, again by an airship, this time a German one. Piloted by Dr Hugo Eckener, who was helped by a crew of thirty-three, the Z-R3 left Friedrichshafen on 12 October 1924, and finished up three days later at Lakehurst, New Jersey.

The most tedious flight was that accomplished by a Dornier Wal flying boat, which was aloft (well, most of the time) between 23 January and 5 February, 1926; because it meandered from Palos—the Spanish port from which Columbus sailed, eventually to come across America—to Buenos Aires, Ramon Franco, the leader in a quartet of fliers, was dubbed, at least by frenzied Latins, the Columbus of the Air.

Next year, between 13 and 24 February, Francesco Marquis

de Pinedo and two other Italians flew a Savoia-Marchetti flying boat from Sardinia to Pernambuco, in Brazil. Soon afterwards, during a Fascist flag-waving jaunt, the *Santa Maria* settled on a lake in Arizona, a member of the crew jettisoned fuel, a local volunteer helper lit a cigarette and threw the match in the water, and the aircraft caught fire and sank; the Italian government, believing that the accident was not an accident at all but a fiendish American plot, screamed threats of reprisal—but the anger simmered down, and it wasn't until 11 December 1941 that the two countries went to war.

Brooks, Louise

The American actress who, after a squabble with Hollywood studio executives, accepted an offer from G(eorg) W(ilhelm) Pabst to go to Germany to play Lulu—destined to be a victim of Jack the Ripper—in his production of *Die Büchse der Pandora* (*Pandora's Box*; 1928), based on two plays by the German dramatist Frank Wedekind. Without seeming to be trying, she gave one of the great screen performances of all time; it has been said that 'her calm, pale face framed by smooth, bobbed hair has become part of the iconography of cinema'. After making another film for Pabst, she returned to Hollywood; but the speaking of lines diminished the impact of her acting, and she soon ceased to work.

Before the part of Lulu was given to Louise Brooks, Pabst had considered offering it to Marlene Dietrich (◊ Marie Magdelene von Losch).

Brown, James

Though now merely a link in a corporate chain, Brown's (the too-good-to-be-true setting of Agatha Christie's *At Bertram's Hotel*) is still the superior hotel of Mayfair; perhaps of London.

It was in 1837, the year of Queen Victoria's accession, that James Brown, a former gentleman's gentleman, took possession of 23 Dover Street:[1] to the consternation, no doubt, of the neighbours—eight lords, three baronets, the Bishop of Ely, and the Tsar's Ambassador to the Court of St James—who must have believed that an hotel would lower the tone of the place. Only months before, Brown had married Sarah Willis at St George's, in nearby Hanover Square. Clearly, he married her, not for *her* money, but because of the promise of some belonging to Lady Byron, the poet's widow, whom Sarah had served as a maid for several years; circumstantial evidence that Anne Byron was Brown's financial angel came to light when the hotel changed hands, and the new owner, going through the rooms, found a small bust of Lord Byron in almost all of them.[2] Brown's venture was a success from the start: a year after opening, he acquired the house next door, and in the two succeeding years, two more houses, thus making an uninterrupted row of four (which still make up the front of the hotel); long afterwards, five houses at the rear, facing on to Albemarle Street, were tagged on. Brown's business boomed in 1851, as a result of the Great Exhibition in Hyde Park, and he used £3,000 of the extra revenue to buy the freehold of the original house. Eight years later, extremely wealthy but dog-tired, he sold the hotel to the owner of Ford's Hotel in Manchester Square. The transaction was completed within hours of Brown's mooting it. Sarah, who seems to have been a prime cause of her husband's tiredness (she was described as 'a very tiresome woman'), wasn't told of the sale until the papers had been signed and a deposit paid. She was furious with James, and remained caterwaulingly so right up until he died in the following year. She did her best to cancel the transaction, and, failing, peppered Mr Ford with pettifogging law-suits. He must have breathed a sigh of relief, even offered drinks on the house, when Sarah died in 1875; but she had bequeathed him problems in a twenty-page will, the executors of which were to be dismissed if they proved at all inefficient, and it took him some time to obtain the freehold of No. 23, which Sarah had grimly but delightedly refused to part with.

At the start of this century, the Ford family turned the hotel into a private limited company. Eventually, it was controlled by the Swiss family Bon, owners of several hotels on and around the Alps, who continued to run Brown's until soon after the Second World War, when it was taken over by the present owners, now called Trusthouse Forte.

There are several 'private function rooms', each named after a person or event associated with Brown's. Predictably, there is the Byron Room. Among the others are:

The *Graham Bell* Room. It was from here that the first telephone call in Britain was made in 1876. The Scots-born American, Alexander Graham Bell, was in London, hoping to interest the government in his invention for carrying voices through a pair of wires; at the suggestion of the American financier John Pierpoint Morgan, who had been a guest at Brown's, he put up there—unaware, it seems, that the Fords had installed a telegraph line between the hotel and their home at Ravenscourt Park, four or five miles away. A telegraph line was just what Bell needed for trying out, then demonstrating, his newfangled 'telephone'. He persuaded the teen-aged Henry Ford (who later became manager of Brown's) to sit at home while he tried to get through to him from the hotel; after hours of crackling non-intercourse (*plus ça change*), he succeeded.

The *Kipling* Room; so called because it is part of the suite that (Joseph) Rudyard Kipling occupied, and did much writing in (seated, so it is said, at a leather-topped desk that is now an exhibit), whenever he was in London between 1892 and 1936, the year of his death.

The *Roosevelt* Room. On 2 December 1886, when Theodore Roosevelt married Edith Kermit Carow at St George's, Hanover Square, he stated that he was a ranchman by occupation and that his address was Brown's Hotel, Dover Street. Nowadays, a portrait of him hangs above the fireplace in the Roosevelt Room; given to Brown's by his daughter Mrs Richard Derby,[3] it carries the inscription,

> Theodore Roosevelt
> 26th President of the United States of America 1901–1909
> Life 1858–1909

Nearly twenty years after Theodore Roosevelt's stay at the hotel, two other Roosevelts, the honeymooning Franklin Delano (born at Hyde Park, New York State) and Anna Eleanor, booked in. In her autobiography, Mrs Roosevelt recalled:

> We went first to London and were horrified to find that in some way we had been identified with Uncle Ted and were given the royal suite at Brown's Hotel, with a sitting room so large that I could not find anything that I put down. We had to explain that our pocketbook was not equal to such grandeur, but that made no difference. We lived in it for those first few days in London.

1 Many of the thoroughfares of Mayfair bear the names of titled persons who once owned the land or who speculated with property developments on it at the end of the seventeenth and beginning of the eighteenth centuries. For instance, Burlington Gardens and Arcade and Cork Street got their names from respective entrepreneurial earls, 'Mayfair's high street' was called after its developer, Sir Thomas Bond, and Dover Street was, to all intents and purposes, created by the first Earl of Dover, who had settled down after a life of lechery, gambling, military campaigning and political lobbying as plain Henry Jermyn: hence Jermyn Street, south of Piccadilly—the setting of a set of Eskimo-Nell-type verses, the first of which begins:

> Lady Elizabeth Anne Shell-Mex
> Had an astonishing urge for sex,
> So they bought her a most expensive beat
> On the sunny side of Jermyn Street.

2 A few of the busts were retained. No one seems to know what became of the rest. Perhaps they were sold en masse to that

secondhand merchant who provided the Ecuadorian town of Guayaquil with a statue of Lord Byron as a stand-in for one of (◊) José Joaquin de Olmedo, and, the merchant having made up a Byronesque job-lot, are even now distributed among Guayaquil's municipal offices, abetting the masquerader in the town square.

3 *Née* Ethel Roosevelt. Dr Richard Derby, whom she married in 1913, was a cousin of Helen Derby Elwell, wife of Joseph Bowne Elwell (◊ Max Gerlach and Willard Huntingdon Wright).

Brown, Lancelot

A man of the earth, and earthy, but during his working life in the middle of the eighteenth century, able to pick and choose among the rich people, some of whom were aristocrats, who pleaded with him to landscape their gardens. 'There are great capabilities here, my lord, great capabilities,' he would mutter as he cast his eye over a dull stretch of land, and it was thus that he got to be called Capability Brown. Shortly before he retired—by then richer than some of those who had hired him—to his own country seat in Huntingdonshire, the Duke of Leinster offered him an especially large fee to travel to Ireland to look at some estates. 'Ireland?' he replied, bemusedly scratching his behind. 'But I haven't finished England yet.' Several of his landscapes have survived or remain not much altered: at Kew, for instance, and in such stately places as Blenheim, Chatsworth, Harewood, and Nuneham Courtenay.

Brugnon, Toto

The least celebrated member of the French Davis Cup team of the 1920s, known—yes, of course—as the Four Musketeers. The others were Jean Borotra ('the bounding Basque'), Henri Cochet, and René Lacoste.

Burke, William

The only murderer with an entry to himself in the English dictionary: *burke*, *v.t.*, to murder, especially by stifling: hence (*figuratively*) to put an end to quietly. In 1828, he and his partner William Hare, who was also Irish, provided Dr Robert Knox, the anatomist, with at least sixteen subjects for his dissecting table at 10 Surgeons' Square, Edinburgh (average price for a 'subject', £10 in winter, £8 in summer). Over-confidence making them slipshod, they were arrested on 1 November 1828; so was Burke's mistress Helen M'Dougal. Hare turned king's evidence, and was the chief prosecution witness at the trial, which began at 9.30 a.m. on Christmas Eve and went on non-stop for twenty-four hours. The jury found that the case against Helen M'Dougal was not proven, but they returned a verdict of 'guilty' against Burke, who was hanged in the Lawnmarket a month later. (Long before the body had been carted away, the hangman's assistants sold pieces of the rope at 2/6d an inch[1]). Edinburgh's only memorial to Burke and Hare (apart from the former's skeleton in the anatomical museum of the university) is a pub named after them which stands almost opposite the site of their crimes in the West Port. Of the many chapbook and broadsheet verses on the case, the best-remembered is

> Up the close and doun the stair,
> But and ben[2] with Burke and Hare;
> Burke's the butcher, Hare's the thief,
> Knox the boy that buys the beef.

1 A high price: three years later, following the execution of John Holloway, the first Brighton 'trunk murderer', a gentleman of Lewes paid half a crown for the whole rope.

2 Out and in.

Carney, Kate

A music-hall star until just after the First World War—during which her name became Cockney rhyming (well, almost) slang for 'army'. A sort of female equivalent of Albert Chevalier, who sang coster songs such as 'Knocked 'em in the Old Kent Road' and 'My Old Dutch', Kate Carney appeared as a pearlie queen, her most famous numbers being 'Three Pots a Shilling' and 'Liza Johnson'. (◊ Andrew Miller.)

Castro, Thomas

In 1866, when Thomas Castro (or whatever his real name was) became known to newspaper readers the world over as The Tichborne Claimant, he weighed more than twenty stone—roughly twice what the twenty-five-year-old Roger Charles Tichborne,[1] heir to the Tichborne baronetcy and the riches that went with the title, had weighed when, a dozen years before, he had set sail from Rio de Janeiro on a ship called the *Bella*; three days out of port, the vessel had gone down in a storm, and it had generally been assumed that everyone on board had perished.

But the French-born, rather dotty Dowager Lady Tichborne never wavered in her hope—indeed, belief—that her son Roger was alive.

In 1863, she inserted an advertisement, in three languages, in *The Times*, pleading for clues to Roger's whereabouts. Despite her offer of a 'handsome reward for any well-authenticated particulars', the advertisement drew a blank.

Two years passed. Then, acting on a hunch that Roger had been rescued by a ship bound for Australia, Lady Tichborne wrote to an advertising agent in Sydney. Using some of the details in the letter, the agent, a Mr Cubitt, concocted an advertisement and placed it in three Sydney newspapers.

As it happened, at about that time a man named Walter Gibbes, a solicitor in the gold-mining and farming community of Wagga Wagga, 250 miles from Sydney, was managing the bankruptcy of a local butcher, Thomas Castro, whose girth indicated that he had eaten more meat than he had sold. In the course of their discussions, Castro let slip that he was 'entitled to some property in England'. And—quite beside the point, it seemed—that he had once been shipwrecked. Intrigued, the solicitor spoke to his wife about the bankrupt butcher—and she recalled an advertisement she had seen in a Sydney paper.

Gibbes found a copy of the paper, read the advertisement, and made some discreet inquiries about Castro. As far as he could make out, Castro had turned up in Australia some time during the 1850s. At the next interview, Gibbes asked one or two veiled questions, then a direct one: 'Shall I call you out loud by your real name?'

Castro held out the pipe he was smoking. Carved under the bowl were the initials R.C.T.

The excited solicitor wrote to Mr Cubitt, the advertising agent. Both men became convinced that Castro was the missing heir when he volunteered information, some of which Cubitt knew to be true, about the Tichborne family. A letter was despatched to Lady Tichborne.

Her reply was guarded: she would need more than just a few morsels of evidence before accepting that Thomas Castro was her long-lost son, Roger Charles; and she would not part with any cash, either to pay Castro's debts in Wagga Wagga or to enable him to sail to England.

After getting Castro to make a will, signing himself 'Roger Charles Tichborne', Walter Gibbes advanced him some money, and the failed butcher travelled to Sydney, hoping that there he would drum up the money for his passage 'home'.

The claimant's stay in the city turned out to be even more productive. An elderly Negro named Andrew Bogle was living there. Before emigrating to Australia, he had been employed for many years by the Tichbornes. Hearing that Master Roger had 'returned from the dead' and was staying at the Metropolitan Hotel, the Negro went to see him. The claimant was out, so Bogle sat down in the courtyard. After a while, Castro lumbered across the yard. Seeing the old Negro, he said, 'Hello, Bogle, is that you?' Though taken aback, Bogle answered, 'Is that you, sir?' 'Yes, I'll see you presently,' Castro said coolly, continuing his ungainly progress into the hotel.

During the subsequent interview, the claimant recalled so much about home and early days that Bogle, at first very doubtful indeed, finished up calling him 'Sir Roger'.

Word soon got round that a positive identification had been made. And, in no time at all, there were adequate funds for the trip to England.

The claimant, with a sizeable entourage, arrived in London on Christmas Day, 1866. Over the next few months, he visited, or was visited by persons who had known Roger Tichborne. Some declared him an impostor; others supported him; and one or two just couldn't make up their minds. Saliently, Lady Tichborne had a brief chat with him and was left in no doubt that he was her son. As an expression of her certainty, the old lady gave the claimant an allowance of £1,000 a year.

If he were to win, certain members of the Tichborne family would have to adjust to a much lower standard of living. Finding that prospect unappealing, they banded together and spent lavishly in defending the case.

Of course, it was not up to the family to disprove the claimant's case, but for him to prove it. The difficulty of that task was greatly increased by the death of his main champion, the Dowager Lady Tichborne. After 102 days of testimony either for or against the claimant, the jury decided that enough was enough: they could stand the boredom, the discomfort, **no** longer. They stopped the case, thereby branding Thomas **Castro** as a massive liar. The decision also meant that he was responsible for the family's costs as well as his own.

But he had another worry. Before he left the court, the judge directed that he be tried for perjury.

It may be hard to credit this, but the criminal case took even longer than the civil action—partly because Castro was defended by a chatterbox Irishman, Dr Edward Vaughan Kenealy. Of the 188 days of the trial, 23 were taken up by Kenealy's closing speech. Despite—or perhaps to some extent because of—the Irishman's prodigal expenditure of words, the jury returned a verdict of guilty. The foreman added that he and his fellows believed the prosecution's submission that, quite apart from the fact that the defendant was not Sir Roger Tichborne, he was not Thomas Castro either—but someone called Arthur Orton, a native of the East End of London. The jury's rider prompted an anagram (not quite an exact fit):

> Sir Roger Charles Doughty Tichborne, Baronet
> You horrid butcher, Orton; biggest rascal here

Orton, Castro or Tichborne—or whoever he was—earned remission from sentences totalling fourteen years, and was released from prison after a decade. He died in poverty in 1898. His few remaining supporters clubbed together to buy a decent oak coffin, on the lid of which was a brass plaque with the name and title he had claimed were his.

---

1 An ancestor, Chidiock Tichborne (1558?–86) was convicted of being a member of the Babington (Roman Catholic) conspiracy against Queen Elizabeth I. He wrote this poem in the Tower of London shortly before his execution:

Tichborne's Elegy
My prime of youth is but a frost of cares;
    My feast of joy is but a dish of pain;
My crop of corn is but a field of tares;
    And all my good is but vain hope of gain:
The day is past, and yet I saw no sun;
And now I live, and now my life is done.

My tale was heard, and yet it was not told;
   My fruit is fall'n, and yet my leaves are green;
My youth is spent, and yet I am not old;
   I saw the world, and yet I was not seen:
My thread is cut, and yet it is not spun;
And now I live, and now my life is done.

I sought my death, and found it in my womb;
   I looked for life, and saw it was a shade;
I trod the earth, and knew it was my tomb;
   And now I die, and now I was but made:
My glass is full, and now my glass is run;
And now I live, and now my life is done.

Chang and Eng

As far as is known, they were the first conjoined (in their case, by a thick, flexible band at the breastbone) identical twins to survive. Born in 1811 in Siam to a Malay-Chinese mother and Chinese father, they were, all things considered, quite agile. Billed as the Siamese Twins, they became a celebrated double-act at exhibitions: so celebrated, in fact, that their show-business name came to be attached to their condition. At the age of thirty, having made a small fortune, they assumed the name of Bunker and settled down in the farming community of Mount Airy, North Carolina. Two years later, they married a couple of sisters from a nearby farm. Each of the twins purchased a house, and, turn and turn about, roughly on a weekly basis, was either host to or guest of the other. To answer the question uppermost in your mind: yes, excessively—one couple produced a dozen children, the other ten. It is reckoned that, by now, almost two thousand descendants have come from the two Bunker unions; the branches of the family tree bear a president of the Union Pacific Railway and a major-general of the United States Air Force. In 1874, one of the twins suffered a fatal stroke, and the other died a few hours later—either from shock or fright, it was believed, though another possible explanation emerged during an autopsy, when it was found that the livers of Chang and Eng were connected.

Perhaps it had something to do with the second part of his pen-name, but Mark Twain (◊ Samuel Langhorne Clemens) was intrigued by twins. He sometimes pretended to be one himself, so as to lead conversation towards a joke, and he used the look-alike theme in several of his works: in *The Prince and the Pauper*, in *Pudd'nhead Wilson*, which contains doppel-gängers as well as a pair of true identical twins, and in the shorter satire 'These Extraordinary Twins', which was inspired by Chang and Eng.

Chapman, John

In 1961, he was the drama critic for the New York *Daily News*; the other half-dozen 'butchers of Broadway' were Robert Coleman (*Daily Mirror*), Walter Kerr (*Herald Tribune*), John McClain (*Journal American*), Norman Nadel (*World Telegram*), Howard Taubman (*Times*), and Richard Watts (*Post*).

Two days after the opening of a musical, *Subways Are For Sleeping*, which had tottered into New York after dispiriting try-out weeks in Philadelphia and Boston, the first edition of the *Herald Tribune* carried a large advertisement, the headlines of which read:

**7 OUT OF 7
ARE ECSTATICALLY
UNANIMOUS ABOUT
SUBWAYS ARE FOR SLEEPING**

Beneath the bold type was a vertical line of portrait photographs, each followed by the name of a critic and a quote about the show. All the quotes were fulsomely admiring, but the most complimentary was the one ascribed to John Chapman:

NO DOUBT ABOUT IT, 'SUBWAYS ARE FOR SLEEPING' IS THE BEST MUSICAL OF THE CENTURY. Consider yourself lucky if you can buy or steal a ticket for 'Subways Are For Sleeping' over the next few years.

The advertisement had been submitted to the other papers, but someone on the *Times*, smelling a rat, had checked the Howard Taubman quote against what Mr Taubman had actually written and, finding no resemblance, had not only spiked the copy but had alerted the *Times*'s rivals. The warning had come too late for the *Herald Tribune*—and only just in time for the *Post*, whose advertising manager had delayed the setting until the picture of a Negro next to the name of Richard Watts had been replaced by a photograph of the paper's white drama critic.

Later that day, David Merrick, the producer of *Subways Are For Sleeping*, admitted—no, proclaimed—a 'prank'. At his instigation, his press agent, using a telephone book, had found people with the same names as those of the critics, invited them to previews, and, while wining and dining them afterwards, persuaded them to say flattering things about the show and obtained their permission to quote the comments. There had been one small hitch: the John Chapman chosen by the press agent had walked out at the end of the first act, muttering unquotably, 'I think it stinks.' Another John Chapman, far less discerning than his namesake, had been hooked from among the Manhattan telephone subscribers.

It didn't matter to Merrick that only one of the papers had printed the advertisement. He drummed up an enormous amount of free publicity from the prank—which probably accounts for the fact that *Subways Are For Sleeping* ran for six months: at least five and three-quarter months longer than it deserved.

One of the chorus boys of the show was Michael Bennett. Fourteen years later, he directed and choreographed *A Chorus Line*, an innovative musical that he himself had conceived. First presented Off-Broadway, at Joseph Papp's Public Theatre, where it opened on 21 May 1975, it moved to the Shubert Theatre (the management of which must have been unhappy that it was played without an intermission, thus reducing their profits from the sale of drinks, ice-cream, and souvenir programmes, T-shirts, key-rings, and heaven knows what else) and ran record-breakingly.

When the songs (music by Marvin Hamlisch, lyrics by Edward Kleban) are heard out of context, only two prove to be self-supporting: 'One', which is a parody of slick chorus-numbers, and the haunting torch-song 'What I Did for Love'. (The latter makes a not-inconsiderable contribution to the plot of my whodunit[1] *The Last Sentence*, published 1978, which is based on the real-life Wallace murder case [◊ Richard Gordon Parry].)

1 Information provided by Jacques Barzun and Wendell Hertig Taylor in *A Catalogue of Crime* (published 1971):

> WHODUNIT. This vocable was invented by the late Wolfe Kaufman when on the staff of *Variety*, the New York newspaper written for actors, which has long had a policy of substituting new terms for existing words and locutions. Whatever the inventor's first intention, *whodunit* now refers indiscriminately to any story of crime.

Charles Pooter

The 'nobody' of *The Diary of a Nobody*. On a page before the entries, he enquired:

> Why should I not publish my diary? I have often seen reminiscences of people I have never heard of, and I fail to see—because I do not happen to be a 'Somebody'—why my diary should not be interesting. My only regret is that I did not commence it when I was a youth.
> *The Laurels*
>   *Brickfield Terrace*
>   *Holloway.*

The diary—most of which first appeared in *Punch*—is a chronicle of English suburban life in Victorian times. It was written on Mr Pooter's behalf by George and Weedon Grossmith. The former, who died in 1912, was a prolific writer of sketches and songs, and a star of Gilbert & Sullivan operas. The latter, who died in 1919, was a popular comedy actor and a playwright; as well as sharing in the writing of the *Diary*, he did the drawings.

Checkers

A cocker spaniel who became famous on 23 September 1952, when Senator Richard Milhous Nixon appeared on television in an attempt to salvage his candidacy for the vice-presidency of the United States following the revelation that he had a fund of more than $18,000, donated mostly by oilmen, at his disposal. After speaking of his humble background, Nixon denied any impropriety, saying that the fund was for 'necessary political expenses' and 'to fight communism'. Then, wanting to be completely frank, he reported another gift from a fan, a cocker spaniel that had been sent in a crate from Texas:

> Black and white spotted. And our little girl—Tricia, the six-year-old—named it Checkers. And, you know, the kids love the dog, and I just want to say this right now—that, regardless of what they say about it, we're gonna keep it!

Following the direction on the cue-card, he BLINKED BACK TEARS; and throughout the land, Republican viewers, and even some Democrats, reached for their hankies, sobbing the while that a man who loved dogs and children just had to be an all-right guy. Unfortunately for Nixon, he seems to have been dogless when another scandal, that of Watergate, was exposed.

Clanton, Ike

The only member of the Clanton gang left alive after the gunfight at the OK Corral, in Tombstone, Arizona, on 25 October 1881; his colleagues, Billy Clanton and Frank and Tom McLowery, had been shot to death by US Marshal Virgil Earp, his brothers Wyatt and Morgan (created deputies by Virgil), and the consumptive dentist and gambler James Henry 'Doc' Holliday. There seems no doubt that the gunfight was the culmination of a long-standing feud, but there are conflicting accounts of what happened in the corral—one suggesting that the fight was hardly fair, considering that none of the Clanton gang was armed.

Clemens, Samuel Langhorne

Born in Hannibal, Missouri, he was a steamboat pilot on the Mississippi for a couple of years before the Civil War, and it was from river slang for 'two fathoms deep' that he acquired his pen-name of Mark Twain, under which he became famous, not just as a story-teller but as an inexhaustible cracker-barrel of sayings. Here are just three apropos of named persons:

It seems such a pity that Noah and his party did not miss the boat.

The Creator made Italy from designs by Michelangelo.

Wagner's music is better than it sounds.

He died in 1910. A premature obituary, published while he was in Europe, prompted him to send a cable to the Press Association: 'The report of my death was an exaggeration.'

Clyde Wynant

It would be unfair on people who have neither read Dashiell Hammett's novel *The Thin Man*, published 1932, nor seen the film, based on the book, that was released two years later, to let slip who Clyde Wynant, the thin man, is. He is *not* the detective. No; the case is solved by a New York socialite named Nick Charles (played in the film by William Powell), assisted in a scatterbrain sort of way by his wife Nora (Myrna Loy; real surname, Williams), and interrupted every so often by their pet dog, a schnauzer bitch called Asta (who, despite the fact that Hammett states emphatically that 'she was a Schnauzer and not a cross between a Scottie and an Irish terrier,' is played in the film by a male wire-haired fox terrier whose real name was Skippy).

The immense—and deserved—success of the film tempted Metro-Goldwyn-Mayer to produce sequels:[1] and in these 'the thin man' is the nickname for Nick Charles (still played by the not specially thin William Powell).

Similarly, Universal Pictures had no qualms about role-reversal in the umpteen follow-ups to *Frankenstein*, made in 1931 with Colin Clive (real name, Clive Greig) as the creator of the monster, and Boris Karloff (real name, William Henry Pratt) as the creation: in the sequels—and, probably resultantly, in many people's minds—it is the monster who is called Frankenstein. The best-known, and best, of the sequels is *Bride of Frankenstein* (1935), in which Elsa Lanchester (real name, Elizabeth Sullivan), as well as being the concoction topped by an Afro hair-style, played the part of Mary Wollstonecraft Shelley, the second wife of the poet, who published *Frankenstein, or The Modern Prometheus*, in 1818. By the time *Lady Frankenstein*, bearing no relation to the Bride, was released in 1970, Frankenstein himself—or, considering the make-up, themselves—had, among other things, met the Wolf Man (1943), been met by Abbot and Costello (really Cristillo) in 1948, and, nine years later, been rejuvenated as a Teenage Frankenstein.

1 *After the Thin Man* (1937), *Another Thin Man* (1938), *Shadow of the Thin Man* (1942), *The Thin Man Goes Home* (1944), *Song of the Thin Man* (1946). William Powell and Myrna Loy starred in all of these, but in the later ones Asta was played by Skippy's grandson, whose name I don't know.

Collins, Floyd

Hoping to find something that might attract tourists, this young Kentuckian explored an underground passage called Sand Cave, near Louisville. When he was 125 feet from the surface, the roof collapsed, and his foot was pinned under a large rock.

In *Only Yesterday: An Informal History of the Nineteen-Twenties* (published in 1931), Frederick Lewis Allen wrote:

Few people might have heard of Collins's predicament if W. B. Miller of the *Louisville Courier-Journal* had not been slight of stature, daring, and an able reporter. Miller wormed his way down the slippery, tortuous passageway to interview Collins, became engrossed in the efforts to rescue the man, described them in vivid dispatches—and to his amazement found that the entire country was turning to watch the struggle. Collins's plight contained those elements of dramatic suspense and individual conflict with fate which make a great news story, and every city editor, day after day, planted it on page one. When Miller arrived at Sand Cave he had found only three men at the entrance, warming themselves at a fire and wondering, without excitement, how soon their friend would extricate himself. A fortnight later there was a city of a hundred or more tents there and the milling crowds had to be restrained by barbed-wire barriers and State troops with drawn bayonets; and on February 17, 1925, even the *New York Times* gave a three-column page-one headline to the news of the denouement:

> FIND FLOYD COLLINS DEAD IN
> CAVE TRAP ON 18TH DAY;
> LIFELESS AT LEAST 24 HOURS;
> FOOT MUST BE AMPUTATED
> TO GET BODY OUT

Within a month, as Charles Merz later reminded the readers of the *New Republic*, there was a cave-in in a North Carolina mine in which 71 men were caught and 53 actually lost. It attracted no great notice. It was 'just a mine disaster'. Yet for more than two weeks the plight of a single commonplace prospector for tourists rivetted the attention of the nation on Sand Cave, Kentucky. It was an exciting show to watch. . . .

In 1951, Billy Wilder made the film *Ace in the Hole* (or *The Big Carnival*), which is clearly based on events in and around Sand Cave in February 1925. The character of a reporter, Charles Tatum, was played by Kirk Douglas; a trapped man, Herbie Cook, by Bob Arthur. In the film, the reporter deliberately delayed the rescue so as to keep the story going: but, rumours aside, there is nothing to suggest that the real reporter, W. B. Miller, did such a thing.

Coutts, Thomas

The son of a banking lord-provost (Scots equivalent of an English lord mayor) of Edinburgh, he and his younger brother

James came south in the early 1760s to join, as partners, the banking firm of Middleton & Campbell in the Strand, London; Thomas brought in £4,000, and presumably the price paid by James for his partnership was much the same. In 1763, the brothers fell out because of Thomas's marriage to James's servant Susannah, whose 'amiable disposition' was seen by Thomas as one of at least two virtues overweighing the fact that she was near-illiterate (she signed herself 'Susanh' in the marriage register of St Martin-in-the-Fields, just round the corner from the bank). Fifteen years later, following James's death, Thomas was left as sole partner of what was now Coutts & Co. He throve by assiduous and sycophantic cultivation of the rich: in particular, of the Prince of Wales, whose custom he acquired in 1800, taking over from Andrew Berkeley Drummond, the banker at Charing Cross, who had been persuaded by George III not to lend the First Gentleman[1] a penny more. When the prince became king, Drummonds (now the Drummonds branch of the Royal Bank of Scotland) ceased to be the royal bankers; since then, Coutts & Co. have been bankers to every monarch apart from Edward VII, who from the age of three weeks was a client of the Cocks, Biddulph branch of the bank that is now called Barclays, in Whitehall.

Susannah bore Thomas three daughters, each of whom was married for her father's money: Susan by the third earl of Guilford, Frances by the first marquess of Bute, and Sophia by Sir Francis Burdett, Bt. When Susannah died, Thomas Coutts almost straightway married an actress called Harriot Mellon, and when *he* died in 1822, leaving his entire fortune to Harriot, she remained a widow for five years before marrying the ninth duke of St Albans. Harriot became much attached to Angela Georgina, youngest of the six children of Francis and Sophia Burdett: so much so that on her death in 1837 she made Angela, who was then twenty-three, heiress to the considerable amount that remained of her grandfather Thomas Coutts's fortune. Angela, who not unnaturally extended her surname to Burdett-Coutts (◊ John Gray, Alice Grey, and Joseph Carey Merrick), was the wealthiest, and therefore most eligible, spinster in the country; but she stayed single until 1881, when at the age of sixty-six she married the Brooklyn-born William Ashmead-Bartlett, member of parliament for the 'pocket borough' of Eye, in Suffolk, who was her junior by thirty-five years: a discrepancy that was considered excessive by many commentators, employed as such or not. By then, Queen Victoria had conferred a peerage on her under the title of Baroness Burdett-Coutts; it was the first time that a woman had received a peerage for public achievement. And it was richly deserved, for she had been (and would continue to be) extravagantly generous to an extraordinarily diverse collation of causes that she thought to be good; or that others (among them Charles Dickens, who, incidentally, dedicated *Martin Chuzzlewit* to her) pestered her to support.

In the sublime last act of *The Merchant of Venice*, Portia exclaims: 'How far that little candle throws his beams!/So shines a good deed in a naughty world.' Well, then, one could say that Angela Burdett-Coutts' good deeds resembled the top of a birthday cake for Methuselah (who, according to the fifth chapter of the Book of Genesis, lived 969 years). Numbering the arts among deserving causes, she helped to establish Henry Irving (◊ Alice Grey) at the Lyceum Theatre in 1870, and subsequently commissioned several paintings of him, most by Edwin Long. She subsidised David Livingstone's expeditions to Africa, and later those of Henry Morton Stanley.

When she died, at the age of ninety-two, at her London home, 1 Stratton Street, in Mayfair, her body lay in state for two days, and it is reckoned that 30,000 people of all conditions and creeds came to the house to pay their respects. She was accorded burial in Westminster Abbey on 5 January 1907.

1 Proposed epitaph by W(inthrop) M(ackworth) Praed:

> A noble, hasty race he ran,
> Superbly filthy and fastidious;
> He was the world's first gentleman,
> And made the appellation hideous.

Crapper, Thomas

No; though this gentleman, born at Thorne, near Doncaster, in 1837, *was* a sanitary engineer and *did* invent the Valveless Water Waste Preventor, the first flush lavatory to be sold in Great Britain, his name, complete or in part, did *not* become a slang word to do with the act of defecation. 'Crap', with its variations, was part of common English speech centuries before Thomas outcommoded the chamber pot.[1] The circumstantial evidence that he was an eponym is bogus. So is the biography of him, entitled *Flushed with Pride*. That issued from the pen of a japester who, as Otto Titsling, completed a double of hoaxes with *Bust Up*, a short history of the brassiere (an appliance that actually arose stealthily in France towards the end of the sixteenth century, and, crossing the Channel, caught on with royal and noble women, including Elizabeth I, who was uplifted before her death in 1603).

1 Or jerry, a slang-word that may be derived from jeroboam, a large bowl (or a bottle four times the size of a normal champagne one) that gets its name from Jeroboam I, a king of Israel in the ninth century BC, who, according to the eleventh chapter of the first Book of Kings, 'made Israel to sin'. There seems no doubt that the jerrycan, used by servicemen to carry petrol, is so called because of some sort of chamber-pot association.

The critical epithet 'jerry-built', often but not invariably applied to cheap and nasty houses, may have been coined from Jericho, the walls of which came tumbling down when Joshua blew his trumpet. Certainly, things were described as being jerry-built before the Jerry brothers set up as house-builders in Liverpool early in the nineteenth century; perhaps their work nudged the expression into common usage.

Some people spell gerrymander with a j. Wrongly. The

word, first of all meaning to rearrange voting districts in the interests of a particular party or candidate, but now applied to any attempt to bend the truth, is formed from the name of Governor Elbridge *Gerry* (1744–1814) and sala*mander*, near-relation of the newt, whose outline was thought to be similar to the gerrymandered map of Massachusetts in 1811.

Creasey, John

A prolific writer, mainly of detective tales, who, as well as using his own name, employed the pseudonyms of Gordon Ashe, Margaret Cooke, M. E. Cooke, Norman Deane, Elise Fecamps, Robert Caine Frazer, Patrick Gill, Michael Halliday, Charles Hogarth, Brian Hope, Colin Hughes, Kyle Hunt, Abel Mann, Peter Manton, J. J. Marric, James Marsden, Richard Martin, Rodney Mattheson, Anthony Morton, Ken Ranger, Tex Riley, William K. Riley, Henry St John, Jimmy Wilde, and Jeremy Yorke. It is reckoned that he completed 565 books between 1932, when he was twenty-four, just getting into his stride, and 1972, the year before his death.

Crum, George

The almost aptly named cook who, as long ago as 1853, created the potato crisp, a savoury morsel that is now sometimes contaminated with flavours ranging from bacon-and-beans to, I shouldn't be surprised, rhubarb-and-custard, but which, pristine, was initially gingerly offered to and noisily munched by the railroad tycoon Cornelius Vanderbilt, who, in the little spare time he allowed himself, sired thirteen millionaires, and who was nick-named Commodore because of his early interest—financial, of course—in ships. A descendant, Harold Stirling Vanderbilt, won fame as a yachtsman (he successfully defended the America's Cup three times), revised right-of-way rules for sailing vessels (the revisions still apply and are still known as the Vanderbilt Rules), was an expert player of auction bridge[1] (his favourite partner was Joseph Bowne Elwell: (◊ Max Gerlach and Willard Huntingdon Wright), invented a variant on that game, called contract bridge, which he first tried out during a cruise on board the steamship *Finland*, en route from California to Havana via the Panama Canal, in November 1925, and subsequently gave his name to a cup he donated for a national team-of-four contract bridge championship and to a system of bidding.

1 The successor to bridge-whist, which was itself the offspring of common-or-cardroom whist—one of whose early devotees, Lord de Ros, hurriedly left London for the Continent when he was caught fiddling high-value trump-cards into his hand; when he died a few years later, it was suggested that his epitaph should read:

HERE LIES LORD DE ROS—
in confident expectation
of the last trump.

Two other card-playing lords are more relevant to this book.
The second Earl of Yarborough (whose family seat, Brocklesby Park in Lincolnshire, is said to have been the model for Bleak House; ◊ Inspector Charles Frederick Field and Marie Manning) frittered away much of his life, from 1809 until 1862, playing whist; as a side-gamble, he laid odds of 1000–1 against members of his school being dealt a hand containing no card higher than a nine. Now such a hand—or, in some circles, a hand sans trumps—is called a yarborough.
During a marathon card-playing session in 1762, the corrupt and immoral John Montagu, fourth Earl of Sandwich, had his valet bring him supplies of roast beef between slices of bread; although the use of bread in place of cutlery or to prevent greasy fingers was not novel, it was only after stories about the session began to circulate that the sandwich got its name.

Czolgosz, Leon

Booking in at an hotel in Buffalo, New York State, on 6 September 1901, this Polish–American anarchist signed the register as John Doe, presumably choosing that name because he had heard of the old legal fiction of referring to plaintiffs in actions for ejectment (recovery of land) as such, their opponents as Richard Roe; later that day, he assassinated William McKinley of Ohio,[1] twenty-fifth President of the United States. The name John Doe (feminine, Jane) is employed by American policemen, medical examiners and the like as a designation for an unidentified person or corpse.

1 The state that, from soon after the Civil War until the early 1920s, provided Presidents galore: 18th, Ulysses Simpson Grant; 19th, Rutherford Birchard Hayes; 20th, James Abram Garfield (assassinated at Washington railroad station on 2 July 1881 by a disappointed office-seeker, Charles Guiteau); 23rd, Benjamin Harrison; 27th, William Howard Taft; 29th, Warren Gamaliel Harding (whose term of office was, thank the Lord, curtailed— though not before he had littered the English language with Gamalielisms, the most infamous of which was 'normalcy').

Davis, Dwight

A tennis player, renowned for his 'twist' serve, who had the idea of, and donated the silverware for, the Davis Cup, an annual national-team championship based on four singles matches and a doubles. It was contested for the first time in 1900 at Longwood Cricket Club, Boston, Massachusetts, between the United States and Great Britain. The latter team lost.

DeSalvo, Albert Henry

Thirteen times between June 1962 and January 1964, he inveigled his way into the apartments of women living alone in Boston, Massachusetts, and then raped and strangled the occupants, for the latter purpose using a ligature that he subsequently tied in a neat bow beneath the chin. Long before he reached the total of thirteen, he was called, for want of his real name, the Boston Strangler. This was the third of his sobriquets: a month or so before he began murdering for pleasure, he had been released from prison, where he had spent nearly a year for having, as the Measuring Man, conned women in the Harvard area, across the Cambridge River from Boston, into letting him traverse their bodies with a tape-measure, which, so he told the women, was a tool of his trade as a tout for a model agency; and for years, before and during his period as the Measuring Man, and even while he was the Boston Strangler, he was the Green Man—so called because of the green overalls he wore on many of the 300-odd occasions when he attacked women in at least four New England states. In October 1964, DeSalvo—probably as the Green Man rather than as the Boston Strangler—curtailed molestation of a victim, apologised for any inconvenience, and hurriedly made off; as soon as the woman was able to do so, she gave an adequate description of her attacker to the police, and DeSalvo was arrested. The publicity-craving lawyer who volunteered to defend him used a ploy, the result of which was that DeSalvo, instead of being charged with being the Boston Strangler, 'copped a plea' under his Green-Man guise, and was sent to prison for life. The sentence was terminated extrajudicially, probably by a fellow-convict at Walpole State Prison: on 26 November 1973, DeSalvo was found dead in his cell, stabbed through the heart.

Whereas DeSalvo had his nicknames foisted on him, David Berkowitz, a young, apparently father-obsessed resident of Yonkers, New York State, chose his own—either Mr Monster or (the one that pricked the press's fancy) Son of Sam—and used them in catch-me-if-you-can letters to the police while he was on the rampage, indiscriminately knifing and haphazardly firing a .44-calibre gun, in New York City between Christmas Eve of 1975 and 10 August 1977, when he was at last arrested; during that period, he killed six persons and wounded seven more. Like DeSalvo, Berkowitz did not stand trial for murder; he pleaded guilty to various offences, and was sentenced to 365 years in gaol—which, because of the quaint American legal arithmetic, could be diminished to twenty-two years.

Come to think of it, American mass-murderers rarely need to invent their nicknames themselves; newspaper reporters do it for them. For instance, considering only multicidal persons **who** have enjoyed entire impunity, the man who cut up at least ten bodies and distributed the parts in and around Cleveland, Ohio, between 1935 and 1937 was dubbed the Mad Butcher of Kingsbury Run (that place being a gorge, unsavoury long before the first evidences of the butchery were observed there); and the man who in 1968 and '69 killed five persons and left two others dreadfully wounded in San Francisco was given the title of Zodiac on account of the sign, which looked vaguely astrological, that he appended to cryptograms that he sent to local papers, and so approved of the title that he straightway signed himself as such on slightly less incomprehensible messages.

The Yorkshire Ripper (Peter Sutcliffe, who in 1981 was sentenced to life imprisonment for several murders and attempts to murder during the previous six years) is the notable exception to the British journalists' way of giving a name to a series of murders rather than to the unknown person who has committed them. An example is the flurry of eight murders, all of prostitutes, in West London between 1963 and 1965, which were variously christened the Thames-side, Towpath, and Nude-Torso murders. And the uxoricidal George Joseph Smith (also known by the surname of Love), who drowned one wife too many in 1913, received no appellation from Fleet Street, though his crimes were soon headlined as THE BRIDES-IN-THE-BATH CASE.

Donna Lucia d'Alvadorez

A lady from Brazil ('where the nuts come from') who is impersonated by Lord Fancourt Babberley, forced into drag by his fellow Oxford undergraduates Jack Chesney and Charles Wykeham, in Brandon Thomas's farce *Charley's Aunt*, which was first produced at Bury St Edmunds, Suffolk, on 29 February 1892, and in London, at the Royalty Theatre, on 21 December of the same year.

Dufrene, Maurice

In 1919, he and another French interior designer, Paul Follot, founded *Décoration Intérieure Moderne*, which came to be known as DIM. A year or so later, each of them was given control of a decorating department of a Parisian store: Dufrene set up *La Maîtrise* at the Galeries Lafayette, while Follot directed *Pomone* at the Bon Marché. Examples of their work, and that of designers who had boarded their band-wagon, were shown off at the *Exposition des Arts décoratifs* in 1925. The term Art Deco, plucked from the name of the exhibition, was applied to the style; or to what people considered the style to be. In the 1960s, 'art deco' enjoyed a revival, sparked off by junk-merchants in Portobello Road and sustained by those who, not being quite sure of the difference between chic and kitsch, relied on *House & Garden* magazine to say what were the 'in' replacements for a mantel-piece clock that chimed 'Danny Boy' or a flock of plaster geese that winged diagonally over an ex-living-room, now lounge, wall.

Dukinfield, William Claude

Calling himself W. C. Fields, he became a star of vaudeville (at first as a comedy juggler) and musical comedy, and then, in the mid-1920s, began making films, many of which he wrote himself, using such pseudonyms as Mahatma Kane Jeeves and

Otis Criblecoblis. In many respects, he played himself (he said that he smiled as soon as he got up in the morning: 'Get it over'), creating humour from a hatred of children and pets and from paranoia about policemen and bank managers (he claimed to have some seven hundred bank accounts, many in fictitious names). Since Christmas was one of his hates, there is a certain irony in the fact that he died on Christmas Day, 1946. He had chosen an epitaph: 'On the whole, I'd rather be in Philadelphia.'

Duplessis, Marie

A French woman who, after earning a meagre living as, successively, a corset-maker and a sales assistant in a milliner's shop, found her true vocation as a whore, initially indiscriminately to the Parisian hoi polloi, and then, when word filtered upwards as to the satisfaction she gave, to aristocrats and successful artists, who kept her in fine style and allowed her to over-indulge her true passion, which was for flowers, specially camellias. Despite the apartmental flora, she had a grey life. And a short one: she died, either from consumption (the romantics' diagnosis) or from a Gallic[1] disease (syphilis?[2]), in 1847, when she was twenty-three. One of her bereaved clients, Alexandre Dumas *fils*,[3] straightway settled down to immortalise her as Marguerite[4] Gautier in *La Dame aux Camélias*, a novel that was published a year after her death. The story was set to music by Giuseppe Verdi, whose opera *La Traviata* ('The Lady Gone Astray'), libretto by Francesco Maria Piave, was first performed, in Venice, in 1853, and has formed the basis of several films: the first (1912) starring Sarah Bernhardt (real name, Bernard), repeating bits and pieces of her stage portrayal of Marguerite; the most memorable, the 1936 version, with Greta Garbo (◊ Greta Gustafsson) as the dame and Robert Taylor (who was actually Spangler Arlington Brough) playing Armand Duval, Dumas *fils*' fictionalisation of himself; and the most detestable, something called *Camille 2000* (1969), in which Marguerite was modernised into a junkie.

The camellia flower, and the evergreen shrub that bears it, is named after Georg Josef Kamel, also known as Camellis, a Moravian Jesuit who, towards the end of the eighteenth century, went to the Philippines as a missionary, created a garden of indigenous flowers and herbs, and sent records of the plants' growth to London, for publication in the *Philosophical Transactions* of the Royal Society. The camellia was one of the many plants christened and classified by the Swedish naturalist Carl von Linné (latinised to Carolus Linnaeus), whose system of biological nomenclature, giving both a generic and a specific name to species, is still used.

1 A wag has described the Eiffel Tower as the supreme Gallic symbol. It was built by Gustave Eiffel, who earlier, in 1874, had designed the framework for the Statue of Liberty—which is the work of the Alsatian sculptor Frédéric-August Bartholdi, who used his mother as the model. The idea for the statue came from the French, who wanted to commemorate their alliance with the United States during the War for Independence; the French promised to underwrite the statue itself, the Americans the pedestal, but funds ran out during the construction, and completion of the work was only due to a fund-raising campaign led by (◊)Joseph Pulitzer, the owner and editor of the New York *World*.

2 The title of Fracastoro's Latin poem of 1530, whose hero Syphilus is infected.

3 Alexandre Dumas *père*'s doctor, a firm believer that 'early to bed and early to rise/makes a man healthy, wealthy and wise' (rather than that, as James Thurber had it, 'early to rise and early to bed/makes a male healthy and wealthy and dead'), persuaded him to eat an apple a day at seven o'clock in the morning under the Arc de Triomphe.

4 In case you are wondering, the ox-eye daisy and other single chrysanthemums are not named after a particular Marguerite. The French name for the daisy is *marguerite*, derived, via the Latin, from the Greek *margarītēs*: pearl.

Edalji, George

Peter Shaffer's play *Equus* (Latin for horse) was first produced by the English National Theatre at the Old Vic in 1973; three years later, that production, a brilliant one, was re-created by its director John Dexter for presentation in the West End, and ran successfully at the Albery Theatre.[1] The production was even more successful on Broadway, where it notched up 1,209 performances, the play itself having become the first to win all four of the major annual awards: the Tony (◊ Oscar Pierce), the New York Critics' Award, the Outer Circle Critics' Award, and the Drama Desk Award. The play has been performed in most other civilised countries, and an unsatisfactory film of it was released in 1977. In 'A Note on the Play', printed in the programmes of the London presentations, and no doubt elsewhere, Peter Shaffer wrote:

> One weekend over two years ago, I was driving with a friend through bleak countryside. We passed a stable. Suddenly he was reminded by it of an alarming crime which he had heard about recently at a dinner party in London. He knew only one horrible detail, and his complete mention of it could barely have lasted a minute—but it was enough to arouse in me an intense fascination.

The act had been committed several years before by a highly disturbed young man. It had deeply shocked a local bench of magistrates. It lacked, finally, any coherent explanation. A few months later my friend died. I could not verify what he had said, or ask him to expand it. He had given me no name, no place, and no time. I don't think he knew them. All I possessed was his report of a dreadful event, and the feeling it engendered in me. I knew very strongly that I wanted to interpret it in some entirely personal way. I had to create a mental world in which the deed could be made comprehensible. Every person and incident in *Equus* is of my own invention, save the crime itself: and even that I modified to accord with what I feel to be acceptable theatrical proportion. I am grateful now that I have never received confirmed details of the 'real' story, since my concern has been more and more with a different kind of exploration. . . .

Perhaps the 'real' story—many times more than second-hand, and therefore amended from the source by the time it reached the ears of Mr Shaffer's friend—is that concerning George Edalji. With this sort of story, it is hard, foolhardy even, to assign a starting date. For convenience, let us say 1903. By then, George Edalji's father, a Parsee converted to Christianity, had been for nearly thirty years the vicar of Great Wyrley, a village in a mining district of Staffordshire. During that time, Shapurji Edalji, his English wife, and their three children had suffered from practical jokes—for instance, the insertion of bogus advertisements under their name in a local paper—and had received poison-pen letters; for some reason, almost certainly racialist and probably having something to do with the fact that George Edalji, the eldest of the children, had curiously bulging eyes that made him look rather like a goblin, the Chief Constable of Staffordshire, Captain the Hon. George Alexander Anson, was convinced, despite the absence of supporting evidence, that George was the culprit. Early in 1903, there was a spate of horrifying killings and maimings of horses and cattle in fields around Great Wyrley; some kind of sharp shallow instrument was used to rip open the animals' stomachs. Anonymous letters sent to the police and to local residents named the criminal as George Edalji, who was then twenty-seven, employed as a solicitor by a practice in Birmingham, whither he travelled from his father's vicarage each working day. The local police, egged on by Captain Anson, came to the paradoxical conclusion that the letter-writer was George Edalji himself, and got a charlatan graphologist to confirm that conclusion; there is reason to believe that some of the evidence tenuously linking Edalji with the crimes, found during a search of the vicarage, was not present prior to the searchers' arrival. Edalji was charged, found guilty, and sentenced to seven years' imprisonment. While he was in gaol, crimes similar to those for which he was being punished plagued the farmers of Great Wyrley. When he had served three years, he was suddenly released; no explanation was given; his name had not been cleared.

Soon afterwards, he published an account of what had happened to him in a paper called the *Umpire*, and this was seen by Arthur Conan Doyle: 'As I read, the unmistakable accent of truth forced itself upon my attention, and I realised that I was in the presence of an appalling tragedy, and that I was called upon to do what I could to set it right.'

And so, nature imitating art, Conan Doyle became Sherlock Holmes (♢ Dr Joseph Bell). After reading accounts of the outrages and of the trial, he visited the scenes of the crimes, and in January 1907 arranged to meet Edalji in the foyer of the Grand Hotel, Charing Cross:

> The first sight which I ever had of Mr George Edalji was enough to convince me of the extreme improbability of his being guilty, and to suggest some of the reasons why he had been suspected.
>
> He had come to my hotel by appointment; but I had been delayed, and he was passing the time by reading the paper. I recognised my man by his dark face, so I stood and observed him. He held the paper close to his eyes and rather sideways, proving not only a high degree of myopia but marked astigmatism. The idea of such a man scouring fields at night and assaulting cattle while avoiding the watching police was ludicrous to anyone who can imagine what the world looks like to eyes with myopia of eight dioptres.

A few days later, on 12 January, Conan Doyle published the first of a series of articles on the case in the *Daily Telegraph*: 'As I bargained that they should be non-copyright, they were largely transferred to other papers, sold for a penny at street kerbs and generally had a very wide circulation, so that England soon rang with the wrongs of George Edalji.'

The articles, which left the police case in tatters, caused

some of the mighty in the land to side with Conan Doyle; to seek redress for Edalji. The government set up a commission to examine the case and report. Meanwhile, Conan Doyle was collecting evidence against the man he believed to be the true culprit. Though the case he built was strong—and was, in his mind, made stronger by the fact that he began to receive anonymous letters similar in handwriting and style to those that had implicated Edalji—even he was constrained by the laws of libel, and so never named the man but referred to him simply as X. As the man has been dead for some years, he can now be identified as Royden Sharp, a native of Great Wyrley, several years younger than George Edalji, and, at the time the mutilations began, apprenticed to a butcher.

The three commissioners (one of whom was a cousin of Captain Anson) decided that, although George Edalji had been wrongly convicted of horse-maiming, and therefore should be pardoned, there was insufficient evidence to show that he had *not* written the letters—and anyway he had 'to some extent brought his troubles on himself'—and so he was to receive no compensation for his years in prison. Conan Doyle considered this 'a wretched decision'; likewise, the Law Society, the body governing solicitors, who at once re-admitted George Edalji to the Roll, with leave to practise.

Conan Doyle had more success, though it took him many years and much money to achieve, in putting right the apparent wrong of the conviction and confinement of Oscar Slater for the murder of Miss Marion Gilchrist in her flat in Glasgow on the night of 21 December 1908. The crime was committed in the space of ten minutes or so, while Miss Gilchrist's servant Helen Lambie was out, buying an evening paper. Lambie returned to find another tenant of the house standing by the closed door of the flat, concerned about the commotion he had heard from within. As Lambie opened the door, a man, seemingly calm, walked past her and the other tenant, and left the house. Miss Gilchrist, who was eighty-two, reputedly wealthy, lay dead on the floor of the living-room, which was stippled with blood that had coursed from the wounds on her scalp and face.

The policemen who investigated the crime sought to trace a crescent-shaped diamond brooch that, according to Helen Lambie, was missing from the flat, and on Christmas Day they learnt that a thirty-seven-year-old German-Jew named Leschziner, more widely known under the alias of Oscar Slater, had been trying to sell a pawn-ticket for such a brooch. Visiting Slater's lodgings, used by him in his trade as a pimp, they found that he had left for Liverpool, to embark for America on Boxing Day. The Liverpool police were not alerted soon enough to forestall what their Glasgow brethren were already calling 'Slater's flight from justice'. Actually, if someone had bothered to check, it would have been discovered that Slater had made arrangements for the trip to America long before the murder; also that his transaction with a pawn-broker had taken place a whole month prior to the crime: his 'flight' was not a flight at all, and it was unlikely that the brooch he had pawned had ever been in the possession of Marion Gilchrist. Following his arrival in New York, the Glasgow police began extradition proceedings; these were attended by, among other Glaswegians, Helen Lambie—who, 'going by [Slater's] walk and height, his dark hair, and the side of his face', identified him as the man she had seen leaving the flat. He was returned to Scotland, tried for the murder, found guilty by a majority of the jurors, and sentenced to death; reprieved from that penalty, he was ordered to be detained in prison for the rest of his natural life.

After his experience with the Edalji case, Conan Doyle had no wish to be involved in anything similar. But in 1910, following the appearance of *Trial of Oscar Slater*, edited by William Roughead and printed and published by William Hodge & Co. of Edinburgh as a title in the series of 'Notable Scottish Trials',[2] he 'went into the matter most reluctantly . . . When I glanced at the facts, I saw that it was an even worse case than the Edalji one, and that this unhappy man had in all probability no more to do with the murder for which he had been condemned than I had.'

With William Roughead and a Glasgow newspaper reporter named William Park, Conan Doyle sought to remedy the apparent miscarriage of justice; one of his first important actions was the publication in 1912 of a slim volume called *The Case of Oscar Slater*. Assistance came from an unexpected source: John Thompson Trench, a detective-lieutenant of the Glasgow police force, who had taken part in the murder investigation. He stated that, shortly after the discovery of the crime, Helen Lambie had told senior officers that the man she had seen leaving the flat was known to her: *known by name*, for he was one of Miss Gilchrist's most frequent visitors. For some reason, the officers involved had ignored this information; more than that, according to Trench, they had virtually dictated Lambie's written statement. Trench was ordered to disavow what he had said, and when he refused to do so, was dismissed from the force without a pension.

The name of the man referred to by Lambie (who in 1927, when she was living in America, confirmed Trench's statement) was never divulged in reports of hearings; nor, of course, in any of the several and diverse writings on the case by Conan Doyle, Roughead, and Park. Invariably, the letters A.B. were substituted. But since 4 July 1964, when the man died, aged eighty-eight, there has been no reason of law for keeping his identity secret. A scion of a wealthy Glasgow family, he was Dr Francis James Charteris; in the period around Marion Gilchrist's murder, he ran a general practice from his home in Great Western Road, close to the scene of the crime. In 1920 he was made professor of materia medica at St Andrew's University, where he remained until his retirement in 1948, having been for twenty years dean of the faculty of medicine.

I have said that in 1927 John Trench's statement was confirmed by Helen Lambie. This sparked off press activity, as a result of which another important prosecution witness recanted much of her evidence. Within a fortnight, Slater was released. The official announcement carried no suggestion that he had been wrongly convicted; there was no mention of compensation for the eighteen and a half years he had spent in Peterhead Prison. Conan Doyle instigated, and guaranteed the costs of, an appeal within the High Court of Justiciary, Edinburgh. He must have experienced *déjà vu* of a most depressing kind when the appeal judges, like the commissioners in the Edalji affair, came up with a compromise decision—illustrating, it seemed to him, 'the determination to admit nothing which inculpates another official'. They concluded that the jury's verdict had been reasonable and that none of the new evidence affected the issue—but they discerned sufficient misdirection in the instructions given to the jury by the presiding judge Lord Guthrie (who was now dead) to warrant the setting aside of the verdict.

Slater received £6,000 as compensation. Directly after his discharge from prison, he had written a note of gratitude that began, 'Sir Conan Doyle, you breaker of my shackels, you lover of truth for justice sake, I thank you from the bottom of my heart. . . .', but when Conan Doyle suggested repayment of money that he and others had spent during the long fight, Slater refused to part with a penny.

The Slater affair ended not with a bang but with rancour. Conan Doyle's final communication with the man he had helped to free was an abrupt note: 'If you are indeed quite responsible for your actions, then you are the most ungrateful as well as the most foolish person whom I have ever known.'

1 Standing back-to-back with Wyndham's, it too was built by Sir Charles Wyndham (◊ Harvey's note 1), who used the same architect, W. G. R. Sprague, for both theatres. It was called the New Theatre from when it opened in 1903 until the end of 1972, when it was renamed as a tribute to the late Sir Bronson Albery, a son of Lady Wyndham (Mary Moore) by a previous marriage, who was the manager for many years. In the early 20s, the theatre was leased by Sybil Thorndike for a series of productions which included the first (March 1924) of Shaw's *Saint Joan*; and later in that decade, *The Constant Nymph*, adapted from the best-selling novel by its author Margaret Kennedy and the play's director Basil Dean, ran for nearly 600 performances, first with Noël Coward and later with John Gielgud in the role of Lewis Dodd. Gielgud was again associated with the New in the 30s: for instance, as Richard II in *Richard of Bordeaux* by Gordon Daviot (the playwriting pseudonym of Elizabeth MacKintosh, who used her great- great-grand-mother's name, Josephine Tey, for all but the first of her detective novels, the most ingenious of which is *The Daughter of Time*, which treats Richard III as a suspect in a whodunit); as Hamlet in what may have been the longest run of Shakespeare's play; and as Romeo or Mercutio, alternating the roles with Laurence Olivier, in the 1935 production of *Romeo and Juliet*. In 1941, when the Old Vic Theatre in Waterloo Road was damaged by German bombing, the New became the London headquarters of the Old Vic Company and of the opera and ballet companies of Sadler's Wells; from 1944 until 1950, the theatre was the home solely of the Old Vic Company, headed by Olivier and Ralph Richardson. Subsequent notable productions include T(homas) S(tearns) Eliot's *The Cocktail Party*, which ran for more than 300 performances from May 1950, and *Oliver!*, Lionel Bart's musical version of *Oliver Twist*, which occupied the theatre for most of the 60s.

2 Inaugurated in 1905 by Harry Hodge, son of the founder of the printing firm, and himself an official shorthand-writer in the Scottish courts; by 1911, eleven volumes, each cased in green

cloth, had been published. It was during that year that Hodge—prompted, no doubt, by an awareness that the number of truly notable Scottish trials was relatively small—started a series of 'Notable *English* Trials' which differed in appearance from the Scottish series by being cased in red cloth. Nine 'Notable English Trials' appeared in just over three years; then came the First World War, during which only one title, *Trial of Sir Roger Casement*, was added to the series. (Conan Doyle was a leader of an unsuccessful campaign to save Casement from execution for treachery.) 1920 saw the appearance of three more 'Notable English Trials', including *Trial of the Wainwrights*, which was published after the death of its editor H(enry) B(rodribb) Irving, the actor, crime historian, and founder member of Our Society (◊ Richard Gordon Parry). The series title was rather a misnomer in relation to one or two of the cases that were covered. Lord Lovat's trial for treason in 1747, though held at Westminster Hall, was far more notable to the Scots, as marking the end of the clan period in the Highlands, than to the English; and as for the Annesley case (1742–5), which consisted of the long-drawn-out attempt by James Annesley to convince *Irish* courts that he was the legitimate son and heir of Arthur Lord Altham, some ingenuity, not to say sophistry, was required of Andrew Lang, the editor of the volume, to explain its inclusion in the series: 'As the nature of the law and its administration was not that of the Brehons, those ancient Hibernian jurists, but that of the English Courts, it is hoped that the circumstances may plead in favour of the appearance of the case among English Trials.'

In 1921, Hodge decided that unification was the answer to his demarcation problems, and the 'Notable *British* Trials' were born, with the red binding of the English series preferred to the Scottish green. Between the wars, forty-four titles were published; in addition, most of the titles that had appeared in the Scottish and English series were rechristened 'Notable British Trials'. No titles were published during the Second World War, but in 1946 the series continued with *Trial of William Joyce* ('Lord Haw-Haw' to British radio-listeners to whom he had broadcast German propaganda from Nazi-occupied territory). Harry Hodge died in the following year, but his son James, who had been responsible for the series since 1937, added fifteen more titles. The eighty-third, and last, new title, *Trial of August Sangret*, was published in 1959. Harry Hodge's wish that 'in the end there would be a valuable record of the development of the criminal law and of the progress of science, especially medical science,' was certainly realised.

Einstein, Isadore

An interminably long-running television series that, week after week, year after year, recounted adventures that had never befallen Eliot Ness and his Untouchable[1] posse of FBI agents during the latter years of the 'noble experiment' of Prohibition must have given millions of viewers the impression that the real Untouchables were the upholders of the Volstead[2] Act most celebrated in the public prints of the time; also that, man for man, Mr Ness and his confederates achieved greater success in the war against booze than other Prohibition agents. Both impressions were as false as the stories cobbled together by the television script-writers.

Right at the start of Prohibition, which came into effect on 16 January 1920, Isadore Einstein, a forty-year-old, bald-headed denizen of New York's Lower East Side, only five foot five inches tall but tipping the scales at 225 pounds, gave up his job as a clerk in a post office to become a Prohibition agent; and, a few weeks later, he persuaded his friend Morris Smith, who was ten pounds heavier but a mite less short than himself, to put a relative in charge of his cigar store and join him. Izzy and Moe became perhaps the most picturesque, probably the most successful, and certainly the most publicised law-enforcing double-act of all time. During one twelve-hour Sunday shift, they established a record by raiding seventy-one speakeasies: an achievement made all the more remarkable by the fact that their progress from one establishment to another was impeded by an accompanying horde of newspaper reporters—who had been apprised of the record-breaking attempt by the record attempters, both of whom revelled in their shared celebrity. Over a period of five years, The Exploits of Izzy and Moe engrossed miles of newspaper columns, devoured gallons of ink, and tickled dry and wet readers alike. Admittedly, they concentrated most of their efforts on small-time bootleggers; but still the statistics of their purge are staggering: 4,392 arrests, and confiscation of five million bottles of booze, valued at $15m, besides an uncounted, being uncountable, multitude of kegs and barrels. They must, at times, have been exhausted, yet, loving their work, they never let up for a minute, not even when they were supposed to be off-duty. It is hard to say which of their swoops most caught the public fancy: perhaps the one that, starting in the Columbus-Circle area of Broadway and finishing up at the other end of the Great White Way, caused the temporary closure (chiefly for repairs) of such swell-elegant establishments as the Beaux Arts, Reisenweber's, Shanley's, and the Ted Lewis Club. But, as with that of other great folk-heroes, their success, when it went to their Heads, created envy and resentment. In the summer of 1925, Izzy and Moe were summoned to Washington to appear before a board of high Prohibition enforcement officials, none of whom had been mentioned in the press except in connection with his birth or marriage. They were told that if they didn't assume a low profile, they would be sacked. Subsequently, they tried, really they did, to stay out of the papers. But it was no good: when they kept their intentions secret and refused to give interviews after the event, reporters simply fabricated Izzy-and-Moe stories. In November, it was announced that they had turned in their gold badges—'thereby firing ourselves,' muttered Izzy. They both went into the insurance business, though not as a team, and prospered: especially Izzy, who by the time he died in 1938, owned a fine house and a large portfolio of high-yielding shares, and was happy in the knowledge that all four of his sons were successful lawyers.

Perhaps, in terms of public esteem, Izzy and Moe were fortunate that they did not survive longer in the civil service, for not long after they fired themselves, the anti-Prohibition movement got into full swing, and the press, bending with the wind, more often criticised than glamorised the activities of enforcement agents. In 1929, the New York *Times* published a verse applauding the sacking of fourteen Prohibition administrators in New Jersey:

> One by one they interfere
> With those Jersey tides of beer;
> Manfully they face the flood,

Then, alas! their name is mud.[3]
Heroes for a little day,
One by one they pass away.

1 In the sense of *incorruptible*—which, prefixed by 'sea-green', was the word used by Thomas Carlyle (◊ William Weare) to describe Maximilien-François-Marie-Isidore de Robespierre, a leader of the French Revolution, particularly in the period (1793–4) of the Jacobin republic.

2 Andrew Joseph Volstead, a tobacco-chewing, shoebrush-moustached Republican Congressman from Yellow Medicine County, Minnesota, wrote the National Prohibition Act.

3 ◊ Dr Samuel Mudd.

Elgar, Caroline Alice

The subject, under her initials, of the first of the *Enigma Variations*, composed by her husband in 1899, when he was forty-two. The Variation, carrying on from the theme without a break, includes romantic and delicate airs. Elgar said that 'those who knew C.A.E. will understand this reference to one whose life was a romantic and delicate inspiration'.

The other Variations:

II:H.D.S.-P. Hew David Steuart-Powell, an amateur pianist who for many years played chamber music with Elgar (violin) and Basil G. Nevinson (cello). 'His characteristic diatonic run over the keys before beginning to play is here humorously travestied in the semi-quaver passages; these should suggest a Toccata, but chromatic beyond H.D.S.-P.'s liking.'

III:R.B.T. Richard Baxter Townshend, a writer of children's books, several of which feature a character known as Tenderfoot. 'The Variation has a reference to R.B.T.'s presenta-

tion of an old man in some amateur theatricals—the low voice
flying off occasionally into "soprano" timbre.'

IV:W.M.B. W. M. Baker, a country squire. 'In the days of
horses and carriages it was more difficult than in these days of
petrol to arrange the carriages for the day to suit a large number
of guests. This variation was written after the host had, with a
slip of paper in his hand, *forcibly* read out the arrangements for
the day and hurriedly left the music-room with an inadvertent
bang of the door.'

V:R.P.A. Richard Penrose Arnold, son of Matthew Arnold,
the poet and critic, and grandson of Thomas Arnold, headmaster
of Rugby School. 'A great lover of music which he played (on
the pianoforte) in a self-taught manner, evading difficulties but
suggesting in a mysterious way the real feeling. His serious
conversation was continually broken up by whimsical and witty
remarks.'

VI:Ysobel. Isabel Fitton, an amateur viola player living in
Malvern, close to the Elgar's home.

VII:Troyte. Arthur Troyte Griffith, a Malvern architect.
'The uncouth rhythm of the drums and lower strings was really
suggested by some maladroit essays to play the pianoforte; later
the strong rhythm suggests the attempts of the instructor [Elgar]
to make something like order out of the chaos, and the final
despairing "slam" records that the effort proved to be vain.'

VIII:W.N. Winifred Norbury: 'Really suggested by an
eighteenth-century house. The gracious personalities of the ladies
are sedately shown. W.N. was more connected with music than
others of the family, and her initials head the movement; to justify
this position a little suggestion of a characteristic laugh is given.'

IX:Nimrod. 'The variations are not all "portraits"; some
represent only a mood, while others recall an incident known
only to two persons. Something ardent and mercurial, in addition to the slow movement (no. IX), would have been needful to
portray the character and temperament of A[ugust] J[ohannes]
Jaeger (*Nimrod*). [In the tenth chapter of the Book of Genesis,
Nimrod, son of Cush, is called 'the mighty hunter before the
Lord'; the German for hunter is Jäger.]

'The variation bearing this name is the record of a long
summer evening talk, when my friend discoursed eloquently on
the slow movements of Beethoven, and said that no one could
approach Beethoven at his best in this field, a view with which I

cordially concurred. It will be noticed that the opening bars are made to suggest the slow movement of the Eighth Sonata (*Pathétique*).

'Jaeger was for years the dear friend, the valued adviser and the stern critic of many musicians besides the writer; his place has been occupied but never filled.'

X:Dorabella. Dora Penny. 'Intermezzo. The pseudonym is adopted from Mozart's *Cosi fan tutti*. The movement suggests a dance-like lightness.'

XI: G. R. S. George Robertson Sinclair, Mus. D., once organist of Hereford Cathedral. 'The variation, however, has nothing to do with organs or cathedrals, or, except remotely, with G. R. S. The first few bars were suggested by his great bulldog Dan (a well-known character) falling down the steep bank into the river Wye (bar 1); his paddling up stream to find a landing place (bars 2 and 3); and his rejoicing bark on landing (2nd half of bar 5). G. R. S. said, "Set that to music." I did.'

XII: B. G. N. Basil G. Nevinson (see II). 'The variation is a tribute to a very dear friend whose scientific and artistic attainments, and the whole-hearted way they were put at the disposal of his friends, particularly endeared him to the writer.'

*XIII: ***.* Lady Mary Lygon.[1] 'The asterisks take the place of the name of a lady who was, at the time of the composition, on a sea voyage. [Probably Helen Weaver, with whom Elgar had had an ill-fated love affair fifteen years earlier.] The drums suggest the distant throb of the engines of a liner, over which the clarinet quotes a phrase from Mendelssohn's "Calm Sea and Prosperous Voyage".'

XIV: E. D. U. Elgar himself. 'Written at a time when friends were dubious and generally discouraging as to the composer's musical future, this variation is merely to show what E. D. U. (a paraphrase of a fond name) intended to do. References made to Var. I (C. A. E.) and to Var. IX (Nimrod), two great influences on the life and art of the composer, are entirely fitting to the intention of the piece.'

'The whole of the work is summed up in the triumphant, broad presentation of the theme in the major.'

The Variations were composed between 5 and 9 February 1899, and given their first performance, conducted by Hans Richter, at St James's Hall, on 19 June of that year.

1 Of the Beauchamp family, later members of which may have become the Marchmains in Evelyn Waugh's *Brideshead Revisited* (◊ Rayner Heppenstall note).

Enos, William Berkeley

A dance director, under the name of Busby Berkeley, whose fill-the-screen production numbers in Hollywood musicals of the 1930s and early '40s are treasured by kitsch enthusiasts. His most renowned effect was created by treating chorus girls or swimmers as bits in a kaleidoscope, and filming their movements with an overhead camera.

Everest, Sir George

Until 1865, the highest mountain in the world was known—to the British, at any rate—simply as Peak XV; but in that year, Sir Andrew Waugh, Surveyor-General of India, suggested that it should be named after his immediate predecessor. The suggestion didn't meet with unanimous approval. Even Sir George Everest himself had qualms, which he expressed at a meeting of the Royal Geographical Society in 1857:

He must confess there were objections to his name being given to this mountain which did not strike everybody. One was that his name was not pronounceable by the native of India. The name could not be written in Persian or Hindu.

A number of influential mountaineers and geographers felt that one of the local names for the peak should be adopted; but they were at odds, some arguing for one local name, others for another. Devadhunga, meaning 'the abode of deity', was mooted; then some German explorers reported that the peak was called Gaurisankar in Nepal and Chingopamari in Tibet. The anti-'Everest' mutterings continued until 1903, when it was established that none of the natives referred to the mountain as Devadhunga and that the peak called Gaurisankar or Chingopamari was thirty-six miles away. The mutterings started up again a few years later, when it was learned that, without much doubt, the natives called the mountain Chomolungma. By then, however, Everest was indelibly on the map—though a few latterday cartographers compromise, calling the massif Chomolungma and the peak Mount Everest.

No one can be sure of the height of the mountain; the present 'official' figure is 29,028 feet, but that will almost certainly be amended as more refined measuring equipment and techniques are introduced. These may, by the way, show that, after all the fuss about climbing Everest (◊ George Herbert Leigh Mallory), it isn't the highest mountain in the world.

Field, Inspector Charles Frederick

Charles Dickens was an enthusiastic public relations man for the Metropolitan Police, set up in 1829 by Sir Robert Peel (and therefore known as bobbies or peelers). He hero-worshipped detectives: one in particular, Inspector Field, who appeared undisguised or wearing the flimsy pseudonym of 'Wield' in articles in *Household Words*, and as Inspector Bucket, probably the first police-detective in English fiction,[1] in *Bleak House*. No one who has read that novel will have forgotten Mr Bucket and his fat forefinger:

> When Mr Bucket has a matter of pressing interest under his consideration, the fat forefinger seems to rise to the dignity of a familiar demon. He puts it to his ears, and it whispers information; he puts it to his lips, and it enjoins him to secrecy; he rubs it over his nose, and it sharpens his scent; he shakes it before a guilty man, and it charms him to destruction. The Augurs of the Detective Temple invariably predict that when Mr Bucket and that finger are in much conference, a terrible avenger will be heard of before long.
>
> Otherwise mildly studious in his observation of human nature, on the whole a benignant philosopher not disposed to be severe upon the follies of mankind, Mr Bucket pervades a vast

number of houses, and strolls about an infinity of streets: to outward appearance rather languishing for want of an object. He is in the friendliest condition towards his species, and will drink with most of them. He is free with his money, affable in his manners, innocent in his conversation—but, through the placid stream of his life, there glides an under-current of forefinger.

1 In 1856, four years after *Bleak House* began to appear, William Russell published his *Recollections of a Detective Police Office*, which purported to be the autobiography of a detective of the Metropolitan Police, but which was, in fact, fiction: probably the first detective novel in the English language.

Fielding, Fred

According to H. R. Haldeman, an authority on the Watergate scandal, Mr Fielding, a White House aide on the legal counsel's staff, was the man who, secretly in an underground garage, gave information on the dirty tricks of the Nixon administration to the *Washington Post* reporter Bob Woodward, who referred to him as Deep Throat—that being the title of a pornographic film that Woodward's partner Carl Bernstein had paid to see as relaxation from the task of President-toppling.

Flanagan, Monsignor Edward

In 1917, he founded Boys' Town, a variation on reformatories for young delinquents, near Omaha, Nebraska. A wag has suggested that his motto, 'There is no such thing as a bad boy', was coined by Oscar Wilde. Spencer Tracy won an Oscar for his portrayal of Flanagan in the 1938 film *Boys' Town*. (Tracy, winner in 1937 for his performance in *Captains Courageous*—based on Rudyard Kipling's novel—is the only actor to have received the award in consecutive years; his friend and most frequent co-star, Katharine Hepburn, is the only actress to have done so, with *Guess Who's Coming to Dinner* in 1967 and *The Lion in Winter* the following year.)

Flegenheimer, Arthur

From *The Pleasures of Murder*, an anthology published in 1983:

Mr Flegenheimer, who was a native of the Bronx,[1] New York City, preferred to be called after Dutch Schultz, the most notorious member of the Frog Hollow gang of ruffians that had caused trouble in the borough towards the end of the nineteenth century.

Taking advantage of Prohibition, Mr Flegenheimer prospered exceedingly as a vintner to the denizens of the Bronx and Manhattan; his bank balances were augmented by other illegal trades. He took a Draconian[2] attitude towards those who rubbed him up the wrong way, and was responsible for the untimely deaths of Jack 'Legs' Diamond ('Just another punk caught with his hands in my pocket' was his post-Legs'-mortem comment), Vincent 'Mad Dog' Coll, Bo Weinberg, *et al.*

However, in 1935, when he insisted on ridding the city of Thomas E. Dewey, the special prosecutor for organised crime who was actually doing some prosecuting, certain exalted members of the newly-constituted 'national crime syndicate', each no more entrancing than Mr Flegenheimer, felt that the proposed execution would be bad for business, so prevented it by arranging for the biter to be bit while he was dining (to be precise, he was in the lavatory when the shooting occurred) at the Palace Chophouse in Newark, New Jersey. But for the poetry of their names, it would not be worth mentioning that his companions, Lulu Rosencranz, Abe 'Misfit' Landau and Otto 'Abbadabba' Berman, were slain by other bullets from the same gun, wielded by an enthusiastic marksman called Charlie 'The Bug' Workman.

Mr Flegenheimer, being not yet deceased, was trundled to a nearby hospital, where a prodigal amount of perfectly good blood was transfused into him. Here are some of his dying words—which, as Dwight MacDonald has observed, are an unwitting parody of the style of Gertrude Stein.[3]

Oh oh dog biscuit. And when he is happy he doesn't get snappy. Please please to do this. Then Henry, Frankie, you didn't meet him. You didn't even meet me. The glove will fit what I say. Oh! Kai-Yi, Kai-Yi. Sure, who cares when you are through? How do you know this? Well, then, oh cocoa know, thinks he is a grandpa again. He is jumping around. No hoboe and phoboe. I think it means the same thing. . . . Oh mamma I can't go on through with it. Please oh! And then he clips me. Come on. Cut that out. We don't owe a nickel. Hold it instead hold it against him. . . . How many good ones and how many bad ones? Please I had nothing with him. He was a cowboy in one of the seven days a week fights. No business no hangout no friends nothing. Just what you pick up and what you need . . . This is a habit I get. Sometimes I give it up and sometimes I don't. . . . The sidewalk was in trouble and the bears were in trouble and I broke it up. Please put me in that room. Please keep him in control . . . Please mother don't tear don't rip. That is something that shouldn't be spoken about. Please get me up, my friends, please look out, the shooting is a bit wild and that kind of shooting saved a man's life . . . Please mother you pick me up now. Do you know me? No, you don't scare me. They are Englishmen and they are a type I don't know who is best they or us. Oh sir get the doll a roofing. You can play jacks and girls do that with a soft ball and play tricks with it. No no and it is no. It is confused and it says no. A boy has never wept nor dashed a thousand kim. And you hear me? . . . All right look out look out. Oh my memory is all gone. A work relief. Police. Who gets it? I don't know and I don't want to know but look out. It can be traced. He changed for the worst. Please look out. My fortunes have changed and come back and went back since that. . . . They dyed my shoes. Open those shoes. . . . Police mamma Helen mother please take me out. I will settle the indictment. Come on open the soap duckets. The chimney sweeps. Talk to the sword. Shut up you got a big mouth! Please help me get up. Henry Max come over here. French Canadian bean soup. I want to pay. Let them leave me alone.

Insisting on that final wish, Arthur Flegenheimer, a man who by taking another's name had given all Dutchmen a bad one, said no more before he expired, two hours later, at twenty minutes to nine. A rogue was a rogue was a dead rogue.

1 Named after Johannes Bronck, a Danish émigré employed by the Dutch West India Company, who in 1639 became the first settler in the area.

2 Draco, an archon (one of the nine chief magistrates) at Athens in 621 BC, had no time for namby-pamby things like suspended sentences and small fines. (And namby-pamby was the nickname applied to Ambrose Philips, whose simple odes to children were considered wishy-washy by eighteenth-century Tories; there is some uncertainty, but it appears that the nickname was applied to Philips by the poet and musician Henry Carey, who claimed to be the composer of 'Sally in Our Alley', and of 'Namby-Pamby', which ridiculed Philips. By the way, Wishy-Washy is the name of a character in the pantomime *Aladdin*, which is based on a burlesque by H. J. Byron which bestowed on the hero's mother the name of Widow Twankey—derived from twankay green tea, the cargo of many of the clippers that at that time, the 1860s, raced home from the East.)

3 ◊ Alice Babette Toklas.

Flush

A red cocker spaniel who in 1842, or thereabouts, was presented by the novelist Miss (Mary Russell) Mitford to her friend, the semi-invalid poetess Elizabeth Barrett, who doted upon him, often mentioned him in correspondence, and portrayed him in a couple of poems that did not enhance her literary prestige. For the first three or four years, Flush spent most of his time lying at his mistress's feet in the dark third-floor bedroom at 50 Wimpole Street. ('Flush's breathing is my loudest sound,' Elizabeth wrote in a letter, 'and then the watch's tickings, and then my own heart when it beats too turbulently.') He was dognapped during three of his infrequent outings, being returned only after ransom money (£20 in all) had been paid. When Robert Browning began courting Elizabeth in 1845, Flush manifested his jealousy in several ways—most painfully, by biting the poet-suitor, alighting on a different leg each time; but Flush came to accept Browning, and Browning Flush, and it was a threesome that travelled to Italy after the wedding. Flush got to know Florence better than did Elizabeth, who wrote: 'He goes out every day and speaks Italian to the little dogs.' He and she died, and were buried, in the city.

On 16 September 1931, Virginia Woolf wrote to Vita Sackville-West:

> Have you a photograph of Henry? I ask for a special reason, connected with a little escapade by means of wh. I hope to stem the ruin we shall suffer from the failure of The Waves [the novel that she had written, and rewritten, forsaking most other activities, over a period of two years].

Vita Sackville-West, who had been Virginia Woolf's lover, was married to Harold Nicolson, who had a cocker spaniel called Henry. The picture of Henry was some help to Virginia Woolf in the writing of *Flush*, her short biography of the dog from his point of view, which she completed in January 1933. A month later, she explained in a letter to Lady Ottoline Morrell:

> Flush is only by way of a joke. I was so tired after the Waves, that I lay in the garden and read the Browning love letters, and the figure of their dog made me laugh so I couldn't resist making him a Life. I wanted to play a joke on Lytton [Strachey; author of *Eminent Victorians*, published 1918]—it was to parody him. But then it grew too long, and I dont think its up to much now. But this is all very egotistical.

During Virginia Woolf's life, *Flush* had greater commercial success than any of her other books.

Fortnum, William

A present-day rhapsodist employed by Fortnum & Mason, the general merchandisers of Piccadilly, London, goes so far as to say that, back in 1707, William Fortnum and Hugh Mason 'created a union surpassed in its importance to the human race only by the meeting of Adam with Eve'. Shielding one's eyes from the purple patches, one learns that William Fortnum—whose ancestors, variously called Fortanon, Fortynham, Fortnane, and, getting close now, Fortnam, were yeoman farmers in Oxfordshire—came to London at the suggestion of a cousin, who was prospering there as a builder, having taken advantage of the sites made vacant by the Great Fire of 1666. While seeking employment, William lodged with Hugh Mason, proprietor of a small shop in St James's Market. It was a short stay, ended when William was taken on as a footman in the household of Queen Anne. As a perquisite, he could keep part-used candles. Leaving none for the other servants, he began moonlighting as a purveyor of secondhand nightlights: so successfully that within a matter of months he had money put by—enough to buy stock for a grocery stall which, set up in a doorway in Piccadilly, he and Hugh Mason tended, turn and turn about, William doing his stints when he was allowed away from St James's Palace. Meanwhile, Mason set up another sideline: catering for the many saddle, pack and dray horses, he established stables in a yard (now called Mason's Yard) off Duke Street, within a stone's throw of where the grocery stall was tethered. Mason's shop and stables prospered; so did the joint venture of the stall; likewise, Fortnum's touting of the discarded royal candles. Fortnum gave in his notice, Mason gave up his small shop, and then, putting their profits together, they opened a shop at the corner of Piccadilly and Duke Street. Much enlarged over the years—first by the founders, then by their descendants—the shop is still on the site: the building graced, since 1964, by an ornamental three-faced clock from which, as it chimes the hour, then dinglings gavottes, figures representing Mr Fortnum and Mr Mason emerge to bow to each other.

Franceschini, Count Guido

On a day in June 1860, Robert Browning left his ailing wife Elizabeth at their home in Florence and took a stroll to the Piazza San Lorenzo, which was filled with stalls peddling 'odds and ends of ravage, picture frames. . . . Bronze angel-heads once knobs attached to chests. . . . Modern chalk drawings, studies from the nude. . . .' Seeing on one of the stalls a vellum-bound collection of pamphlets, legal briefs and manuscript letters pertaining to a forgotten *cause célèbre*, he picked it up and, after only a cursory glance, purchased it for one lira—'eightpence English'.

Hand-lettered on the title-page of the Old Yellow Book, as he subsequently called his prize, was the following information:

Posizione Di Tutta La Causa Criminale,
Contro Guido Franceschini. . . .
'A Setting-forth of the entire Criminal Cause against Guido
Franceschini, Nobleman of Arezzo, and his Bravoes, who were
put to death in Rome, 22 February 1698. The first by beheading,
the other four by the Gallows. Roman Murder Case. In which it is
disputed whether and when a Husband may kill his Adulterous
Wife without incurring the ordinary penalty.'

Straightway, Browning was fascinated:

> Still read I on, from written title-page
> To written index, on, through street and street,
> At the Strozzi, at the Pillar, at the Bridge. . . .

'My plan was at once settled,' Browning told a friend many
years afterwards. 'I went for a walk, gathered twelve pebbles
from the road, and put them at equal distances on the parapet
that bordered it. Those represented the twelve chapters into
which the poem is divided; and I adhered to that arrangement to
the last.' The poem was his greatest: *The Ring and the Book*.

Browning's recollection that he immediately decided to put
the Old Yellow Book to poetic purpose seems to have been at
fault. There is evidence that he offered the book as the basis for
an historical narrative to a writer named W. C. Cartwright, who
declined it; to a Miss Ogle, author of 'that very pretty book' *A
Lost Love*, who could make 'nothing out of it'; to a leading
fellow-poet—probably Tennyson; and, according to an entry in
a friend's diary, to Anthony Trollope 'to turn into a novel; but T.
couldn't manage it'.

One must be grateful that his generosity was turned down,
leaving him with the thought, 'Why not take it myself?'

(The Hon.) Freddie Threepwood

His *Memoirs*—so scarce as to be unobtainable—are mentioned a number of times in the works of P(elham) G(renville) Wodehouse. So is he. And so are many other Threepwoods.[1] Freddie is the unfavourite son of Lord Emsworth, who was much discountenanced by his early behaviour: 'a heavy, loutish-looking youth', he was expelled from Eton, sent down from Oxford, and, among other indications of his amoral nature, caught stealing from his kin. But he is a changed man, or seems to be, since he married Niagara ('Aggie') Donaldson, daughter of the founder of Donaldson's Dog Biscuits Inc. of Long Island, NY, and became a dog-biscuit salesman for his father-in-law's firm.

1 Doubly coincidental, P. G. Wodehouse once lived in a house called Threepwood, close to Emsworth House, a preparatory school in the village of Emsworth, on the A27 road between Havant, Hampshire, and Chichester, Sussex.

Gandhi

A dachshund, full name Mahatma Coatma Collar Gandhi; perhaps the least expensive of the gifts showered upon the actress Marion Davies by the newspaper tycoon William Randolph Hearst, with whom she lived, sometimes at San Simeon, his castle on the coast of California. Whatever Orson Welles may have said to the contrary, Hearst was his and/or Herman Mankiewicz's inspiration for the character of Charles Foster Kane in the best film that has ever been made, and the castle of Xanadu in *Citizen Kane* is a caricature of San Simeon. From the shooting script:

NARRATOR

Legendary was the Xanadu where Kubla Khan decreed his stately pleasure dome (With quotes in his voice):

'Where twice five miles of fertile ground
With walls and towers were girdled round.'

(Dropping the quotes) Today, almost as legendary is Florida's Xanadu—world's largest private pleasure ground. Here, on the deserts of the Gulf Coast, a private mountain was commissioned, successfully built for its landlord . . . Here for Xanadu's landlord will be held 1940's

biggest, strangest funeral; here this week is laid to rest a potent figure of our century—America's Kubla Khan—Charles Foster Kane.

The relationship between Kane and Susan Alexander bears some resemblance to that between Hearst and Marion Davies (for instance, Kane financed Susan's operatic debut in *Thais* at the new Chicago Opera House, and Hearst financed films starring his ex-chorus-girl mistress); but the notion that Hearst would have been at all nostalgic about a toy 'Rosebud' sledge—or anything else, for that matter—is grotesquely unlikely.

Gerlach, Max

The *in memoriam* column of *The Times* of 19 December 1970 contained an entry for GATSBY, that name alone, with a snatch of verse. No one on the paper knew that the entry related to a cocker spaniel, a paragon among dogs, who died young.

With *The Great Gatsby*, published 1925, F(rancis) Scott (Key) Fitzgerald probably came closer than any other novelist this century to achieving what he should have set out to do. According to Matthew J. Bruccoli, author of the most detailed Fitzgerald biography (*Some Sort of Epic Grandeur*, published 1981):

Long Island provided material for Fitzgerald's third novel as impressions from that 'riotous island' went into the writer's process of cerebration. Jay Gatsby was partly inspired by a local figure, Max Gerlach. Near the end of her life Zelda Fitzgerald said that Gatsby was based on 'a neighbor named Von Guerlach or something who was said to be General Pershing's nephew and was in trouble over bootlegging'. This identification is supported by a newspaper photo of the Fitzgeralds in their scrapbook, with a note dated 7/20/23: 'En route from the coast—Here for a few days on business—How are you and the family old Sport? Gerlach.' Here is Gatsby's characterising expression, *old sport*, from the hand of

Gerlach. Attempts to fill in the history of Max Gerlach have failed; the only clue is a 1930 newspaper reference to him as a 'wealthy yachtsman'. ('Yachtsman' was sometimes a euphemism for rum-runner.)

I don't disagree; but I would add my belief that bits and pieces of Gatsby were derived, not from Joseph Bowne Elwell himself (◊ Willard Huntingdon Wright), but from the impression of him as a fascinatingly shady romantic egotist that was created by newspaper reporters after he was murdered at his home in Manhattan on 11 June 1920: for two or three weeks, startling revelations about the great bridge player's extra-professional activities—as, for instance, race-horse owner, police informer, bootlegger, indiscriminate masher—appeared on the front page of newspapers, even the New York *Times*. The murder was committed eleven weeks after the publication of Fitzgerald's first novel *This Side of Paradise*; ten weeks after his marriage to Zelda Sayre at St Patrick's Cathedral, Manhattan. In reading the papers, just about all the papers, for items about himself and Zelda, he must, many times, have been sidetracked into reading about the fabulous Elwell. At the end of *Through the Looking-Glass*, Alice says of the Red King: 'He was part of my dream, of course.' To me, it seems probable that when Fitzgerald looked back on the heady spring and summer of 1920, Elwell was part of *his* dream.

That snatch of verse that I mentioned at the start: It was the second line of the epigraph of *The Great Gatsby*:

> Then wear the gold hat, if that will move her;
> If you can bounce high, bounce for her too,
> Till she cry 'Lover, gold-hatted, high-bouncing lover,
>   I must have you!'
>
> *Thomas Parke D'Invilliers*

The name of the author was Fitzgerald's pseudonym for himself. It is said that on one of the three occasions when the novel was bought for filming,[1] the executive dealing with the contract, sure that the epigraph would not be needed but determined to prevent any problem involving copyright, paid Fitzgerald's agent an extra amount for the few lines, asking him to pass it on to Mr or M. D'Invilliers.

1 In 1926, 1949 and 1974; with, respectively, Warner Baxter, Alan Ladd and Robert Redford playing Gatsby.

Gibson, Charles Dana

The American cartoonist and illustrator who, around about 1890, when he was twenty-three, created and shortly made masses of money from a creature of his imagination, promptly christened the Gibson Girl, whom he portrayed in manifold costumes, poses and pursuits. Tall, radiant, always looking towards a far horizon, her nose almost imperceptibly retroussé, her lips delicately moulded, she became an epitome of the Gay Nineties and of Art Nouveau (◊ Arthur Lasenby Liberty). She supported lamp-shades, gave a touch of class to crockery, was serenaded in countless songs, and ran for some time as a musical comedy. Nature imitated art: her hats and gowns were copied, and whenever she actually did anything, such as play lawn-tennis or ride a bicycle, thousands of young ladies became energetic too, keeping their eyes on a far horizon the while. She continued her exemplary progress until the First World War; but after the sinking of the *Lusitania* on 7 May 1915, Gibson transformed her into Miss Columbia, a militant detester of Kaiser Wilhelm II in particular and of the Boche in general. (◊ Harvey for the Gibson variation on the Martini cocktail.)

Gillette, King Camp

Having appropriated the idea from his inspired but unperceptive employer, William Painter, inventor of a disposable crown cork, he patented the first safety-razor with disposable blades in 1901.

Goldenberg, Emanuel

The real name of the art-loving film-actor Edward G. Robinson, whose career spanned half a century, from 1923 until 1973, the year of his death. He never gave a poor performance, and twice gave great ones: as Rico Bandell (in some respects, like Al Capone) in *Little Caesar*, the 1930 screen adaptation of W. R. Burnett's novel, which is one of the two best gangster movies (the other is *The Roaring Twenties*, 1939, a film made splendid by Gladys George[1] and James Cagney, the finest film-*star* of all time), and as Burton Keyes, the match-less insurance investigator, in the best *filme noir*, *Double Indemnity* (1943), the script of which was based on a story by James M. Cain and written by Billy Wilder, the director, and Raymond Chandler.

1 Who modelled her performance on Mary Louise 'Texas' Guinan, the Queen of the Speakeasies in the Prohibition era of mass drunkenness (1920–34). A former bronco-rider in circuses and a star of two-reel silent Westerns, billed as 'The Female Two-Gun Bill Hart', Texas Guinan was the proprietor of, and mistress of

ceremonies at, the El Fey Club—so called because it was backed by the racketeer Larry Fay—at 107 West 45th Street, Manhattan. In his book *Ardent Spirits: The Rise and Fall of Prohibition* (published 1973), John Kobler writes:

> Though El Fey featured a variety of bizarre entertainers, among them a girl calling herself Nerida, who danced with an eight-foot python twined about her nude torso, the stellar attraction was Texas herself, a calliope-voiced dyed blonde, sheathed in ermine and flashing a bracelet encrusted with almost 600 diamonds. Her *shtick* consisted of chafing the customers. 'Hello, sucker!' she would bellow at them as they entered, a greeting that became a catchphrase of the dry decade . . . A 'big butter-and-egg man,' meaning a big spender from a small town, was another Guinan coinage. If the cash register failed to ring often enough, Texas would blow a whistle and raise her gravelly voice above the jazz band and the wooden clappers: 'Come on, suckers, open up and spend some jack!' Texas Guinan's fortunes were already on the decline when, in 1933, a disgruntled doorman employed by Larry Fay at another speakeasy, Club Napoleon, put four bullets in him.

Goldfish, Samuel

Not until 1918, when he had been producing films for eight years, latterly for Goldwyn Pictures, a company that *Gold*fish had formed with the Sel*wyn* Brothers, did he change his name to Goldwyn. (Granting him permission to do so, Judge Learned Hand remarked that 'a self-made man may prefer a self-made name.') By 1925 he was an independent producer, owning a studio and supporting a stable of stars (and female contract players, called 'Goldwyn Girls'). His most successful period was round about the Second World War: *Wuthering Heights* (1939), *The Little Foxes* (1941), and *The Best Years of Our Lives* (1946)[1]—speaking of which, he said, 'I don't care whether it makes money as long as everybody in the United States sees it.'

He made—or is said to have made—many other convoluted comments: Goldwynisms. A sampler:

'Include me out.'

'Let's have some new clichés.'

'I read part of the book right the way through.'

'Every director bites the hand that lays the golden egg.'

When told that a novel bought for screen adaptation contained Lesbian characters: 'Can't we change their nationality?'

'If Roosevelt were alive, he'd turn in his grave.'

'A verbal contract isn't worth the paper it's written on.'

'I'll give you a definite maybe.'

'Anybody who goes to see a psychiatrist ought to have his head examined.'

1 All three films have speeches that are memorable for one reason or another.

In *Wuthering Heights* (script by Ben Hecht and Charles MacArthur), Merle Oberon, whose real name was Estelle O'Brien Merle Thomson, dies in Laurence Olivier's arms—but not before she has enquired, 'Heathcliff, can you see the grey over there where our castle is?', and, without pausing for a reply, promised: 'I'll wait for you until you come.'

In *The Little Foxes* (script chiefly by Lillian Hellman from her play), Herbert Marshall, who is none too well all the way through the picture, and whose demise is hastened by Bette Davis, tells her:

Maybe it's easy for the dying to be honest. I'm sick of you, sick of this house, sick of my unhappy life with you. I'm sick of your brothers and their dirty tricks to make a dime. There must be better ways of getting rich than building sweatshops and pounding the bones of the town to make dividends for you to spend. You'll wreck the town, you and your brothers. You'll wreck the country, you and your kind, if they let you. But not me. I'll die my own way, and I'll do it without making the world any worse. I leave that to you.

And in *The Best Years of Our Lives* (script by Robert E. Sherwood, working on the basis of McKinlay Kantor's verse novel *Glory for Me*), Fredric March, recently demobilised from the army, waxes sarcastic to fellow-bankers:

I want to tell you all that the reason for my success as a sergeant is due primarily to my previous training in the Cornbelt Loan & Trust Company. The knowledge I acquired in the good old bank I applied to my problems in the infantry. For instance, one day in Okinawa, a major comes up to me, and he says, 'Stephenson, you see that hill?' 'Yes, sir, I see it.' 'All right,' he said, 'you and your platoon will attack said hill and take it.' So I said to the major, 'But that operation involves considerable risk. We haven't sufficient collateral.' 'I'm aware of that,' said the major, 'but the fact remains that there is the hill and you are the guys who are going to take it.' So I said to him, 'I'm sorry, Major: no collateral, no hill.' So we didn't take the hill, and we lost the war.

Gray, John

In 1858, on the day after 'Auld Jock' Gray, a shepherd, was buried in Greyfriars Churchyard, Edinburgh, his Skye terrier Bobby was found asleep on the grave. Paying no heed to the sexton, who evicted him, the dog returned night after night; and each day, as soon as the one o'clock gun was fired from the castle, he trotted into a local inn for his lunch. He continued the nightly vigil until his own death on 14 January 1872, when officials of the kirk agreed to his being buried next to his master. Americans contributed a headstone, and a memorial, paid for by the Baroness Burdett-Coutts (◊ Thomas Coutts), was erected on Candlemaker Row, near the church. It is still there—surprisingly, unblemished by louts: a drinking fountain for dogs, with a bronze statue of Greyfriars Bobby seated on a central pillar.

Griffo, Francesco

This book is set in Bembo (called Griffo by some printers who believe in giving credit to whom it is due), which is the modern version of a manuscript typeface designed by Francesco Griffo, a goldsmith from Bologna, for the Venetian printer Aldus Manutius Romanus, and first used in 1495 in a pamphlet by the then-humanistic scholar and writer Pietro Bembo. Staying with Bembo for a moment: at subsequent times in his life (1470–1547) he was secretary to Pope Leo X, historiographer of Venice, and librarian of St Mark's. When—Leo and his successors, Hadrian VI and Clement VII, having died—Paul became the third pope of that name, Bembo was offered a cardinal's hat on condition that he renounce the study of classical literature and concentrate on theology, and he accepted like a shot. Soon afterwards, the convert cardinal's virtue was rewarded with bishoprics.

Until 1500, typefaces were either gothic or roman; each based on a scribes' style of handwriting, the former was used for text-books, the latter for literary works. Feeling that there was a need for a third type, for use in inexpensive books in small formats, Aldus commissioned Griffo to cut punches of a lower-case fount following a style of handwriting used for everyday business purposes: the style was called chancery script from its development in the Vatican chancery.

The new letter form, which came to be known as *italic*, was tried out as the title of a woodcut illustration in the *Epistole* of Saint Catherine of Siena, published by Aldus in September 1500; the following April, Aldus used italic throughout an edition of the works of Vergil (228 octavo leaves), and he afterwards used it extensively in a series of pocket-sized editions of Latin and Italian texts.

As Griffo's letters had only a slight forward slant, they blended reasonably well with capitals of a roman (upright) fount.

When other printers copied the 'Aldine italic', the mixed-fount convention was followed, and it was not until the 1530s, by which time designers were giving italics a more pronounced slant, that upper-case italics appeared. The italic fount cut in Rome by Ludovico degli Arrighi was the model for those designed by Claude Garamond and other French designers of the sixteenth century.

Gumm, Frances

As a small child, she appeared with her sisters, Virginia and Suzanne, in a vaudeville singing act, but in 1935, when she was thirteen, she was put under contract by Metro-Goldwyn-Mayer, at whose behest she changed her name to Judy Garland. She scored a hit in *Broadway Melody of 1938* by singing a version of 'You Made Me Love You', rewritten as a birthday greeting to Clark Gable. Soon after making the first of the Hardy-family films with Mickey Rooney, she was given the role of Dorothy in *The Wizard of Oz* (1939), based on the book by Frank L. Baum. After a sneak preview, the producers cut the scene in which she sang 'Over the Rainbow', because they felt that it slowed the action—but then had second thoughts. The song received an Academy Award, and it is reckoned that Judy Garland sang it over 12,000 times during the thirty years before she died from an overdose of sleeping pills.

Gustafsson, Greta

She became Greta Garbo at the insistence of Maurice Stiller, a leading film-director in her native country of Sweden. Unarguably, the most beautiful film-star of all time, and probably the most reserved, she spoke the line, 'I want to be alone', in *Grand Hotel*, which was made in 1932. Before that, she had appeared as Anna Karenina (silently) and as Anna Christie, and subsequently she played Queen Christina, Anna Karenina again, and Camille (◊ Marie Duplessis), thus virtually cornering the market for portrayals of ladies with irregular love-lives and sad ends.

Harpick, Peter J.

A transvestite sculptor, innovative in his use of Plasticine, whose mother Adascha Harpick, *née* Schmidt, was a keen cricketer (collections of sport statistics, though not (♭) *Wisden*, record that she scored a half-century on behalf of a Women of Kent XI during a friendly match with the Ladies of South Kensington at Fontwell Park in 1860) and whose father Wally is said to have been descended from the Romanovs by way of a Brighton peer. In early manhood, after studying under Dr Wilhelm Bunbury at the Chorlton-cum-Hardy Polytechnic, Harpick developed an obsession that his mother was a surrogate, standing in, as it were, for a woman of Whitechapel's unfortunate class who had actually borne him. In the autumn of 1888, he determined to put an end to all prostitutes in that area, and, being methodical, started off with those who were unfortunate enough to have an 'a' in their names. After doing away with half a dozen, between times writing provocatively to the press, signing the messages with an anagram of his name, he became bored with the whole idea, and retired to south-east London, where he died in obscurity soon after publishing his monumental work, *Statues to be Observed in Penge and Its Environs: a Rambler's Guide* (1903), which was dedicated to 'my only true begetter, Mr W.H.' (his late father, of course).

As far as I know, this is the first time that Harpick has been identified as 'Jack the Ripper', whose tally of victims is sometimes put at ten but more often includes only Martha Turner, or Tabram (7 August 1888), Mary Ann ('Polly') Nicholls (31 August 1888), Annie Chapman (8 September 1888), Elizabeth ('Long Liz') Stride and Catharine Eddowes (the 'double event' of 30 September 1888), and Mary Jane ('Jeannette') Kelly (9 November 1888). Harpick is, I submit, quite as likely to have committed the crimes as are any of the people previously accused in books and articles:

Joseph Barnett, a porter at Billingsgate fish market who at one time lived with Mary Jane Kelly; Prince Albert Victor, Duke of Clarence; Dr Thomas Neill Cream—or a doppel-gänger, since Cream appears to have been in an American prison when the murders were committed; Montague John Druitt, a cricket-playing lawyer turned schoolmaster who committed suicide a month or so after the murder of Mary Jane Kelly; Sir William Withey Gull, physician in ordinary to Queen Victoria, and accomplices in the persons of Sir Robert Anderson, the head of the Criminal Investigation Department of the Metropolitan Police, and John Netley, who had been the Duke of Clarence's carriage driver; 'Jill the Ripper', a psychopathic midwife; Severin Klosowski, otherwise known as George Chapman, an innkeeper who was hanged for triple-murder by poisoning in 1903; Alexander Pedachenko, also known as Vassily Konovalov, Andrey Luiskovo and Mikhail Ostrong (or Ostrog), an insane Russian doctor working for the Okhrana, the Tsarist secret police; Jack Pizer, or Kosminski ('Leather Apron'), an insane Polish Jew; an unnamed secretary of General William Booth, founder of the Salvation Army; an unnamed shochet, employed to slaughter animals by the Jewish ritual method; 'Dr Stanley', a Harley Street surgeon; James Kenneth Stephen, a writer of parodies and doggerel, and, incidentally, a relative of Virginia Woolf (◊ Flush).

Harrod, Henry Charles

A tea merchant, not specially successful at the trade, in 1849 he took over a grocery shop in Middle Queen's Buildings (now Brompton Road) from his friend P. H. Burden. The locus, called Knightsbridge, was undesirable, infamous for an excess of highway robberies, and the turnover of the shop, in which two assistants were employed, amounted to no more than £20 a week. But Mr Harrod was fortunate in the timing of the take-over: eighteen months later, when the Great Exhibition opened in Hyde Park, just to the north, tourists and trippers bumped up the shop's takings, and it wasn't long afterwards that so-called mansion-blocks of flats began to rise in and off the nearby Cromwell Road; museums, too. Still, by 1861, when Mr Harrod passed control of the shop to his son Charles Digby, little had been done to enhance it, nothing to enlarge it. Charles Harrod took things in hand, over the next few years adding, first, patent medicines, stationery and perfumes to the range of goods; then (presumably not all at once) game, fruit and vegetables, china, confectionery and flowers; in 1874—by which time he had built an extension in the back-garden, bought two adjoining shops, and replaced the original shingle by one among several others that read 'C. D. Harrod, Grocer'—he had nearly a hundred assistants, working from seven in the morning (and encouraged to be on time by fines of three-ha'pence for each unpunctual quarter of an hour) till eight at night. On 6 December 1883 the store was destroyed by fire; Charles Harrod straightway opened an office in the back-room of a local pub, and on 7 December wrote to customers, assuming that all were ladies or at least women:[1]

Harrods Stores

Madam,
    I greatly regret to inform you that, in consequence of the

above premises being burnt down, your order will be delayed in
the execution a day or two. I hope, in the course of Tuesday or
Wednesday next, to be able to forward it.

In the meantime, may I ask you for your kind indulgence.
Your Obedient Servant

C. D. Harrod

Rebuilding took nine months. Shortly after the grand re-
opening, Harrod decided to allow credit. Lillie Langtry and Ellen
Terry (◊ respectively Thomas Rule and Alice Grey) were among
the first account-customers; and, perhaps amending Harrod's
unisex view of his patrons, so was Oscar Wilde (◊ Charles
Thomas Wooldridge). Ill health symptomatic of exhaustion
forced Harrod to retire in 1891, but the company was now
growing almost of its own volition, soon to become a group of
stores that included Dickins & Jones and D. H. Evans in London,
Kendal Milne in Manchester, and J. F. Rockley down in Tor-
quay. And 1894 saw the completion of a furniture depository,
several of the floors of which were made from material disman-
tled from the original but superseded Piccadilly tube station, on a
bank of the Thames, at Barnes. (It is—with Fulham Football
Ground,[2] Duke[3]'s Meadows, and the Mortlake Brewery[4]—
known to millions of radio listeners as a landmark of the Oxford
and Cambridge Boat Race,[5] rowed each spring between the
respective vicinities of the bridges of Putney and Chiswick.) In
1901, adjacent land having been purchased, the present store
began to take shape.

Agreeable yardstones in the store's recent history, of more
interest than the squabbles about who should own and run it,
include:

1980   The release of a record, called 'A Touch of Harrods',
        of a medley played by the resident pianist in one of
        the several restaurants.
1981   The introduction of Harrods cigarettes.
        The opening of a Long Hair Clinic.
1982   The opening of a mother-to-be department called
        Great Expectations.
1983   Reverting (well, sort of) to the original Mr Harrod's
        original occupation, the devotion of an entire counter
        — tastings on request—to 'teas' made from fruit.

1 Gwen Raverat (in *Period Piece*, published in 1952): 'I have defined Ladies as people who did not do things for themselves.'

2 Known as Craven Cottage because of the house of that name, now used for dressing rooms and offices, that diagonally faces a corner of the pitch. Built about 1780 by the sixth Baron Craven, in 1840 it was taken by Edward (George Earle Lytton) Bulwer-Lytton (first Baron Lytton), the novelist, orator, and statesman; he wrote three novels at the riparian retreat (*Night and Morning, The Last of the Barons, The New Timon*), and in 1846, shortly before he left, there entertained Prince Louis Napoleon, who had just escaped from the fortress of Ham.

3 Of Devonshire, perhaps; Dukes of Devonshire—members of the Cavendish family—once owned fields opposite the Meadows.

4 There has been a Mortlake Brewery since 1487, when the first was built on the site of a manor belonging to the Archbishops of Canterbury; although the present one is owned by Watney's, the pub it partly encompasses, called The Jolly Gardeners, is owned by Young's, who stock it with ale from their Ram Brewery at Wandsworth, farther downstream.

5 First rowed in 1829.

Harry Gattling-Fenn

The most expert—or perhaps one should say most publicised—exponent of Upmanship, the system of cut-throat affability (subdivided into Gamesmanship, Lifemanship, One-Upmanship, and Supermanship) that was promulgated by Stephen Potter, 'the Master of 681 Station Road, Yeovil'.

Soon after the publication of *One-Upmanship* in 1952, *Time* magazine coined the word 'one-yupmanship' to describe the acting, or non-acting, style of Gary Cooper in cowboy films.

Harvey

By November 1944, when he made his inaugural non-appearance on Broadway in the play of the same name,[1] winner of the Pulitzer Prize for Drama that year, he was a white rabbit who, though 6 feet 1½ inches tall, was invisible to everyone save an aimless, amiable, bibulous character called Elwood P. Dowd—but when, two and a half years before, Mary Coyle Chase, a housewife in Denver, Colorado, had got the idea for the play and started on the first of thirty versions, Harvey had existed in her mind first as a canary, then as a penguin. The plot of the play is splendidly simple: Elwood's social-climbing sister and her daughter Myrtle Mae (who in the first scene is 'looking charming in a Rancho-Rose toned crepe picked out at the girdle with a touch of magenta on emerald') try to get him committed to a sanitarium, but when the sister explains that he never goes anywhere without his bosum-friend the rabbit—whose favourite author, incidentally, is Jane Austen—the doctors conclude that it is she who should be immured.

The part of Elwood was created by the actor and vaudeville singer Frank Fay (once the husband of the film-star Barbara Stanwyck—real name, Ruby Stevens—who, after divorcing him, married Robert Taylor [◊ Marie Duplessis]), but was subsequently played during the 1,775 performances at the 48th Street Theatre by a succession of actors, among whom the most miscast was the debonaire, very English song-and-dance man Jack Buchanan, who tended to look uncomfortable in any costume other than top hat and tails.

When the play opened in London, at the Prince of Wales Theatre, in January 1949, Elwood was played by the music-hall comedian Sid Field, who had never before appeared in legitimate drama. Field was certainly the greatest English-born comedian since Charlie Chaplin; he may have been the funniest performer of all time. (One can get some idea of his quality from the film *London Town*, 1946, in which he re-created his music-hall performances as the Cockney, the Golfer, the Man about Town, the Musician, and the Photographer.) In *Ego 9*, published 1948, James Agate (◊ Michael William Balfe) wrote:

> Field is in the great tradition. He cannot put hand, foot, eyebrow, or tongue-tip wrong, is immensely and unendingly funny, and as a great comedian he cannot escape the law which insists that performers in this kind shall be known for something outside their comedy. With Leno[2] it was swell of soul, with Grock[3] it is logic, and with Charlie Chaplin pathos. Field has a quality I have not seen on the stage since Hawtrey,[4] of whom Henry Maxwell wrote:
>
> 'Whoever—man, woman, or child—has *pouted* to such effect as Hawtrey? He would pout to indicate a certain type of displeasure. Babies are often given to it, but Hawtrey—contriving to look more like a baby than any infant in its cradle—could yet impart something additional, piquant and pertinent; he could impart to it just that element of pathos which it is the rare achievement of the lovable to command, even when they are being as difficult as only the lovable know how to be.'
>
> Sid Field is always a great baby, and never more than when he is being, as he thinks, sophisticated.

He was chosen to play Elwood by Mary Coyle Chase. It was inspired casting. He was, of course, very funny; but his performance was, at times, sad—particularly, perhaps, in the scene in which Sanderson, a young doctor, asks Elwood why he calls his rabbit Harvey.

ELWOOD: *(proudly) Harvey is his name.*
SANDERSON: *Yes; but how do you know that?*
ELWOOD: *Ah!—now that's a very interesting coincidence. One night, several years ago, I was walking down Fairfax Street—between Eighteenth and Nineteenth—you know that block?*
SANDERSON: *Yes, Mr Dowd.*
ELWOOD: *I'd just helped Ed Hickey into a taxi. Ed had been minding his drinks—and I felt he needed 'conveying'. I started to walk down the street when I heard a voice saying, 'Good evening, Mr Dowd.' I turned, and there was this great big white rabbit leaning against a lamp-post. Well, I thought nothing of that! Because, when you've lived in a town as long as I've lived in this one, you get used to the fact*

that everybody knows your name. So I went over to chat to him. He said: 'Ed's a little spiffed tonight—or might I be mistaken?' Well, of course, he wasn't mistaken. I think the world of Ed—but he was spiffed! Well, he went on talking, and finally I said: 'You have the advantage over me. You know my name—but I don't know yours.' And right back at me he said: 'What name do you like?' Well, I didn't have to think a minute. 'Harvey' has always been my favourite name; so I said: 'Harvey.' Now this is the most interesting part of the whole thing. He said: 'What a coincidence; my name happens to be—Harvey'!

The play ran for 610 performances in the West End, but Sid Field twice had to leave the cast because of illness; and after his death, at the age of forty-five, on 3 February 1950, Elwood was played by the American comedian Joe E. Brown, who had previously played the part on Broadway.

A film based on the play was released in 1950. It starred James Stewart,[5] who had played the part of Elwood P. Dowd on Broadway and who subsequently played it in the West End.

Changing the subject from comedy to cocktails, round about 1970 a Californian named Thomas Harvey spent his days surfing and his evenings imbibing 'Italian screwdrivers' (concoctions of vodka, Galliano, and orange juice), and then tried to find his way home, his progress made staccatissimo by the number of walls he banged into; shortly, the cause of his sustaining so many injuries became known as a Harvey Wallbanger.

Among other mixtures and/or dilutions of alcohol named after —or said to have been named after—persons are the following:

The *bloody Mary*, which, despite the fact that the sobriquet was applied to Queen Mary I of England, is supposed to be so called as a reminder of Mary, Queen of Scots. Just why it got this name is unclear; perhaps the title followed from someone's description of it as the 'queen among drinks'. There seems no doubt that vodka and tomato juice were first mixed in 1920 by Ferdinand L. Petiot, a barman at Harry's New York Bar in Paris; nor that he subsequently spiced the drink with salt, pepper, lemon, and the all-important Worcestershire sauce, when it became the 'red snapper'. Some time before Petiot thought of complicating the drink, Roy Barton, an American cabaret entertainer, referred to it as the 'bucket of blood', copying the name of a club in Chicago at which he performed.

The *Gibson*. When, circa 1900, (♭)Charles Dana Gibson

requested a Martini (gin, vermouth, bitters, other ingredients according to taste, and a speared olive) at the Players Club, Manhattan, the barman, finding that he had no olives, made necessity the mother of invention by using a pearl onion instead.

The *gin rickey*. Almost certainly, this blending of gin, lime-juice and carbonated water gets its name from someone called Rickey, but there are two schools of thought as to the creator's identity: one favours James K. Rickey, a hard-drinking colonel in the Union Army during the American Civil War; the other supports a different Colonel Rickey, forename unknown, who, according to H(enry) L(ouis) Mencken, was 'a distinguished Washington guzzler', at the peak of his drinking power in the mid-1890s.

The *Rob Roy*, a mixture of Scotch, sweet vermouth and bitters, usually decorated with a cherry, bears the nickname of the eighteenth-century Scots bandit and plunderer Robert Mac-Gregor, whose exploits, mostly legendary, are recounted in Sir Walter Scott's Waverley Novel *Rob Roy* (published 1817).

The *Tom Collins*, a protean drink almost always served in a tall glass, more or less resembles the gin-sling—a mélange of gin, lemon- or lime-juice, soda-water, and sugar—slung by Tom Collins, who was a barman at Limmer's Old House, London, in the nineteenth century.

Unpleasing addenda:

The *Mickey Finn*, a vicious soporific (probably depending upon chloral hydrate for its ill-effect), is said to have been first administered in Chicago round about the turn of the century, the administrant being a criminous barman named Michael Finn who used the 'knockout drops' to facilitate robbery.

Grog, originally diluted rum but later any kind of inferior alcoholic drink (apart from cheap wine, which is 'plonk'), gets its name from Vice-Admiral Sir Edward Vernon (1723–94), who was known as Old Grog because of his penchant for coats of grogram, a mixture of silk and mohair. When, seeking to diminish drunken brawling between decks, he ordered that the mainbrace be spliced less comprehensively, by adding water to the rum rations, the resulting adulterated drink was condemned as grog. Still, it made some seamen groggy.

1 Two other famous modern plays have titles referring to characters that are never seen: at the end of the eccentric conceit by Samuel Beckett, the cast and any remaining members of the audience are left *Waiting for Godot*; and as the final curtain falls on the comedy by Gerald Savory that ran at Wyndham's Theatre, London, for 799 performances from 25 February 1937, delayed guests called *George and Margaret* are ringing the doorbell.

Wyndham's, which opened in 1899, was built by the actor-manager Sir Charles Wyndham (◊ George Edalji's note 1). An early hit at the theatre was *An Englishman's Home*, a play written anonymously by Guy du Maurier that dealt with an invasion of the country; it caused a sensation when it was presented in 1909, and greatly increased recruitment to the newly formed Territorial Army.

2 Dan Leno (1860–1904), whose real name was George Galvin, was a Cockney comedian; from 1888, he appeared year after year as the dame in pantomimes at Drury Lane.

3 Born Adrien Wettach in Switzerland in 1880, he became the supreme clown of his generation: never speaking a word, he created humour from a feigned inability to cope with musical instruments, and pathos from apparently accidental exposure of his baldness (self-imposed by daily shaving of his head); he started in the circus, but from 1911, when he was engaged by C(harles) B(lake) Cochran for a show at the Palace Theatre, London, his appearances were almost exclusively in music halls, usually in the West End.

4 Sir Charles Hawtrey (1858–1923), actor-manager, light comedian, adapter of a German play as the farcical comedy *The Private Secretary*, which he presented and starred in time and time again, keen student of the Bible, with a text for every occasion, and spender of more money than he earned. Once, when he was appearing at Drury Lane, the theatre manager, having grown tired of his regular request for subs, refused him an advance on his salary; wherupon Hawtrey sauntered to the nearest shop displaying the sign of the three balls, pawned himself, and later presented the pledge-ticket to the manager, who was forced to redeem it so that Hawtrey could appear on stage that night.

5 Before becoming a film-actor, English-born James Stewart changed his name to Stewart Granger.

Heinz, Henry John

By 1859, when he was fifteen, he was not only working full hours in his father's brickyard at Sharpsburg, Pennsylvania, but growing vegetables, which he sold in Pittsburg, six miles away, getting up at three o'clock each morning, Sunday excluded, to do so. At twenty-one, he had sufficient capital to buy a half-interest in his father's business; three years later, he and a friend started a firm called Heinz, Noble & Co. But, following a collapse in the stock market, he was declared bankrupt. Though he was a religious man, and one who seems to have tried to live by most Christian precepts, he did not let legalities or the list of his creditors dissuade him from borrowing money to start a new business, ostensibly owned by his brother John and a cousin. He won discharge from bankruptcy in 1885, and presently registered the business under his own name: the H. J. Heinz Company. His main, and soon only, vocations were the preservation of food-stuffs and the purveying of them in cans, bottles or jars.[1]

In 1886, he, his wife, and their sons Clarence and Howard, sailed for Europe. Mixing business with the pleasure of seeing relatives in Germany, Heinz, having thought to include half a dozen cases of his products in the family's luggage, stopped off in London and somehow managed to carry five of the cases through the front entrance of the premises of Fortnum and Mason (◊ William Fortnum) in Piccadilly, and up the preliminarily red-carpeted stairs to the buyer's office. He had not made an appointment; he feared that, even if he were allowed into the sanctum, he would encounter 'conservative resistance' to his sales-talk. And so he was pleasantly surprised when the buyer, after politely ignoring his spiel but perusing the products, announced: 'We will take all of them.' Thus it was that Heinz's mass-market foods were introduced into Great Britain by one of London's most up-market stores.

According to Robert C. Alberts, author of *The Good Provider* (published 1974):

> Heinz personally hit upon the '57 Varieties' slogan in or before 1892 while riding in a New York elevated train. He was studying the car cards and was taken by one that advertised '21 styles' of shoes. He applied the phrase to his own products. There were more than sixty of them at the time, but for occult reasons his mind kept returning to the number 57 and the phrase '57 Varieties'. 'The idea gripped me at once,' he said, 'and I jumped off the train at the 28th Street station and began the work of laying out my advertising plans. Within a week the sign of the green pickle with the "57 Varieties" was appearing in newspapers, on billboards, signboards, and everywhere else I could find a place to stick it.'
>
> He had only two stern restrictions on his advertising: he never posted billboards in or around Pittsburg, and he never advertised in the Sunday newspapers.

The recent advertising campaign, employing the slogan of 'Beanz Meanz Heinz', may have increased the Great British consumption of the company's three products (among some 170) that are basically baked beans; but at the previous count, 730 million beans—each electronically examined for blemishes—were being canned each day.

1 In 1795, the French government, troubled by war, revolution, and, among other concomitants, the difficulty of feeding large numbers of soldiers and sailors, offered a prize of 12,000 francs to anyone who could devise a way of preserving food for long periods of time. Fourteen years later, a Parisian confectioner, Nicolas Appert, came up with an answer that was considered satisfactory, and collected the award from Napoleon himself. Appert's solution—to put food into wide-mouthed, subsequently cork-capped, jars, and then heat the jars so as to expel the air that he thought caused food to go off—remains, apart from its reasoning, valid.

In 1810, the year after Appert collected his prize-money, an Englishman, Peter Durand, fashioned a container not unlike a tea canister (hence the word can); and shortly afterwards, still in 1810, a compatriot named Brian Donkin—who may have filched Durand's idea—set up the first canning company, which lasted as an independent concern for more than half a century. In 1819, yet another Englishman, William Underwood, opened the first food-preserving firm in America—at Boston, Massachusetts—and, about twenty years later, yet another, a man called Thomas Kensett, was the first to go into the business in a big way, by building a plant near Baltimore, Maryland, a location chosen because of its proximity to Chesapeake Bay, which was then abundant with shellfish and other seafoods.

In 1857, Nicolas Appert's notion that air caused food to deteriorate was contradicted by another Frenchman, Louis Pasteur, who discovered that the culprits were the bacteria that exist in all natural food; basically, his method of killing bacteria was no different from Appert's for driving out air—which, unknown to Appert, exterminates the Schizomycetes—but such sterilising came to be called pasteurisation.

Revolution and war, indirectly responsible for the discovery of the principles of canning, also gave the first main impetus to canned food's ubiquity. It is reckoned that when the American Civil War broke out, about five million cans of food were being produced annually—and that when the Confederate forces surrendered four years later, on 9 April 1865, production, spurred on by the need for unperishable rations and speeded up by the discovery that the addition of calcium chloride to the water greatly reduced the time required for sterilisation, had risen to thirty million.

Hentschel, Carl

An expatriate Pole, usually taken for a German, he was the original of Harris in *Three Men in a Boat* (published 1889); George was based on a bank-clerk called George Wingrave, and, of course, the third man was the author of the book, Jerome K(lapka) Jerome; Montmorency was a real dog with a different name.

It was theatre-going that brought the Three Men together. Jerome and Wingrave, already friends, became friendly with Hentschel through meeting him, over and over again, at first nights in the West End.

In 1900, Jerome published a sequel, *Three Men on the Bummel*, in which he waited until the last paragraph before explaining that *bummel* is a German word meaning a journey without a definite purpose: a ramble.

In his memoirs, he wrote: 'I think I may claim to have been, for the first twenty years of my career, the best abused author in England. *Punch* invariably referred to me as "'Arry K'Arry". . . .'

He died in 1927, and is buried in the churchyard of Ewelme, a still-pretty village in the Chilterns.

Heppenstall, Rayner

Extract from Christopher Sykes's biography of Evelyn Waugh[1] (published 1975):

It was the custom then [apparently in 1945] for the Home Service [now Radio 4] to introduce the Sovereign's Christmas broadcast by an hour's 'world round-up' programme. It had been decided to approach Evelyn in the hope that he would take on the task of introducing the programme. It was felt at Broadcasting House that the Corporation should send as their ambassador a literary man. An appointment was made at the Hyde Park Hotel. With singular maladroitness the emissary chosen was a disappointed novelist, a deeply class-conscious man whose self-esteem bordered on mania, and who regarded Evelyn's work as decidedly inferior to his own. Being a man who looked on good manners as servility unworthy of genius, he did not attempt to win Evelyn's agreement by any exercise of charm, wisely perhaps as he had little to exercise. He preferred an attempt at impressing the other.

Evelyn was angered by the incident which he long remembered. He said to me once, 'Why does your Corporation send people like Kurkweiler to me and expect to get anything out of me?' In fact the BBC emissary bore a sturdy English name, but Evelyn always insisted that this man (who later displayed some sympathy with Nazism) was a German Jewish refugee whose real name was Kurkweiler. The proposition came to nothing.

Later in the biography, Sykes claims that 'Kurkweiler' was one of the people at the BBC who tried to thwart his plan to broadcast a dramatisation of Waugh's novel *Helena*.

'Kurkweiler' was Rayner Heppenstall, who did not read the biography until April 1980. He told his side of the story in an entry in his journals (published under the title of *The Master Eccentric* in 1984):

> Whether Sykes's memory or Waugh's original account to him is at fault I do now know, but the meeting took place not at the Hyde Park hotel, but at White's club.
>
> My immediate boss, Laurence Gilliam, was the only man who with certainty knew of the meeting at the time. It was Laurence who, maladroitly or not, had deputed me to arrange the meeting. This was because it was I who had suggested Waugh as an alternative to T. S. Eliot, known or supposed to be unavailable. The great inducement was the amount of foreign currency to be put at the disposal of whoever introduced the round-up from whichever European capital he chose (having visited others during the period before Christmas). Despite certain misgivings about Waugh's social posture, I greatly admired his writing.
>
> I could only be regarded as a 'disappointed' novelist in that I had been lugged into the ranks of the army for four and a half years so soon after the appearance of my first novel [*The Blaze of Noon*], which had been a *succès* both *de scandale* and *d'estime*. At the time of my call-up, I had just begun work on a second novel, which I did indeed finish while in the army, during an exceptionally pleasant interval in that seemingly interminable *servitude*. This had gone pretty well, despite being put out in a limited edition at a high price by publishers who feared repercussions from certain passages. I had not yet begun a third novel, having come out of the army with a gratuity totalling twenty-seven pounds and needing a job at once. I had signed on the first dotted line to appear under my nose and, if the date of my meeting with Evelyn Waugh was indeed in the autumn of 1945, I had been at the BBC for no more than a few months, still finding my way in that complicated world, never having produced a programme, not even a member of staff but under probationary programme contract for some months more. . . .
>
> I don't understand how there can possibly have been a battle of *Helena* in 1951, while Harmon Grisewood still controlled Third

Programme, unless he objected to Sykes's intention of dramatising only the novel's second part. For what I believe was his very first production, he also seems to have insisted on a programme budget which would enable him to employ two such expensive actors as John Gielgud and Flora Robson. I, certainly, had nothing to do with such difficulties as he may have experienced over this wasteful employment by a novice producer on a programme I did not even listen to.

In the difficulties he more probably experienced in placing a talk by Waugh on P. G. Wodehouse in 1961, even Sykes does not pretend that I played any active part, but only says: 'The "Kurkweiler" affair was not forgotten.' As a matter of fact, I thought this talk a thoroughly good idea and believe that it did much to dispel the cloud which had hung far too long over Wodehouse. I had myself just published, in the *Times Literary Supplement*, a middle-page article in praise of P. G. Wodehouse.

Sykes's onslaught has filled me with shocked surprise. The whole time we were colleagues, he had appeared friendly to me. So he had on the one occasion when we had met since. At any moment, he could have asked me for my account of my one meeting with Evelyn Waugh, whom even he shows to have been a frequent mythomaniac. If he had nursed an intense dislike of me for years, he had been guilty of sustained hypocrisy, to say the least. Perhaps his enmity dated only from 1969, when he read my account of him in *Portrait of the Artist as a Professional Man*. It may be that Christopher Sykes is too sensitive about his wobbling jowls and that to see these mentioned may have touched off a streak of paranoia.

1 Like Rayner Heppenstall, among other novelists, Waugh turned people into characters, places into settings. In 1925, he was a master at the Arnold House preparatory school near Colwyn Bay, North Wales: the school, under the alias of Llanabba Castle, is the setting of the opening chapters of his first novel *Decline and Fall*, and one of his teaching colleagues, a man named Young— described by Waugh in his diaries (published 1976) as 'monotonously pederastic'—was the model for Captain Grimes. The classical scholar Maurice Bowra was sketched as Mr Samgrass, the Oxford don in *Brideshead Revisited*; Lady Diana Cooper, wife of (Alfred) Duff Cooper, later Viscount Norwich (◊ Mr X), was the Mrs Stitch of both *Scoop* and *Sword of Honour*; Waugh admitted that Alastair Graham, who retired from the diplomatic service in 1933, when he was twenty-nine, to live reclusively in Wales,

contributed to the character of Sebastian Flyte in *Brideshead Revisited*; Brian Howard, a homosexual aesthete of American parentage who committed suicide by an overdose of drugs in 1958, was the main inspiration for Ambrose Silk in *Put Out More Flags* and contributed in small measure, along with the outlandish and aesthetic Harold Acton, to Anthony Blanche in *Brideshead Revisited*; seven members of the Lygon family, children of the seventh Earl Beauchamp, are supposed to have become the Marchmains in *Brideshead Revisited*, and it has been suggested that Madresfield Court, the Lygon home near Malvern, Worcestershire, is the original of 'Brideshead'; Nancy Mitford's husband, the Hon. Peter Rodd, known to some of his many acquaintances as Prod, and thought by at least one of them to be 'a very superior con man', was the main model for Basil Seal, who casts his shadow over several of Waugh's novels, including *Black Mischief* and *Scoop*. Other persons are considered, or consider themselves, to be the originals of characters in Waugh's fiction.

Hill, Dr Charles

In the 1940s and early '50s, he was known only as the Radio Doctor to the millions of people, no more than ninety per cent of whom were hypochondriacal, who listened to his broadcasts. Speaking in a voice that summoned up the image of a plum-duff, and eschewing long words and medical jargon, he imparted what seemed to be common-sense advice on health in such magazine-programmes as *The World Goes By*, hosted by Freddie Grisewood, and *Kitchen Front*, which was presented by Howard Marshall, whose voice was almost as plumetty (a mixture of plums and suet) as his own. He casually mentioned physical unmentionables,[1] and gave homespun definitions of medical terms and specialities. Some listeners were outraged when he defined a pathologist as 'a man who sits on one stool and examines those of other people'; and others, or perhaps the same ones, protested at his use of the word 'belly'. More censored broadcasters envied the way he got away with words and remarks that would certainly have been expunged if they had dared include them in scripts which they submitted. Hill explained to an envier: 'It's quite easy, my dear chap. All you've got to do with the BBC is to put in two dirty words, and if they find one they won't even look for the other.'[2] In 1963, he was created Baron Hill of Luton, and in the same year was appointed chairman of the Independent Television Authority, a position that he held until 1967; then he returned to the BBC for a five-year stint as chairman of the governors.

Another famous pseudonymous broadcaster, starting before Dr Hill and continuing when radio was doctorless, was Derek McCulloch: Uncle Mac of *Children's Hour*.[3] All the juvenile listeners, millions of them at five o'clock each weekday afternoon, thought of Uncle Mac as a kind and jovial old gent; but McCulloch, who continued to suffer from wounds received during the First World War, was actually withdrawn, inclined towards grumpiness. Under his real name, he was the question-master of *The Brains Trust* (originally called *Any Questions?*), the first of the relatively few intelligent-chat shows; according with the conception of Howard Thomas, the producer, that 'the three key figures should be, respectively, a brain, a tongue, and a heart,' the most regular question-answerers during the early years of the programme were the biologist Julian Huxley, the slightly-charlatan teacher Dr Cyril Joad (who so often prefixed his answers with 'It depends what you mean by' that the words became a catch-phrase), and the Münchausenesque[4] Commander (Archibald Bruce) Campbell.

Among broadcasting dance-band leaders during the war and in the decade that followed, it seems that only one, Gerald Bright, employed a *nom de musique*: Geraldo. A scion of Jewish parents living meagrely in the East End of London, he found it easier to keep his baton waving in time with his musicians' outpourings than to introduce what they intended to play; even though the introductions were rehearsed word by word, they often came out so quaintly that an announcer, usually Bruce Wyndham, had to step in as interpreter.

In their book *Those Vintage Years of Radio* (published 1972), John Snagge—best remembered as the imperturbable, even bored, commentator on the Oxford and Cambridge boat-race—and Michael Barsley tell a story about Geraldo:

Having acquired the trappings of a successful band-leader—a Rolls-Royce, top-hat, astrakhan-collared coat, rings, and cigar—he decided to pay a visit to the place of his birth, Whitechapel Road. He was stalking in some magnificence through his old haunt, when a little man came up to him, and said, 'You're Gerald Bright, aren't you?' Geraldo graciously admitted it. The little man said, 'You were the bloke who was going to go up to the West End and run a big show with a top band and all the stars, so you told us—weren't you?' The great figure nodded again. 'Well,' said the little man, 'wot 'appened?'

1 Now often referred to as naughty bits (a term coined or given currency by members of Monty Python's Flying Circus). Those parts peculiar to the female body that are apparent when such a body is fully clothed are known to some as wobbly bits, to others as Bristols (from Bristol City, one of the two local football clubs), and to still others, a declining minority, as boobs or even simply breasts.

2 An idea that he may have picked up, indirectly, from the crime-writer Dashiell Hammett, who, twice-shy of an editor, submitted a story containing two expressions, one harmless, the other risqué, in the belief—correct, as it turned out—that the editor would delete the harmless one and leave the other, thinking that he was doing just the opposite. The expression struck out was gooseberry lay (American thieves' slang for stealing from a washing-line); the word considered inoffensive was gunsel, which, flowering from the German root of *gänselein* = gosling, denotes a young homosexual killer.

3 In 1933, when members of the Oxford Union created a national stir by voting that they would in no circumstances fight for King and Country, *The Times* published a contemptuous leading article headed 'The Children's Hour'.

4 Rudolf Erich Raspe, author of *Baron Münchausen's Narrative of His Marvellous Travels and Campaigns in Russia*, published in London in 1785, seems to have plagiarised from a series that had appeared in a Berlin journal a few years before; at least some of the anecdotes recounted in those articles were based on tall tales told by a Hanoverian soldier, Karl Friedrich Hieronymus von Münch-hausen, who was in his sixties when the series was printed, and some of the same stories had been going around by word of mouth long before the imaginative, exaggerative warrior was born.

Hobson, Thomas

According to Richard Steele, writing in the *Spectator* in 1712, this well-known Cambridge figure gave birth to the expression 'Hobson's choice' by his insistence that customers wanting to hire one of his hackney horses take the horse nearest the stable door. Hobson's death in 1631, when he was eighty-six, was commemorated in a number of poems, including two, or perhaps three, by John Milton, of which the better, or best, is 'On the University Carrier, who sickened in the time of his vacancy, being forbid to go to London, by reason of the Plague' ('shifter' in line 5 can be taken to mean trickster; a chamberlain—line 14—was an attendant at an inn who looked after the bedchambers):

> Here lies old Hobson, Death hath broke his girt,
> And here alas, hath laid him in the dirt,
> Or else the ways being foul, twenty to one,
> He's here stuck in a slough, and overthrown.
> 'Twas such a shifter, that if truth were known,
> Death was half glad when he had got him down;
> For he had any time this ten years full,
> Dodged with him, betwixt Cambridge and the Bull.
> And surely, Death could never have prevailed,
> Had not his weekly course of carriage failed;
> But lately finding him so long at home,
> And thinking now his journey's end was come,
> And that he had ta'en up his latest inn,
> In the kind office of a chamberlain
> Showed him his room where he must lodge that night,
> Pulled off his boots, and took away the light:
> If any ask for him, it shall be said,
> Hobson has supped, and 's newly gone to bed.

The play *Hobson's Choice*, by Harold Brighouse, was first produced in 1912 at the Gaiety Theatre, Manchester, the first repertory theatre in Great Britain, run by Miss Annie Horniman.

Hooker, General Joseph

Giving a new meaning to Napoleon's adage that an army marches on its stomach, he did his best to ensure that the Union troops he commanded during the American Civil War had prostitutes on call in off-duty periods. Thus, his name became a synonym for a prostitute; or perhaps one should say that he unwittingly increased the circulation of an existing synonym, coined from Corlear's Hook, a brothel-packed part of the city of New York.

Hughes, William

TO.THE.ONLIE.BEGETTER.OF.
THESE.INSVING.SONNETS.
Mr W.H. ALL.HAPPINESSE.
AND.THAT.ETERNITIE.
PROMISED.
BY.
OVR.EVER-LIVING.POT.
WISHETH.
THE.WELL-WISHING.
ADVENTVRER.IN.
SETTING.
FORTH.

T.T.

The identity of Mr W.H., the dedicatee of the First Quarto of Shakespeare's *Sonnets*, edited by the publisher Thomas Thorpe

(T.T.) in 1609, is fascinatingly perplexing to many people, some of whom are not particularly keen on Shakespeare's work, but is cut and dried to a number of scholar detectives, who co-operatively or solitarily insist that he was:

A person called William Hughes. The simple—and sole—reason for his candidacy is the seventh line of Sonnet 20, 'A man in hue, all "hues" in his controlling', which is taken to be a pun on the last name of Mr W.H. The trouble with William Hughes is that he is multifaced: in Oscar Wilde's fictional biography *The Portrait of Mr W.H.* (1889), he is a boy actor, incredibly beautiful, who played leading female roles in Shakespeare's plays until he was tempted away from the company by an offer he just couldn't refuse from a rival impresario; Samuel Butler, the author of *Erewhon* ('nowhere' backwards) and editor of the 1899 edition of the *Sonnets*, nominated a ship's cook named William Hughes; and several authorities plump for William Hewes (they insist on calling him that, although his name usually appears as Howes), who was a musician attached to Robert Devereux, Earl of Essex (himself favoured by others as the dedicatee). There is, by the way, no evidence that Shakespeare was ever acquainted with anyone named Hughes, Hewes or Howes.

William Herbert, Earl of Pembroke. A popular choice on several counts: Shakespeare's early plays, written between 1589 and 1592, were put on by Pembroke's Men, the company patronised by William Herbert's father, and by the time William Herbert had reached his teens, he was a friend of Shakespeare's and a fan of his plays; the First Folio was dedicated by the editors to William Herbert and his brother Philip, Earl of Montgomery.

Henry Wriothesley, Earl of Southampton, whose supporters contend that his initials were transposed by Thomas Thorpe so as to disguise the fact that he was the Fair Youth of the Sonnets. They point out that he was Shakespeare's only acknowledged patron; that it was to him that Shakespeare dedicated his early erotic poems, and that episodal passages in the Sonnets seem to mirror incidents in Southampton's life. All well and good—but there is nothing to show that Southampton remained friendly with Shakespeare, or took any interest in his work, after 1594. And how can the punnings on the name Will in Sonnets 135 and 136 be explained if the Fair Youth was called Henry? And how does one get round the fact that if Shakespeare didn't start on the Sonnets until about 1595, the date accepted by nearly all authorities, Southampton, having attained his majority, could not have been happy to find himself referred to, in Sonnet 126, as a 'lovely boy'? And so on.

William Hatcliffe, of Hatcliffe, Lincolnshire: a fairly recent contender, winkled out of oblivion by the admirably entertaining Leslie Hotson, who set out his credentials in a succinctly-titled book, *Mr W.H.* published 1964. Having noted certain passages in the Sonnets that suggest that the Fair Youth was a prince, Hotson argues that Shakespeare was not referring to an aristocrat but to the Prince of Purpoole, who presided over the Christmas revels at Gray's Inn; he then asserts that the Sonnets were composed in 1588–9 (thus unintentionally abetting the cause of Henry Wriothesley), and reveals that the prince in charge of the revels that year was 'Dominus de Purpoole Hatcliffe'.

Others whose claims have been staked include a same-name cousin of the aforementioned William Herbert, a very minor poet named William Holgate, and Shakespeare's brother-in-law William Hathaway. And Baconians (◊ Francis Bacon) are partial to the notion that the initials stand for 'William Himself'.

But what of the word 'begetter' in the dedication? Few early Shakespearian scholars believed that Mr W.H. was the inspirer of the Sonnets. Most of them assumed that he was the person who begot—procured—the manuscript, and passed it on to Thomas Thorpe. So more names enter the list. Two in particular:

William Hall, a stationer's assistant who, according to Sir Sidney Lee, author of *A Life of William Shakespeare* (published 1898), busily touted for copy for printers.

Sir William Harvey, or Hervey, who was the third and last husband of the Dowager Countess of Southampton, Henry Wriothesley's mother. (In case you are wondering, knights were often addressed as Mister in Elizabethan times.) Harvey, first proposed in the middle of the last century, has been vigorously seconded by A. L. Rowse, a professor of history and author of books on Cornwall and cats, who in 1963 published a volume entitled simply—like the Bible—*William Shakespeare*. The theory—which depends on the idea that Henry Wriothesley was the Fair Youth—is that the countess had a copy of the manuscript of the Sonnets, and that after her death Harvey found it among her papers and presented or sold it to Thomas Thorpe.

As, like Oscar Wilde, I can resist everything except temptation, I must throw a dollop of mud into already muddied waters by suggesting a sort of variation on the idea that the letters W and H are transposed initials, hiding the identity of Henry Wriothesley. It is that Thomas Thorpe set the initials he had in mind upside down, for H.M. stood for none other than Elizabeth I, a Fair Youth in Virgin Queen's clothing.

Humperdinck, Engelbert

A German composer whose most successful work was the opera *Hänsel and Gretel*. First performed in Weimar on 23 December 1893, when it was conducted by Richard Strauss, it was produced at over 50 theatres in the following year, and a *Hänsel and Gretel* touring company was formed.

Ireland, William Henry

A precociously brilliant and delinquent Englishman who in 1794, when he was nineteen, had no difficulty in persuading his father—who was a dealer in prints and rare books—and a number of experts and scholars that documents he had forged were the unliterary work of Shakespeare, found quite by chance in the home of a friend who wished to remain anonymous. Having tested the market and found it wanting more, he dashed off an entire Shakespeare play, *Vortigern and Rowena*, which was accepted by Sheridan, himself deceived, for production at Drury Lane. The premiere was delayed, but Ireland kept himself busy by writing *Henry II*, which he shelved while he got on with *William the Conqueror*—an epic that had progressed to the start of its final act by April Fools' Day, 1796, when Ireland had to break off to attend the dress rehearsal of *Vortigern and Rowena*. Suspicions concerning the authenticity of this play were confirmed on the first night, when members of the audience tittered at some of the opening lines, then guffawed, and finally, bored by an excess of unintended whimsy, turned rather nasty. Ireland never did get to finish *William the Conqueror*; and, as far as is known, he did not turn his hand to that of any dead author other than Shakespeare.

Ireland's works, finished and unfinished, were published by his father, who, blind to related talent, maintained that 'young William is too stupid to have composed them'.

Jack Worthing

The labyrinthine plot is unimportant—merely the excuse for certain lines—to *The Importance of Being Earnest*, Oscar (Fingal O'Flahertie Wills) Wilde's superlative comedy, which was first produced at the St James's Theatre, London, on 14 February 1895, little more than a fortnight before Wilde initiated the libel action against the eighth Marquess of Queensberry that resulted in his own ruin. Of the unimpassioned lines that spring from the story, or assist it along, perhaps the most quoted are:

> I hope you have not been leading a double life, pretending to be wicked, and being really good all the time. That would be hypocrisy.

> A misanthrope I can understand—a womanthrope never.

> All women become like their mothers. That is their tragedy. No man does. That is his.

> To lose one parent . . . may be regarded as a misfortune; to lose both looks like carelessness.

Briefly—and, I fear, incomprehensibly—the plot revolves around a man who has been called Jack Worthing ever since, as a baby, he was found in a handbag at Victoria Station. As an excuse for being away from his country home at weekends, Jack has invented a younger brother, Ernest, whom he needs to visit in London. Jack's chum Algy introduces himself as Ernest to Jack's ward Cecily, and soon afterwards Jack proposes to Algy's cousin Gwendolyn, passing himself off as an Ernest since she feels that she is fated to marry someone of that name. When it seems that both girls are engaged to Ernest, Jack and Algy decide to be re-christened. Subsequent to further complications, Jack turns out to be Algy's long-lost brother, actually named Ernest. Soon after this discovery, the final curtain descends.

Jacquet, Richard

From about 1678 until 1686, shortly before he died in bed at his home in London, he was the most publicised of England's several public executioners. Not under his own name, though. As is explained in Lloyd's *MS Collection of English Pedigrees* in the British Museum, 'The Manor of Tyburn, where felons for a long time were executed, was formerly held by Richard Jacquet, whence we have the name Jack Ketch as a corruption.'

That nickname, tagged to all executioners, is far more circumscribed of usage than the real name of an earlier hangman: at the start of the same century, a man called Derrick, a servant of the Earl of Essex, was sentenced to death but then pardoned on condition that he hang a job-lot of twenty-three other delinquents, and he carried out the assignment with a type of hoist that was subsequently called after him.

The longest-serving executioner was William Calcraft, whose reign began in 1829 and ended forty-five years later, by which time hangings had become private affairs, the last public one in Great Britain being outside Newgate Prison on 25 May 1868, when Michael Barrett was executed for his part in a Fenian bomb outrage.

In 1972, I topped and tailed a facsimile edition of *My Experiences as an Executioner*, the memoirs of James Berry, whose services were engaged on 200 occasions between 1884 and 1892, when he retired so as to have the liberty and the time to deliver lectures opposing capital punishment. I recall that a bookseller asked the publisher for 'My Experiments as an Executioner'—a title that would have been appropriate to William Marwood, who was the immediate predecessor of Berry and the immediate successor of Calcraft (by coincidence, all three were in the footwear trade before turning to neckware: Marwood was a cobbler, Berry sold shoes, and Calcraft made them). It was Marwood who conceived, and claimed to have perfected, the weight-of-body/distance-of-fall equation of the 'long drop'. He was the answer to a ubiquitously posed conundrum: 'If pa hanged ma, who would hang pa?'

Hanging has run in a few English families: for instance, James Billington, who took over from Berry, was succeeded by his sons William and John, operating in tandem; and there have been three Pierrepoints—Henry, his brother Thomas, and Henry's son Albert (who, after resigning his office in 1956, became landlord of a pub called 'Pity the Poor Struggler'—the last word of which was altered to Strangler by regular customers). But none of the English hanging lines is anywhere near as long as the cutting line of the French Sansons, who were the head decapitators in that country from 1688 until 1847, when the last of them was dismissed for pawning a guillotine.

In Great Britain, the last execution of a woman was on 13 July 1955, when Ruth Ellis was hanged at Holloway Prison, ostensibly[1] for the murder of her lover David Blakely on the previous Easter Sunday. The final executions of all were carried out on 13 August 1964, one at Walton Gaol, Liverpool, the other at Strangeways, Manchester, the victims being, respectively, Peter Allen and John Welby (better known as 'Ginger' Owen Evans), who, together, had been found guilty of the murder of John West, who was employed as a van-driver by a firm of launderers in Workington, Cumberland.

Perhaps it is considered a breach of taste to enjoy any executional anecdotes, let alone to have a favourite among them; but I do, and I have. The story that most appeals to me may be apocryphal. It concerns an axeman of Elizabethan times who had mastered his trade: indeed, had become past-master of it, having introduced subtleties, making it akin to art. Once, he was called upon to despatch a noble miscreant. The latter, pinioned uncomfortably to the block, became impatient, and muttered: 'Get a move on, man.' To which the axeman replied, deferentially of course: 'It is done, my Lord. You have but to nod your head.'

1 I use that word for this reason: one of the bullets Mrs Ellis fired at Blakely ricocheted and struck a passer-by in the thumb, and it was because of this that the Home Secretary, Gwilym Lloyd George, believing that people should be able to walk the streets without fear, refused to grant a reprieve.

Judson, Edward Zane Carroll

For some thirty years from the middle of the nineteenth century, he had the highest literary income in America: proceeds of the pulp-magazine serials and dime novels, recounting acts of derring-do on battlefields, on the high seas, and in the still-extremely-wild West, that he churned out under the pen-name of Ned Buntline. A rabid WASP (White Anglo-Saxon Protestant; the acronym hadn't yet been created, but never mind), he spent much of his sparse spare time propagandising for, successively, the Native American Association, the Native American Party, and the Know-Nothing (American) Party; in 1849, deciding that actions spoke louder than words, he helped to disorganise the Astor Place riot, protesting against the appearance of an English actor in an American theatre (◊ William Charles Macready), and consequently languished a year in a New York jail.

He went west in the summer of 1869, searching for material for a series of novels, and, fetching up at North Platte, Nebraska, tried to wheedle stories from a cavalry officer, Major Frank North. But the major, not liking the look of him (his deeply-pouched eyes were shifty, and his handkerchief-pocket was obscured by an undergrowth of medals that no army had ever awarded), got rid of him by pointing to a wagon and advising him to have a word with the man sleeping off a hangover beneath it. The man was a twenty-three-year-old frontier roustabout who had worked as an Indian scout before and after serving as a private in the Union forces during the Civil War; he had certainly fired a gun at Indians on a number of occasions, and some of the shots may have landed on their target; he was acquainted with James Butler 'Wild Bill' Hickok—sometime outlaw, sometime lawman—and manifested his admiration for him by recounting episodes in the Hickok saga as if they had involved himself; he was handsome of face and figure, with brown eyes, long dark hair, and a goatee beard; and he was garrulous and keen to be quoted, publicised, made up into a legend. His name was William Frederick Cody.

The story of his life, as told to and embellished by Ned Buntline, soon appeared as a serial in Street & Smith's *New York Weekly*, with the title of BUFFALO BILL: THE KING OF THE BORDER MEN—to which Buntline appended a personal-comment subtitle: *The Wildest and Truest Story I Ever Wrote*. Wild it was; and wildly astray of the truth. Still, Cody wasn't concerned. Nor did he mind being called Buffalo Bill, though that nickname, quite new to him, was applied to several frontiersmen whose lives had been more adventurous than his. Neither did he complain at being portrayed as a militant teetotaller, as great a foe of the Demon Drink as he was of the Plains Indians.

The serial, and subsequent Buntline bunkum,[1] was the foundation of Buffalo Bill's fame. With impressive speed, other literary hacks got in on the act; the most prolific of these was a writing machine called Colonel Prentiss Ingraham. Cody himself was happy to labour on behalf of the legend—first, by submitting to lionisation by swank Easterners, then by touring theatres, appearing as 'himself' in hastily cobbled dramatic vehicles (during gaps in the action, Buntline stomped on to the stage to rant temperance lectures—so stentoriously[2] that when he staggered back to his dressing-room, hoarse and sweating, he felt entitled to a medicinal swig or two or three of whisky). When, in 1873 or thereabouts, the Buntline/Buffalo-Bill partnership petered out (chiefly because Cody was dissatisfied with his share of the takings), Cody went solo. He was extremely fortunate in that one of his most adoring fans, a man named John Burke—

who called himself Major, though he had never been commissioned, and was nicknamed Arizona John, contradicting the fact that he had never visited that state—was seeking employment at the time, and was not merely glad but honoured to accept Cody's offer of a job as factotum. Burke, who had been a journalist, an actor, and the manager of a troupe of acrobats, proved to be a more than adequate replacement of Ned Buntline as the publicist of Buffalo Bill; a salesman who believed in his product, he dreamed up methods of advertising and promotion that, decades later, were imitated on Madison Avenue.

In 1882, financed by a showman called Nate Salsbury, Cody took an outdoor extravaganza, Buffalo Bill's Wild West Show, on the road. After a shaky start, the show began to make money— not a great amount until the season of 1885–86, when the company was augmented by the sharp-shooting Annie Oakley (◊ Phoebe Anne Oakley Mozee) and by Sitting Bull, one of the chiefs of the Sioux Indians, some of whom had annihilated General George Custer and a contingent of 264 men at the Battle of the Little Big Horn on 26 June 1876. Sitting Bull was paid $50 a week, plus expenses, simply for sitting on a horse and staring impassively at the spectators; made shrewd by previous dealings with impresarios, he insisted on having the sole right to sell pictures of himself and on being allowed to charge people who wanted to be photographed with him. In addition to its profitable traipsing about North America, the Wild West Show was several times transported to Great Britain and countries in Europe.

A numerate bibliographer has reckoned that between 1869 and 1917, the year of Cody's death (John Burke died six weeks after his hero—of a broken heart, according to some amateur diagnosticians), 1,700 Buffalo Bill books, mostly dime novels, were published. The town of Cody, in the Big Horn Basin of Wyoming, was founded by Cody as an investment; it never paid its way during his lifetime, but it is now a leading tourist attraction, jam-packed with stores selling gimcrack mementoes. There is a Buffalo Bill Dam, 328 feet high, in the proximate Shoshone Canyon: just one of heaven knows how many monuments to Ned Buntline's creation.

---

1 A word derived not from a person but from a place: Buncombe, North Carolina. In 1820, near the end of the debate on

the 'Missouri Question' in Congress, Felix Walker, the member
for Buncombe, rose to speak, totally ignoring calls for the
'Question'. Several congressmen converged on him, imploring
him to shut up; but having explained that he was bound to *make a
speech for Buncombe* because the electorate of the district expected
him to, he carried on talking.

2 Stentor was a Greek warrior in the Trojan war 'whose voice
was as powerful as fifty voices of other men'.

Judson, Whitcomb

A Chicagoan who, having invented a zip-fastener, showed it off
at the Chicago Exposition of 1893, where it caught the eye of
Colonel Lewis Walker. After many ups and downs, the colonel
made and tried to market an improved version in 1902. But his
C-Curity wasn't improved enough, and so didn't catch on.
Success of a sort was achieved by a Swedish engineer, Gideon
Sundback, who was granted a patent for a 'separable fastener' in
1913.

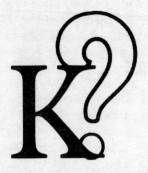

Kafka, Franz

An Austrian writer of Czech origin, only forty-one when he died in 1924, whose fictional heroes find the world incomprehensible, and whose readers (well, most of them) are similarly perplexed by his work, a central theme of which seems to be encapsulated within the latter-day comment: 'Just because I'm paranoid doesn't mean that someone isn't following me.' Among people who read literary reviews, the phrase 'a Kafkaesque situation' has definitely lost ground to the much-the- same-meaning 'Catch-22[1] syndrome', but is still spoken, in the sense of 'you can't beat the system', by those who cannot abide non-medical use of the word 'syndrome'.

In *Ego 9*, published in 1948, James Agate (◊ Michael William Balfe) reprinted An Alphabet of Literary Prejudice that he had compiled for a journal called *The Windmill*. The entry for K was about Kafka:

> Am thinking of starting a movement to be called 'Kafka is Balls', with a club of which I propose to make myself Perpetual President. Not on the strength of having read Kafka—indeed, I have never opened him—but because of what the highbrow magazines tell me about him. Am considering a button with the letters P.P.K.I.B.C. Perpetual President Kafka is Balls Club.[2]

Agate's idea was the obverse of a fan club, the first of which was the Keen Order of Wallerites, founded round about the turn of the century by admirers of the actor-manager Lewis Waller (really William Waller Lewis), who was known to non-fans as 'the high-priest of dignified tushery'—an unfair description, for although he made lots of money by playing Monsieur Beaucaire, Brigadier Gérard, and D'Artagnan, he was admired as Brutus, Faulconbridge, and Henry V (called Hank Cinque by some Americans). One side of the KOW badge showed Waller in powdered peruke as Monsieur Beaucaire; on the other was a picture of his favourite flower, which, perhaps unhelpfully to his image, was the pansy. Not to be outdone, fans of Herbert Beerbohm Tree (◊ Beatrice Stella Tanner) banded together as the True-to-Trees.

1 From Joseph Heller's novel of the same name, published 1962. The catch is illustrated by an air-force officer's explanation that 'anyone who wants to get out of combat isn't really crazy, so I can't ground him'.

2 Even if it were not sort of relevant to this book, I should want to quote the entry for C:

CORTEZ. 'Silent, upon a peak in Darien.' But of course. He was stout and out of breath. On the other hand, Vasco da Gama, according to Meyerbeer, was excessively vocal in similar circumstances.

Kemmler, William

He eloped with Tillie Ziegler, another man's wife; but in 1889, when they were living at Buffalo, New York State, Kemmler, having grown tired of Tillie, sought to dispel his ennui by murdering her with an axe. As a result of his unsubtle crime, he became the first 'electrocide'—a word coined by the New York

World, an organ owned by (↻)Joseph Pulitzer that had supported the campaign against the replacement of hanging by electrical execution. The inaugural use of the electric chair revealed defects in the theory. Anyone desiring details of William Kemmler's unsudden death can consult the issue of the *World* published the day after the execution, which was conducted on 6 August 1890 at Sing-Sing Prison.

The first authorised[1] use of a gas chamber for killing a human being was at the Nevada State Prison, Carson City, on 8 February 1924, when a Chinaman called Gee Jon was executed for the murder of a member of a rival tong gang; a time-keeper noted that death ensued some six minutes after hydrocyanic gas had been admitted to the chamber.

> 1 In 1891, Herman Webster Mudgett (who used at least eleven aliases, his favourite being Henry Howard Holmes) opened an hotel, built to his own specifications, in Chicago; local people dubbed the Gothic-style building Holmes's Castle. Some of the guests never checked out. Five years after the opening, police visited the hotel, intending to quiz Mudgett about an insurance fraud; but he had fled—to Philadelphia, as it transpired. Searching the building, the police found that it contained all modern murderous conveniences, including air-tight rooms with gas inlets. Mudgett conducted his own defence at his trial for the murder of a business associate, Benjamin Pitezel; found guilty and sentenced to death, he confessed to twenty-seven killings. He was hanged at Moyamensing Prison, Philadelphia, on 7 May 1896.

Koenigstein, Claudius-François

A French murderer and anarchist, known by his mother's maiden name of 'Ravachol', who proclaimed, 'There are no innocent *bourgeois*.' No doubt he felt that this belief was confirmed when he went to the guillotine (↻ Lady Mallowan's note 6) in 1892.

Konigsberg, Allen Stewart

The real name of Woody Allen, the bespectacled, Jewish–
American comedian, comic actor, and writer of comedy films
(usually vehicles for himself and, until recently, Diane Keaton).
To paraphrase Henry Wadsworth Longfellow: when Allen is
funny, he is very very funny, but when he is unfunny he is very
unfunny indeed.[1] His Broadway success *Play It Again Sam*,[2]
which unsolemnises the Bogart cult, was filmed in 1972.

1 The nursery song goes like this:

> There was a little girl, and she had a little curl
> Right in the middle of her forehead;
> When she was good, she was very very good
> But when she was bad she was horrid.

The lines were only attributed to Longfellow until 1882, the
year of his death, when it was revealed that he had acknowledged
the authorship.

2 A misquotation from the 1942 Warner Brothers film *Casablanca*, which almost had the misfortune to star Ronald Reagan and
Ann Sheridan instead of Humphrey Bogart and Ingrid Bergman,
and in which the song 'As Time Goes By', sung by Dooley
Wilson, was slipped in as an afterthought.

Some three years later, when the Marx Brothers (◊ Leonard
Marx) were about to make *A Night in Casablanca*, the Warner
Brothers threatened legal action, claiming that the use of the name
Casablanca would constitute an esoteric breach of copyright.
Groucho, speaking on behalf of himself and his siblings, wrote a
letter which read, in part:

Dear Warner Brothers,

Apparently there is more than one way of conquering a city and holding it as your own. For example, up to the time that we contemplated making this picture, I had no idea that the city of Casablanca belonged exclusively to Warner Brothers. However, it was only a few days after our announcement appeared that we received your long, ominous legal document warning us not to use the name Casablanca.

It seems that in 1471, Ferdinand Balboa Warner, your great-great-grandfather, while looking for a shortcut to the city of Burbank, had stumbled on the shores of Africa and, raising his alpenstock (which he later turned in for a hundred shares of the common), named it Casablanca.

I just don't understand your attitude. Even if you plan on re-releasing your picture, I am sure that the average movie fan could learn in time to distinguish between Ingrid Bergman and Harpo. I don't know whether I could, but I certainly would like to try.

You claim you own Casablanca and that no one else can use that name without your permission. What about 'Warner Brothers'? Do you own that, too? You probably have the right to use the name Warner, but what about Brothers? Professionally, we were brothers long before you were. We were touring the sticks as The Marx Brothers when Vitaphone was still a gleam in the inventor's eye, and even before us there had been other brothers—the Smith Brothers; the Brothers Karamazov; Dan Brothers, an outfielder with Detroit; and 'Brother, Can You Spare a Dime?' (This was originally 'Brothers, Can You Spare a Dime?' but this was spreading a dime pretty thin, so they threw out one brother, gave all the money to the other one and whittled it down to, 'Brother, Can You Spare a Dime?') . . .

The rest of this letter, Groucho's replies to letters he received from the bewildered legal department at Warner Brothers, and much more of his correspondence can be consulted in *The Groucho Letters* (published 1967).

Leach, Alexander Archibald

The real name of the Welsh-born film-actor Cary Grant, who continued to play romantic leads long after he should have been past it. A reporter once sent him a telegram, 'HOW OLD CARY GRANT?', and received the reply: 'OLD CARY GRANT FINE. HOW YOU?' Most impersonators rely on an adenoidal 'Judy, Judy, Judy,' but he never spoke this mortal line on the screen. (Nor did James Cagney ever say, 'You dirty rat.' And, of course, in the literary sphere, Sherlock Holmes never said, 'Elementary, my dear Watson.')

Liberty, Arthur Lasenby

The son of a small-time draper in the small town of Chesham, Buckinghamshire, he failed to get a university scholarship in 1859, when he was sixteen and by which time the family was living in Nottingham, and so was sent to London to make his living as a clerk in a lace warehouse owned by an uncle. Writing home soon after his arrival, Liberty reported that the business made the uncle 'miserable and without spirit'; though he didn't say as much, it is clear from the tenor of the letter that Liberty was similarly dispirited by both the warehouse and the uncle. He soon found another position, this time with a draper in Baker Street; but, as depressed as he had been at the warehouse, gave in his notice after eighteen months or so. Then he moved to the esteemed establishment of Farmer & Rogers' Great Shawl and Cloak Emporium, which occupied three adjoining premises in the 170s on the west side of Regent Street. Happier from the start, and happier still when he was put in charge of the emporium's oriental workshop, which was as favoured a gathering place of apostles of art for art's sake as was La Porte Chinoise in Paris, he stayed with the company until 1875—and would have stayed longer had he not married the daughter of a West End tailor who provided sufficient dowry for him to launch out on his own in a half-shop, 218a Regent Street, to which he gave the grand-sounding name of East India House, hoping to cash in on the vogue for oriental fabrics, ginger-jars, and the tall vases that James McNeill Whistler, one of the artists who transferred their custom from the oriental workshop to Liberty's establishment, called Long Elizas from their Dutch name *Lange Lysen*. Liberty's prosperity was nudged along or boosted unwittingly by some of his celebrated customers.

By the actress Ellen Terry (◊ Alice Grey), for instance. She had been Japan-fixated since 1863, when she had appeared as Titania in a costume of eastern materials, designed by Edward William Godwin (whom she lived with after separating from her first husband, the painter and sculptor George Frederic Watts, four years after the part-oriental production of *A Midsummer Night's Dream*). Whistler gave Ellen Terry a blue-and-white Nankin dinner set, and 'sent my little girl a tiny Japanese kimono when Liberty was hardly a name'. Both presents fitted in with the decor of her house in Bloomsbury, the drawing room of which was recalled many years later by the actor Johnstone Forbes- Robertson:

The floor was covered with straw-coloured matting, and there was a dado of the same material. Above the dado were white walls, and the hangings were of cretonne, with a fine Japanese pattern in delicate grey-blue. The chairs were of wickerwork, cushions like the hangings, and in the centre of the room was a full-sized cast of the Venus of Milo, before which was a small pedestal holding a censer from which rose, curling round the Venus, ribbons of blue smoke. The whole effect was what art students of my time would have called 'awfully jolly'.

'Artistic silks' from Liberty were used for the costumes of the first production of Gilbert and Sullivan's *Patience*, at the Opera Comique, London, in 1881, which caused quite a stir because the actor playing Bunthorne, the fleshly poet, was, even down to the monocle, a counterfeit presentment of Whistler, while the idyllic poet Archibald Grosvenor was played like, and given props associated with, Oscar Wilde (◊ Jack Worthing)—no coincidence, for

> Though the Philistine may jostle, you will rank as an
> apostle in the high aesthetic band,
> If you walk down Piccadilly with a poppy or a lily in
> your mediaeval hand.

In the Savoy Theatre, built from the takings of Gilbert and Sullivan operas and for their presentation, a private room for royal and otherwise distinguished members of the audience was festooned with Liberty silks; soon afterwards, similar rooms in other theatres were similarly garlanded. Arthur Liberty made sure that the private rooms received plenty of publicity; likewise, the mission, ostensibly secret, of 'Liberty's special envoys' to Japan, there to observe the natives and to buy fabrics on behalf of the first production of *The Mikado*.

As Liberty's fame grew (not only among Britons and Americans, but among Continentals, too: in the 1890s, the decorative style that got its name of Art Nouveau from that of the Paris shop of a German art-dealer called Samuel Bing became known to Italians as *Stile Liberty*), the business expanded—from half-shop to full shop, to several shops, not all adjacent, and then to a large store at the corner of Regent Street and Great Marlborough Street. In 1927, ten years after the death of *Sir* Arthur Liberty, a new Tudorbethan store was completed, its timber—oak and teak—taken from two men-of-war, HMSs

Hindustan and *Impregnable*. Liberty's was by then even more associated with the Bloomsbury artistic circle than was free, gender-irrespective love. And it came in for gibes from writers outside the circle. Susan, Lady Tweedsmuir, wife of the author (as John Buchan) and Governor-General of Canada, wrote in *Edwardian Lady* (published 1966) that, even before the war, 'stupid people equated intellectual women with those who wore floppy dark green Liberty dresses, strings of beads, and flat heeled shoes'; in *Cakes and Ale* (published 1930), Somerset Maugham had a character called Alroy Kear, an aspiring novelist who 'joined dining clubs where, in the basement of an hotel in Victoria Street or Holborn, men of letters, young barristers, and ladies in Liberty silks and strings of beads, ate a three-and-sixpenny dinner and discussed art and literature'; and in *The Documents in the Case*, the crime novel by Dorothy L(eigh) Sayers and Robert Eustace that also appeared in 1930, a letter dated 14 October 1923 is quoted: 'I knew we should be asked downstairs to tea. And we've been! Down among the Liberty curtains and the brass Benares ware! Three young women, two bright youths, the local parson and the family . . . Everything too conscientiously bright . . . No sooner had I got there than I was swept into a discussion about "this wonderful man Einstein!"' But for Liberty's—then, before, in the years leading to the Swinging 60s, and even more so since—almost any publicity has been good publicity.

Lincoln, Abraham

A trombonist; one of the comparatively few dead or now aged American exponents of jazz who were legally entitled to their entire dais-names. The trumpeter James Jordan acquired the nomenclative prefix of Taft—presumably from William Howard Taft, twenty-seventh President of the United States—and Lester

Young, saxophonist and clarinettist, was nicknamed Prez, short for president, by Eleanora Holiday, the singer and composer who preferred to be called Billie (after the film-star Billie Dove) but who was sometimes known as Lady Day: a less elevated title than that of the vocalist, pianist and song-writer Victoria Spivey, who, naturally, was called Queen. There was a prevalence of Kings: among them, the singer and pianist Nat Cole (a shortening of Nathaniel Adams Coles), the Puerto Rican trumpeter Louis Garcia, the cornetist and composer Joe Oliver, and the trumpeter and arranger Edwin Swayzee, who during his brief career (he was only thirty-two when he died in 1935) worked with such jazz celebrities as 'Cab' Cabell Calloway and 'Jelly Roll' Ferdinand Morton, and toured Europe with the 'Blackbirds' stage-show. European titles were annexed by the pianist William Basie, who chose to be called Count, and the drummer Joseph Marshall, who reigned as Kaiser (the German version of the Latin *Caesar*) in the company of, among many others, Fletcher 'Smack' Henderson, Mezz Mezzrow (really Milton Mesirow), and the Duke, Edward Kennedy Ellington, who was a good pianist and a sometimes inspired composer (of, for instance, 'Mood Indigo' and 'Sophisticated Lady'—a title that was pluralised into the title of a show using Ellington's music that was successful on Broadway in the early 1980s). Modest compared with most of jazz's dignitaries, the pianist and arranger Charles Phillip Thompson settled for Sir.

Lord Dundreary

Dundreary sidewhiskers got their name from the silly-ass, dandy character in Tom Taylor's *Our American Cousin*, which was the play being presented at Ford's Theatre, Washington, on Good Friday, 1865, when President Lincoln, sitting in a box, was assassinated by John Wilkes Booth, an actor who was not in the cast (♭ Dr Samuel Alexander Mudd). The mortuary joke, 'But apart from that, Mrs Lincoln, how did you enjoy the play?', has been joined by 'But apart from that, Mrs Kennedy, how did you like Dallas?'

Macbeth

An eleventh-century Scots king who probably wouldn't have recognised himself as the eponymous character in Shakespeare's play, which is loosely based on what the sixteenth-century Raphael Holinshed wrote of him in the mainly mythic *Chronicles of Scotland*. The play has a history of misfortune in rehearsal and performance: stabbings, sudden illnesses, falls from rostra, etc. As far as I can tell, the only fatal accident occurred during a performance at the Oldham Coliseum, Lancashire, in March 1947, when Harold Norman, the actor playing the leading part, was stabbed to the bowels by Antony Oakley, playing Macduff, and died from peritonitis. In theatrical circles, the superstition about the play is so strong that most people don't dare even to speak its title but refer to it as 'the Scottish play' or something similar. Noël Coward, determinedly unsuperstitious (except that he drew the line at sleeping thirteen to a bed), asked for a portrait of Lady Macbeth to be included in the decor for his play *Waiting in the Wings* (1960), which is set in a home for aged actresses; in most productions, the portrait is a copy of John Singer Sargent's painting of Ellen Terry as she appeared with Henry Irving (◊ Alice Grey) at the Lyceum in 1888–9, wearing a costume that glowed with the metallic lustre of the wings of green beetles.

Macguffin

Alfred Hitchcock's term for a 'non-plot' around which an elaborate story is created. In *North by Northwest*, the writer Ernest Lehman put together two Macguffins: Roger Thornhill, an advertising agent, is kidnapped by spies, who have mistaken him for a CIA agent—but the latter agent is non-existent, invented by the CIA as a means of trapping the gang.

Incidentally, the most famous scene in that film may be not quite as Hitchcock wanted it. He is quoted as having said, 'I had it all worked out that Cary Grant would slide down Lincoln's nose when he was on Mount Rushmore, then hide in Lincoln's nostril, then have a sneezing fit which gave his position away to his pursuers. It's a shame I was never allowed to do it. The Department of the Interior said that if I used Mount Rushmore, any chase or fight scene had to take place between the heads,[1] not on them. Why? I was told it was a shrine of democracy.'

1 Of Presidents George Washington, Thomas Jefferson, Abraham Lincoln and Theodore Roosevelt.

M'Laughlan, Charles

An Irish actor, under the name of Macklin, who may have been over a hundred when he died in 1797. His main claim to fame is that he was the first actor since the Restoration to play Shylock as a tragic figure, thus drawing from Alexander Pope a rave review in the form of a couplet:

> This is the Jew
> That Shakespeare drew.

Macklin wrote several comedies, two of which outlived him: *Love à la Mode*, in which he himself played Sir Archy McSarcasm, and *The Man of the World*, in which he continued to star as Sir Pertinax McSycophant when he was into his eighties.

McNeile, Herman Cyril

Born in 1888 at the Naval Prison at Bodmin, Cornwall, where his father, a naval officer, was governor, he received most of his education at Cheltenham College, and then, after a spell at the Royal Military Academy at Woolwich, was commissioned into the Royal Engineers (formerly the Royal Sappers and Miners; saps are trenches by which infantrymen approach hostile positions). Though he was keen on writing, the only thing he had published before the First World War was an article in a racing paper, for which the recompense was a tip on a rank outsider, which finished first past the post at gratifyingly long odds. He had what was known as a good war: in the autumn of 1914, shortly after being sent to France with the British Expeditionary Force, he was promoted to captain; he was involved in the first and second battles of Ypres—being gassed at the latter—and, as well as being mentioned in despatches, was awarded the Military Cross and further promoted, to the rank of lieutenant-colonel. When he wasn't fighting, he wrote articles and stories based on thoughts that went through his mind when he was; one of the stories was read by Lord Northcliffe, owner of the *Daily Mail*, who was so taken with it that he not only asked for more but tried, without success, to persuade Lord Kitchener, the thud-and-blunder Secretary of State for War, to release McNeile from the army so that he could become a trench correspondent for the *Mail*. As it wasn't done for a serving officer to write under his own name, Northcliffe turned McNeile's occupation into a pseudonym: Sapper.

An inaugural volume of the stories, called *Sergeant Michael Cassidy, RE*, sold 50,000 copies within nine months of its publication in 1915; other collections followed, and were almost as successful.

In the months just before and shortly after his demobilisation, Sapper completed a novel—a shocker or startler, as he alternatively referred to it. Published in 1920, it caught the public mood to a T: the hero and his chums were ex-soldiers who found peace dull; the villains were Bolsheviks, Jews to boot. In this book, *Bulldog Drummond*, and subsequent ones,[1] Hugh 'Bulldog' Drummond, aided by Algy, Peter, Ted, Toby and Jerry, thwart-ed the dastardly plans of, but never quite managed to exterminate, Carl Petersen[2] and the *femme fatale* Irma, who (the relation-ship was never made clear) was Carl's wife, mistress, daughter, or—least likely—very good friend. Bulldog was a sort of energetic, unaesthetic Philo Vance (◊ Willard Huntingdon Wright); he said—or, more often than not, *cried*—such things as: 'Together we will outwit the knaves. I will write and cancel a visit: glad of the chance. Old Julia Manton—face like a horse: house at Sheffield: roped me in, Tumkins—positively stunned me with her verbosity. Ghastly house—but reeks of boodle.' (From chapter 2, 'In Which Scotland Yard Sits Up and Takes Notice', of *The Black Gang*; the second of the series, published 1922.)

Egged on by his agent A. P. Watt, Sapper turned some of the adventures into stage plays which were produced in the West End with diminishing returns at the box office. The first, called simply by the hero's name, opened at Wyndham's in March 1921, and ran for 430 performances; but the success was due more to Gerald du Maurier's[3] performance as Hugh Drummond than to Sapper's adaptive skill. Subsequent efforts did not pay their way. The final dramatisation, *Bulldog Drummond Hits Out*, was not staged until after his death, from cancer of the throat, at the age of forty-eight; that was in 1937. He left a fortune—which would increase over the years from new impressions and editions of his books and from Bulldog Drummond films—to his wife and two sons.

1 When Sapper died, the saga was prolonged by his old friend and collaborator Gerard Fairlie, a regular soldier, talented at sports, particularly golf and boxing. In a radio broadcast, Sapper said that he had based Drummond on Fairlie. I can think of no other instance of a literary prototype becoming the recounter of adventures of the literary product.

2 About halfway through Sapper's series, Petersen dies in a dirigible—but, as was said after George Gershwin's death in 1937, one doesn't have to believe this if one doesn't want to.

3 His greatest early success came in 1906, when he played the part of Raffles (◊ Captain Joseph Shaw's note 2) in the West End. From then until his death in 1934, he was one of the most adored of London's matinee idols. Du Maurier cigarettes are named after him. (At least two other brands of cigarette have been associated, but less successfully, with stage personalities: De Reszke, named after the Polish tenor Jean [1850–1925], and Olivier, named after the actor Laurence.)

Gerald du Maurier's father George is best remembered as an artist for his work for *Punch*, and as an author for his novel *Trilby*, published in 1894. The following year, Paul Potter's dramatisation of the novel was presented at the Haymarket by Herbert Beerbohm Tree; Gerald du Maurier had a small part in the production. Audiences were much taken by the soft felt hat worn by the heroine Trilby O'Ferrall, an artist's model who is hypnotised into becoming a singer, and such headgear, worn more often by men than women, became known as a trilby; also, the name of the hypnotist, Svengali, came to be applied (more generally than that of the German physician-hypnotist Franz Mesmer, who began expounding his mesmeric notions in 1775) to people with power over others.

Gerald's brother Guy, a regular soldier killed in action in France in 1916, was the anonymous author of the play *An Englishman's Home* (◊ Harvey's note 1).

Gerald's daughter Daphne is a successful author of fiction, including the short story on which Hitchcock's film *The Birds* is based (the pre-release advertising campaign was noticeable—indeed, hardly missable—for the slogan, 'The Birds is Coming'), and *Rebecca* (also filmed by Hitchcock), which has one of the two most-quoted opening lines of twentieth-century novels: 'Last night I dreamt I went to Manderley again.'

The other most-quoted opening line, 'It was a bright cold day in April, and the clocks were striking thirteen,' is from *Nineteen Eighty-Four* by George Orwell (◊ Eric Arthur Blair)— who, in an essay, looked down on middle-aged men who use the novels of Sapper in aid of a fantasy existence.

Macready, William Charles

In theatrical parlance, a Macready is a long pause for dramatic effect (marked in the prompt copy with a half-circle over a dot, signifying to the prompter that his help is not required). For some thirty years after about 1820, Macready, an actor who hated acting, was one of the leading tragedians on the English stage; when Edmund Kean died in 1833, he was virtually unrivalled. However, in 1849, when he played a season at the Astor Place Opera House in Manhattan, his pre-eminence was forcibly questioned by supporters of the American actor Edwin Forrest; aided by anti-British elements, the Forrest fans caused a riot outside the theatre, which was quelled only after twenty-two people had been killed and thirty-six wounded by shots fired by the militia. Macready, who was himself a man of ungovernable temper, decided that discretion was the better part of valour (a misquotation from Shakespeare's *Henry IV, Part 1*), and never again appeared in America.

Macy, Rowland Hussey

The direct descendant of the Thomas Macy who, some time between 1659 and 1661, became the first white man to settle on Nantucket Island, Massachusetts—having chosen to do so because of Baptist repression of Quakers in nearby Salisbury, where he had lived after emigrating from England—Rowland was born on the island in 1822, the fourth of six children of John Macy, who had captained a merchant ship before establishing a small store, devoted mainly to books and magazines.

When he was fifteen, Rowland Macy sailed from New Bedford as a member of the crew of the whaling ship *Emily Morgan*, bound for Cape Horn and the Pacific. The voyage lasted nearly four years.[1] On Sunday, 26 September 1841, the ship dropped anchor at New Bedford, and that night the owner wrote in his diary:

> A strong S. West wind & fine weather. Two good sermons from Mr Osgood. Towards evening the Emily Morgan made her appearance, all full and all well, a capital voyage & capitally conducted. She has also more [than] 250 lbs Ambergris taken from the stomach of one whale—a prize indeed if it proves pure. The E.M. has been absent 45½ mos. & has 3100 bbls. oil.

What Macy did next is unclear. It is said that he went to Boston, and there spent six months or so in a printing office; if the story is true, it indicates where he picked up the rudiments of the advertising skill that he later displayed. He was certainly in Boston in August 1844, when he married Louisa Houghton, the sister of a dry goods retailer in the city. Financed, perhaps, by his new brother-in-law, he set up a thread and needle store at 78½ Hanover Street. By 1846, he had moved his business to

Washington Street; unsuccessfully, it seems, for two years later he was working for his brother-in-law.

In 1849, when the news of the discovery of gold in California reached New England, Macy and his brother Charles—his senior by ten years—straightway set sail for San Francisco. If they tried their hands at gold-mining, it can have been only for a short time, for by July of the following year they were trading in partnership with two other men, doing business under the name of Macy & Co. at Marysville, forty miles north of Sacramento. Advertisements in the Marysville *Herald* described the firm as

> General Dealers in Provisions, Dry Goods, Clothing, &c. &c. Also Agents for Hawley Co's Express. Letters, Packages and Gold Dust forwarded to all parts of the world, through Adams & Co.

One advertisement proclaimed that Macy & Co.

> . . . have just received a large addition to their present stock of goods, and are prepared to furnish just about everything necessary for the use of Miners. They have on hand now a stock amounting to eighty thousand dollars. . . . Country Merchants, Packers, City Traders, MINERS, &c., will do well to give us a call before purchasing elsewhere.

But in the autumn of 1850 Macy & Co. went bust. Charles remained in Marysville as agent for the Adams Express Co., but Rowland travelled back east. Though he had made little money from the California venture, he had learnt much about the practice and perils of general retailing.

He used that knowledge when, in April 1851, he and his brother Robert, younger than himself by two years, opened a dry goods store at Haverhill, a town in Massachusetts with a population of 5,877. Departing from the retail norm, the brothers insisted on GOODS FOR CASH; but Rowland, speaking for himself, announced

> his intention to give this Store such a reputation for NOVELTY AND LOW PRICES, as shall make it a *marked and distinct feature* in the Dry Goods trade of Haverhill. At this store may be found at all times the best stock of FANCY DRY GOODS in town, at prices which defy competition. Most of the time he has a good stock of

heavy DRY GOODS and DOMESTICS, but never, unless bought in such a way as to be sold at LESS THAN THE REGULAR PRICES. . . .

We do not profess to keep a large Stock of Goods, but we *do* keep a FAST one. . . .

It appears that the Haverhillians were none too impressed. During the four weeks immediately preceding Christmas 1851, the store was closed; it re-opened on Christmas Day for Macy's first sale. After several more sales, each publicised by a rather frantic advertisement topped by a crowing rooster, the Haverhill store closed for good in the summer of 1855.

During the following three years, Macy occupied himself as a broker, dealing in shares, money and real estate; he moved from Haverhill to Boston to Superior City, Wisconsin. In 1858, he left the last-named place and headed for New York, where he intended to have one last try at making a success of retailing.

On Wednesday, 27 October, he opened a small fancy dry goods store at 204 Sixth Avenue. The first day's takings amounted to $11.06. Believing that things could only get better, he persevered. Thirteen months later, when he was employing a staff of fifteen, he had spent $2,800 on advertising, and had sold ribbons, laces, embroideries, artificial flowers, feathers, handkerchiefs, cambric flouncings, hosiery and gloves to the total value of $90,000.

In 1866, he leased the ground floor of 66 West 14th Street, the building at the rear of his store: perhaps without knowing it, he had begun to create a department store.[2] More adjoining premises were acquired, and by 1877, the year of his death, his business occupied the ground space of eleven buildings. Three years before, he had granted a crockery and glassware concession to L. Straus & Sons, on the understanding that they would pay him half of their profits. In 1896, the Strauses took complete ownership of the department store, which they continued to call R. H. Macy & Co.

The present store, on Herald Square, was opened on 8 November 1902. It was the retailing wonder of the age: nine storeys tall, it contained thirty-three hydraulic freight and passenger lifts and four escalators; pneumatic tubes were used for shooting cash and sales checks from one part of the building to another. The store continued to grow during the 1920s and early

'30s, and eventually encompassed the entire block from Broadway to Seventh Avenue, and from 34th Street to 35th: 2,012,000 square feet of floor space, making it the largest store in the world. Nowadays the 11,000 employees scattered through 170 departments offering 400,000 different items handle 45 million transactions each year. Using patriotism in aid of publicity, Macy's organises a fireworks display on the Fourth of July and a Broadway- clogging parade on Thanksgiving Day.

1 To get some idea of what Macy went through, read the expository chapters of *Moby Dick*, which recount Herman Melville's experiences on a whaling voyage begun in January 1841, when Macy was still at sea.

2 As far as I can tell, the world's first department store was the Marble Dry Goods Palace, which was opened in 1848; it was also, at that time, the largest shop in the world, for it occupied the whole length of a block on Broadway. The proprietor, Alexander Turney Stewart, had been an Irish schoolmaster or a schoolmaster in Ireland (considering his name, the latter alternative seems more likely) before his emigration to New York in 1823.

Mallory, George Herbert Leigh

'Because it is there,' this unemployed schoolmaster replied when, in 1923, while he was on a lecture tour in America, a reporter asked him why he wanted to climb Mount Everest (◊ Sir George Everest). Mallory had taken part in two Everest expeditions—a reconnaissance in 1921 and, in the following year, a full-fledged but unsuccessful attempt to reach the summit, during which an avalanche killed seven Sherpa porters[1]—and was gathering money in the hope of going on a third in 1924. Though his answer to the reporter is often quoted—and not just in a mountaineering context—there is uncertainty as to what he meant. Perhaps he didn't mean anything very much—but, tired and ill-tempered, sick of hearing the same question over and over again, simply snapped the words, hoping to change the subject. According to Walt Unsworth, the top climb-chronicler, Mallory used the word 'there' for things with a mystical quality, a habit picked up from A(rthur) C(hristopher) Benson, the author and master of Magdalene College, Cambridge, who, writing to him in 1911, had urged him to read a book that achieved high quality 'by being there'; during the war, Mallory had written home, describing privates digging trenches and saying that he would like to draw them like figures from Millet—only 'more there'. Unsworth suggests that Mallory 'was searching for what the poet Franz Wefel put more elegantly: "For those who believe, no explanation is necessary; for those who do not believe, no explanation is possible."'

Mallory was able to take part in the 1924 expedition. He and another member, Andrew Comyn Irvine, were last seen, about a third of the way up the mountain, 'going strong for the top'.

That attempt was unsuccessful; and so were those of six further expeditions and of three solo climbers. The first ascent was made by an expedition led by Colonel Henry Cecil John Hunt in 1953: a New Zealand bee-keeper, Edmund Hillary, and a Sherpa guide named Tenzing Bhotia (or, as he later preferred, Tenzing Norgay) reached the main summit on 29 May.

Hunt, Hillary and Tenzing received much publicity and several honours; but the other members of the expedition were soon forgotten, if they were ever remembered by people with no head for heights. They were Charles Evans, the deputy leader, who was a Liverpool surgeon; George Band, a post-graduate of Cambridge; Tom Bourdillon, a physicist; Alfred Gregory, a Blackpool travel-agent; George Lowe, who in his native New Zealand was a school-teacher; Wilfred Noyce, a schoolmaster and author; L. G. C. ('Griff') Pugh, a physiologist; Michael Ward, a London surgeon; Michael Westmacott, a statistician, and Charles Wylie, an officer in the regiment of Gurkhas.

1 Between 1921 and 1953, ten white climbers and thirteen Nepalese (Sherpa guides, coolies, and a Gurkha) died on the

mountain; the former total includes half a dozen members of a Soviet team that made an unsuccessful, and therefore unpublicised, attempt in 1952.

Mallowan, Dame Agatha Mary Clarissa Miller Christie, Lady

On 6 August 1975, the New York *Times* created a precedent by giving front-page coverage to the death of a fictional character:

HERCULE POIROT IS DEAD; FAMED BELGIAN DETECTIVE

'Hercule Poirot, a Belgian detective who became internationally famous, has died in England. His age was unknown. . . . His career, as chronicled in the novels of Dame Agatha Christie, his creator, was one of the most illustrious in fiction.

Mr Poirot, who was just 5 feet 4 inches tall, went to England from Belgium during World War I as a refugee. He settled in a little town not far from Styles, then an elaborate country estate, where he took on his first private case.[1]

The news of his death, given by Dame Agatha, was not unexpected. Word that he was near death reached here last May. . . . There had been many rumours to the effect that Dame Agatha had locked up two manuscripts— one a Poirot and one a Marple—in a vault and that they were not to be published until her death.[2] Jonathan Dodd, of Dodd, Mead, said that the Poirot was the one now being published.

Although the career of Poirot will no more engage his historian, a spokesman for the author said that Dame Agatha, who will be 85 Sept. 15, intends to continue writing.[3] In her long writing career, one that parallels the literary existence of her detective, she has published 85 full-length novels and collections of short stories, which have sold 350 million copies in hard cover and paperback all over the globe. This figure does not include the pirated editions behind the Iron Curtain, of which no count can be made.

In addition, under the pseudonym of Mary Westmacott she has written a half-dozen romances. . . .

. . . Dame Agatha, who has been described as a large woman looking both kind and capable, is the daughter of a well-to-do American father and English mother. She was tutored at home and attended, as she recalled, innumerable classes: dancing, singing, drawing. In World War I, she worked in a Red Cross hospital, and this experience gave her a good working knowledge of poisons, ingredients that turn up rather frequently in her books.[4]

In 1926, she suffered an attack of amnesia, left home and was discovered some days later in a hotel under another name. The furore stirred up by the newspapers over her disappearance has made her shy of newspapers and reporters ever since. . . . In 1928, she was divorced from her first husband, Archibald Christie, and in 1930 she was married to Max Mallowan, an archaeologist.'

Several of Dame Agatha's stories have been turned into plays, films, or both. At a London first-night of one of the plays, the stage manager, confused by a similarity between a number of lines delivered towards the end of the last act, brought the curtain down after the murderer had been revealed but before his motive had been explained; the audience applauded bewilderedly.[5]

Of course, the most successful of the plays is *The Mousetrap*, based on one of the nine tales in a volume published in 1949 as *Three Blind Mice and Other Stories* and subsequently as *The Mousetrap*; directed by Peter Cotes, and with Richard Attenborough and his wife Sheila Sim playing leading roles, the play opened at the bijou (490-seat) Ambassadors Theatre, London, on 25 November 1952, and, decades later, was transferred to the theatre next door, the slightly larger (600-seat) St Martin's, where it continues to run, having long ago exceeded the number of performances of any play produced anywhere in the world. At the last count, the play had been produced in 41 countries: not in Australia or on Broadway, however, for Dame Agatha forbade productions in those places until six months after the West End run—which, as the London *Mousetrap* has become as much of a tourist attraction as the Tower, Madam Tussaud's,[6] or the Tate Gallery,[7] may mean never. An Off-Broadway production opened towards the end of 1960 but didn't run far into 1961; which is rather surprising, considering that American visitors to London constitute a large proportion of the audiences at the St Martin's. Those travelling to the theatre by taxi are advised to tip the driver well, since disappointed cabbies are likely to drive away, shouting, 'It's the —— wot dun it.'

The quizzical Americans who have banded together as the Institute of Expertology, dedicated to publicising pundits' howlers, will be delighted by an extract from *Crime and the Drama; or Dark Deeds Dramatised*, a book published in 1927 by H. Chance Newton, who was better known as Carados, the opinionative columnist of the London *Referee*. Speaking of plays inspired by the Maybrick poison mystery (Liverpool, 1889), Newton declares:

> The best and most daring of these dramas was by that brilliant playwright Sydney Grundy.[8] He very soon came forth with a very powerful society play which, when he asked me to see it on its trial performance at the Greenwich Theatre, was called, *The Mouse Trap*—a reference, of course, to Hamlet's retort to King Claudius' question at the famous matinee at Elsinore Castle.
>
> I advised Grundy, however, to choose a better title, at least one more understandable by the general public, who might not be supposed to know their Hamlet. Grundy did choose another title. He renamed it, in fact, *A Fool's Paradise*.

1 *The Mysterious Affair at Styles* was rejected by several publishers before being accepted by William Collins & Sons, who neglected it for a whole year, eventually publishing it in 1920.

2 *Curtain* was written in the 1940s. The decision to publish it unposthumously was prompted by the box-office success of the film made in 1974 of *Murder on the Orient Express* (which, when first published in America in 1934, was called *Murder in the Calais Coach*).

The Orient Express ran for the first time—Paris to Constantinople (now Istanbul)—on 1 June 1889, and for the last, or so it was thought, on 17 May 1977; there is now an abridged version, stopping short at Venice.

3 She died on 12 January 1976.

4 On 13 January 1976, Rayner Heppenstall (⚲) wrote in his journal:

> I corresponded once with Agatha Christie. This was over one of her novels in which it seemed to me that she had based her story and the murderess on a real-life French case and, if it were so, wanted to say this in *A Little Pattern of French Crime*, which I was then writing, so that it must have been in 1969. The French murderess had been of a distinctly lower social class than Mrs Christie's.
>
> In opposition to what seems to be the common view, I think that Agatha Christie wrote better towards the end, at any rate in the detail of her writing. She became a better stylist. If she had later revised the dialogue of *The Mousetrap*, it would have become a better play. Her early novels are also disfigured by a crude anti-Semitism.

Dame Agatha's letter to Heppenstall, written from Winterbrook House, Wallingford, Berkshire, on 13 January 1969, read, in part:

> I am afraid I cannot be much help to you in what you want to know, especially as I am just recovering from influenza and feel definitely muzzy in the head.
>
> As far as I can recall I read an article a good many years ago, I think in a medical journal of some kind, dealing with various French cases, on women who had attended patients and frequently children with great devotion. The patients usually died and the devoted neighbour wept bitterly over their demise. As far as I remember the article stressed the pathological side of these cases. Several of them were cited and I should imagine that Jeanne Weber was prominent among them. The medical article was the only thing I remember, but as it was a long time ago I had really forgotten practically all about it, though finding it interesting to include the possibility of such a thing in my last book [*By the Pricking of My Thumbs*, published 1968]. That is the best I can do.

It has been suggested that her literarily innovative use of the poison thallium in her 1961 novel *The Pale Horse* put ideas into the head of Graham Young, who in 1971 compulsively poisoned colleagues at a Hertfordshire photographic firm with thallium.

5 At about the same time, I was on the sidelines of a final-curtain incident as the stage director for a production of Ibsen's *Hedda Gabler* in which, for a reason that I cannot recall, the dark-haired actress playing Hedda wore a blonde, Shirley-Temple-like wig.

The play is performed in a box-set with a draped alcove in the back wall. In the last act, Hedda exits between the drapes and plays a piano as a sort of overture to suicide. The piano, heard but not seen by the audience, is played by an offstage musician. In this particular production, as soon as the musician responded to a cue to stop playing, I fired a pistol at the back of the piano. The report twanged and reverberated; an effect that pleased me. While this was going on, Hedda had to arrange herself on a chaise in the alcove, a hand clutching her heart and steeped in Gordon Moore's red toothpaste, ready to be as still as death when Dr Brock flung wide the drapes.

On the first night, Hedda came offstage, the musician started to play the piano, and I waited with the pistol while an assistant stage manager squeezed the tube of toothpaste over Hedda's hand. She then ran back into the alcove and reclined on the chaise as the musician finished playing and I fired the gun. As she lay back, the blonde wig fell from her head.

Noticing this, I whispered at her. Dr Brock was already on his way upstage to open the drapes.

Hedda lifted her head and stared at me, let out a small exclamation, then scuttled from the alcove into the wings. In her panic, she forgot all about the wig apart from the fact that she was not wearing it. The thing had landed on a cushion on the chaise, the fabric of which was blemished by the red imprint of a hand, and several blobs of toothpaste. An awesome sight.

Dr Brock pulled open the drapes with a flourish. A gasp went up from the auditorium. He stared helplessly, uncomprehendingly, staggered slightly, then, turning to face the audience, cut to the last line of the play: 'My God, people just don't do such things.' The curtain came down amidst thunderous applause. But, unfortunately, the reviews were mixed. One critic expressed puzzlement regarding the calibre of the suicide weapon. 'Perhaps the explosive was fired from an Ack-Ack gun,' he suggested.

6 The founder of the waxworks exhibition was born **Marie** Gresholtz in Berne, Switzerland, in 1760. Her father, a **soldier,** having died before her birth, and her mother, daughter of a **pastor,** six years afterwards, she was adopted by an uncle, Johann **Kurtz** (or Creutz; whichever, he subsequently latinised his name into Curtius), with whom she migrated to Paris in 1770. Curtius was a proficient modeller of figures in wax. Marie assisted him, then practised the art herself; when he set up a Cabinet de Cire in the Palais Royal, some of the exhibits were hers, and she took on commissions that he was too busy to accept. The enterprise flourished; even during the Revolution, when Curtius and Marie, equally expedient, modelled heads decapitated by the guillotine (an instrument perfected by Dr Antoine Louis, who probably based his design on similar gadgets that had been employed in other countries, Scotland among them, but named after Joseph Ignace Guillotin, the member of the Constituent Assembly who proposed its adoption for all executions, thus doing away with the unegalitarian dichotomy of one method of beheading for the rich, another for the poor).

When Marie was thirty-four—by which time Curtius was dead, perhaps murdered by a poisoner—she married a Monsieur Tussaud, son of a well-to-do wine-grower in Mâcon; but in 1800 she separated from her husband, and two years later sailed for England, taking her cero-plastic exhibits and mementoes of the Revolution with her. Peripatetic at first, setting up her exhibition first in one large town, then in another, it was not until 1833 that she acquired premises in Baker Street, London (on a site now occupied by the headquarters of Marks & Spencer). She died there in 1850, shortly after a wax figure of herself had been completed. The effigy of the little (very little) old woman is still displayed in Marylebone Road, whence the waxworks moved in 1884.

7 Created by Sir Henry Tate, who, having started his working iife as a grocer's assistant in Liverpool, made a fortune from another man's invention of a machine for cutting sugar into cubes. But for this idea, patented by Tate, there would be no Tate & Lyle multinational company, no Mr Cube squaring up to Socialists who yearn to nationalise the firm, and no Tate Gallery. About 1890, Tate first spoke of offering his collection of contemporary art, housed in a mansion at Streatham, South London, to the National Gallery. Far from being an offer that couldn't be refused, it was considered too munificent. So Tate approached the Chancellor of the Exchequer, saying that if the government would provide a site in central London, he would erect a building and give it a start as a gallery of national art by providing the bulk of

his paintings by British artists. The Chancellor made overtures to land-owners, but three years passed before the politician Sir William Harvey donated the ground on the Thames Embankment on which stood Millbank Prison, which was about to be demolished; Sir William also promised to maintain the gallery, and to place the foundation in the hands of the National Gallery's trustees. The building, paid for by Tate and designed by Sidney Smith in a 'free classic style', was opened by the Prince and Princess (Alexandra) of Wales in 1897; Tate was knighted in the following year, and died a year later. Recently, the gallery has made some odd acquisitions (most nonsensical, perhaps, a pile of bricks, referred to by a connoisseur as 'art with a capital F'), but these are minor blemishes; there are many fine works, including Sargent's painting of Ellen Terry (◊ Macbeth).

8 A barrister in Manchester until he achieved success as a dramatist, he is remembered, if at all, for his adaptation of a French farce as *A Pair of Spectacles*, first produced on the West End stage (at the Garrick, named after the eighteenth-century actor David Garrick) in 1890, and revived over and over again, even a couple of times after his death in 1914.

Mrs Grundy—from whom sprang grundyism = prudishness —is an unseen character in Thomas Morton's play *Speed the Plough* (1798), of whom another character says: 'Always ding-dinging Dame Grundy into my ears—What will Mrs Grunday say?—or, What will Mrs Grundy think?'

The life of another fictitious Grundy is abstracted in the nursery-rhyme variant on the Seven Ages of Man:

> Solomon Grundy,
> Born on Monday,
> Christened on Tuesday,
> Married on Wednesday,
> Very ill on Thursday,
> Worse on Friday,
> Died on Saturday,
> Buried on Sunday.
> This is the end
> of Solomon Grundy.

Manning, Marie

She, together with her husband Fred—and with Charles Dickens looking on—was hanged on the roof of Horsemonger Lane Gaol, London, in 1849. In some respects, the Manning case resembles the Crippen case,[1] sixty-one years later: the body of the victim, Patrick O'Connor, once Marie's beau, was buried in quicklime beneath the kitchen floor; the Mannings were recklessly eager to dispose of O'Connor's assets; they were frightened into fleeing from justice. (Unlike Dr Crippen and his mistress Ethel Le Neve, who stuck together as 'Mr and Master Robinson', the Mannings fled in different directions, Marie to Scotland, Fred to the Channel Island of Jersey.) A rather ordinary case, it seems today; but it caused great public interest—chiefly because Marie, once she was caught, tried to live up to the romantic picture of her painted by imaginative reporters.

A week or so before the execution, Dickens told his friend John Leech, the *Punch* cartoonist, 'The doleful weather, the beastly nature of the scene, the having no excuse for going (after seeing Courvoisier[2]) and the constantly recurring desire to avoid another such horrible and odious impression, decide me to cry off.' But the attraction of repulsion (Dickens's own term) proved too strong for him. On the eve of the event, he informed Leech: 'We have taken the whole of the roof (and the back kitchen) for the extremely moderate sum of Ten Guineas, or two guineas each.'

In 1852, when *Bleak House* began to appear, scenes of, and incidents in, the Manning case were brought to mind, and 'Hortense', the murderous French maid, was instantly recognised as a domestic version of Marie:

> . . . a large-eyed brown woman with black hair; who would be handsome, but for a certain feline mouth, and general uncomfort-

able tightness of face, rendering the jaws too eager, and the skull too prominent. There is something indefinably keen and wan about her anatomy; and she has a watchful way of looking out of the corners of her eyes without turning her head, which could be pleasantly dispensed with—especially when she is in an ill humour and near knives.

Mrs Manning chose black satin for her hanging gown, and it is said that sales of this material slumped as the result of the bad publicity.

1 The American-born Dr Hawley Harvey Crippen, who was known to friends as Peter, buried parts of his wife's body in the cellar of their home, 39 Hilldrop Crescent, in the Camden Town district of North London, having, prior to the surgery, dosed his wife with the narcotic poison hyoscine. The victim, daughter of a German mother and a Polish father who sold fruit from a stall in Brooklyn, was christened Kunigunde Mackamotzki; when she was in her late teens, living in an apartment paid for by a married Brooklynite, she began calling herself Cora Turner, but soon after marrying Crippen in September 1892 (they had first met a couple of months before, when she had visited the medical practice where Crippen was locum; he subsequently recalled, rather vaguely, 'I believe she had had a miscarriage, or something of that kind'), she assumed the name of Cora Motzki, hoping—forlornly, as it turned out— that it would help to realise her ambition of obtaining soprano roles in grand opera. In 1897, the Crippens came to England—he to open a London branch of a Manhattan cure-all firm called Munyon's Homeopathic Remedies; she, optimistic because American acts were in vogue, to try her luck on the English stage. Though her appearances at music-halls were few and far between, and soon her sole theatrical connection was as honorary treasurer of the Music Hall Ladies' Guild, she preferred to be known by her newish stage-name of Belle Elmore than as Mrs Cora Crippen.

Crippen's motive for murdering his wife was his love for a typist who really was named Ethel Le Neve; he called her Wifie, while her pet-name for him was Hub. But following the demise of Mrs Crippen, Ethel posed as Master Robinson (Crippen as 'his' father) during the voyage to Father's Point, Quebec, where— Captain Henry Kendall, the master of the SS *Montrose*, having seen through her disguise and sent a message to the ship's owners in Liverpool (the first time that wireless telegraphy was used in the cause of criminal detection)—police were waiting to arrest both of them. On the morning of Crippen's execution (Ethel having been acquitted as an accessory to his crime), she again sailed for North America, on this occasion calling herself Miss Allen. By the time she returned to England during the First World War, she had discarded Allen for Nelson. It was under the latter name that she married Stanley Smith, a clerk in a South-London furniture store. The Smiths had two children. In August 1967, Mrs Smith, an eighty-four-year-old widow, died in hospital. She had been reticent about her past, but her last request was that a locket containing a picture of 'Peter' Crippen—Hub to her—should be pinned to her shroud.

2 Twenty years before, Dickens and William Makepeace Thackeray had been in the crowd of 40,000 or so who had watched the execution of François Benjamin Courvoisier, the Swiss valet who had slain his master Lord William Russell. Dickens caught sight of Thackeray, but was unable to attract his attention. Both men were affected by the experience—Thackeray especially. He afterwards wrote the essay, 'Going to See a Man Hanged':

> I feel myself ashamed and degraded at the brutal curiosity which took me to that brutal sight. . . . I pray to Almighty God to cause this disgraceful sin to pass from among us, and to cleanse our land of blood. . . . I fully confess that I came away that morning with a disgust for murder, but it was for *the murder I saw done.*

Marx, Leonard

Nicknamed Chico, he was the first son (born 1891) of Samuel Marx and his wife Minnie, who was a sister of Al Shean, a partner in the famous vaudeville act of Gallagher and Shean.[1] His brothers were Adolph (Harpo), Julius (Groucho), Herbert (Zeppo), and—never a Marx Brother on film—Milton (Gummo).

Groucho's film roles include Professor Quincey Adams Wagstaff (*Horse Feathers*), Rufus T. Firefly (*Duck Soup*), Otis B. Driftwood (*A Night at the Opera*), Dr Hugo Z. Hackenbush (*A Day at the Races*), J. Cheever Loophole (*At the Circus*), and Wolf J. Flywheel (*The Big Store*).

Sample of Marxist humour (from *The Cocoanuts*, the Brothers' first film, made in 1929):

GROUCHO: *We're going to have an auction.*
CHICO: *I came over here on the Atlantic auction.*

The most memorable snatch of dialogue in a Marx Brothers film did not involve any of the Brothers. Right at the start of *Monkey Business*, the mate of a transatlantic liner reports to the captain: 'There are four stowaways in the forward hatch.' 'Four?' queries the captain. 'How do you know there are four?' 'They are singing "Sweet Adeline",' the mate explains.

Groucho is said to have sent the following telegram:

Please accept my resignation. I don't want to belong to any club that will accept me as a member.

1 Extract from a letter written by the journalist Alexander Woollcott to Jerome Kern, the composer of popular songs, on 22 February 1933:

And Al Shean, Jerry. Do you know about him? He and his sister were children of an old German musician named Lafey Schoenberg, who played the small towns of Hanover for fifty years, travelling from one to the other in a cart, and who died in Chicago at the age of one hundred and one. When they came to this country Al went to work as a pants-presser, and the sister made lace in a tenement. Al was known as the fastest presser south of Rivington Street, but he had a passion for singing swipes. He was always organising quartets and being fired for practicing in the can during working hours. Once, when a whole quartet was fired it went right into vaudeville as the Manhattan Comedy Four. This success inflamed the sister. It was too late for her to go on the stage, what with her five children and all, so she decided *they* must, and then pushed them into the theatre, although they and the theatre resisted strenuously. Of course you know they are the Marx brothers. When their star went into the ascendant in 1924 the Gallagher and Shean partnership had broken up, and Mrs Marx was faithless enough to think Al had better go into the ginger ale business. And now look at him. Playing so legitimately. Playing so beautifully. She would have been so proud and happy.

Merrick, Joseph Carey

His 'Autobiography', only a couple of pages long but sold in the form of a pamphlet to patrons of a freak show in which he, billed as The Elephant Man, was the main attraction, begins:

I first saw the light on the 5th of August, 1860. I was born in Lee Street, Wharf Street, Leicester. The deformity which I am now exhibiting was caused by my mother being frightened by an Elephant; my mother was going along the street when a procession of Animals were passing by, there was a terrible crush of people to see them, and unfortunately she was pushed under the

Elephant's feet, which frightened her very much; this occurring
during a time of pregnancy was the cause of my deformity.

The measurement round my head is 36 inches, there is a large
substance of flesh at the back as large as a breakfast cup, the other
part in a manner of speaking is like hills and valleys, all lumped
together, while the face is such a sight that no one could describe
it. The right hand is almost the size and shape of an Elephant's
fore-leg, measuring 12 inches round the wrist and 5 inches round
one of the fingers; the other hand and arm is no larger than that of
a girl ten years of age, although it is well proportioned. My feet
and legs are covered with thick lumpy skin, also my body, like
that of an Elephant, and almost the same colour, in fact, no one
would believe until they saw it, that such a thing could exist. It
was not perceived much at birth, but began to develop itself when
at the age of 5 years.

Not all of that, not even the date of birth, is accurate; and
few doctors of the present day, if any, would accept Merrick's
explanation for his deformity, which seems to have been a severe
manifestation of a disease called neurofibromatosis (neurofib-
roma being the term for a kind of tumour composed of nerve and
fibrous tissue).[1]

In 1886, Merrick was rescued or crimped from his actual or
would-be exhibitors by Frederick Treves,[2] lecturer and demon-
strator in anatomy to the London Hospital Medical School, who
arranged for him to be kept in a private ward, much like a cell, in
a part of the hospital known as Bedstead Square. There, during
the four remaining years of his life, he was observed and
examined by Treves and other medical men, and exhibited to
important personages, including members of the royal family,
who ventured to Whitechapel solely for the display of Merrick or
to see him in addition to other sights. He had one outing: a visit
to the pantomime at Drury Lane, probably in 1887, the year
before Dan Leno (◊ Harvey) made his debut at the theatre. The
visit was arranged by the actress Madge Kendal, and was made
possible by Baroness Burdett-Coutts (◊ Thomas Coutts), who
kept a private box at Drury Lane. Merrick, driven to the theatre
in a closed carriage, was smuggled into the box by way of the
Royal Entrance and the Royal Stairway; he sat with Treves at the
rear of the box, shielded from the view of the rest of the audience
by a phalanx of nurses wearing evening clothes. It is said that he
thoroughly enjoyed the fleeting glimpses of Puss in Boots; but

his usual immurement must have made him an uncritical spectator.

    1 Earlier in the century, a woman whose name may have been
Eleanor Fitzgerald and who suffered from tumours so pendulous
that she might have tripped over them had they not been
supported, appeared as The Elephant Woman in side-shows.

    2 Who became internationally renowned in the summer of
1902. On 24 June, just two days before the date fixed for the
coronation of the Prince of Wales as Edward VII, the heir-
apparent suffered an acute attack of perityphlitis. Treves, who had
come to specialise in that condition and others similarly affecting
the lower part of the stomach and its appendix, was called in by
royal physicians and, after consulting with them, performed an
operation. Edward, making a good recovery, was crowned on 9
August; and Treves was dubbed Sir Frederick soon afterwards.

Miller, Andrew

His press-gang, operating in the Portsmouth (or 'Pompey') area
at the time of the French Revolution and the subsequent
Napoleonic Wars, was so industrious that he was talked of,
whispered about, simply by his first name, and his victims were
said to have been snatched into 'the Andrew'—an appellation
that is still applied to the Royal Navy (◊ Kate Carney) and, by
extension, to the sea.

Milne, Christopher Robin

His birth in 1920 heralded an extraordinarily successful period for his father A(lan) A(lexander) Milne, who had three plays produced in the West End (*Mr Pym Passes By*, 1920; *The Truth About Blayds*, 1921; *The Dover Road*, 1922) and whose brilliant detective novel *The Red House Mystery* was published in 1922. When Christopher Robin was four, his father published *When We Were Very Young*, a series of verses dedicated to him; *Now We Are Six* followed in 1927. In the same genre, but in prose, A. A. Milne wrote *Winnie-the-Pooh* (1926) and *The House at Pooh Corner* (1928). All these books were splendidly illustrated by Ernest H. Shepard.[1] In 1961, five years after the author's death, the New York *Herald Tribune* dubbed *Winnie Ille Pu*, Dr Alexander Lennard's translation of the first Pooh book into Latin, 'the status book of the year'.

However, back in 1928, Dorothy Parker, writing as Constant Reader in *The New Yorker*, had slated Pooh, concentrating her venom on his explanation that he had inserted 'tiddely-pom' in a verse 'to make it more hummy'. Miss Parker concluded her review: 'And it is that word "hummy", my darlings, that marks the first place in *The House at Pooh Corner* at which Tonstant Weader Fwowed up.'

J. B. Morton (who, as Beachcomber, wrote a humorous column in the *Daily Express* from 1924 to 1975) composed one of many Christopher Robin/Pooh parodies:

> Hush, hush,
> Nobody cares!
> Christopher Robin
> Has
> Fallen
> Down-
> Stairs.

Another, by an author who wishes to remain anonymous, notes that

> They're changing sex at Buckingham Palace;
> Christopher Robin turned into Alice.

1 Other illustrators associated with particular authors include:

Hablot Knight Browne, who was first linked with Charles Dickens in 1836, as illustrator of a slim anti-Sabbatarian volume called *Sunday as it is by Timothy Sparks*, and who soon afterwards—briefly as Nemo, then as Phiz (which seemed to go well with Dickens's pen-name of Boz)—began providing the plates for Dickens's popular works, starting with *Pickwick Papers*.

John Tenniel, the *Punch* cartoonist, knighted in 1893, who illustrated the Alice books of Lewis Carroll (a lecturer in mathematics at Christ Church, Oxford, whose real name was Charles Lutwidge Dodgson); Tenniel was ninety-six when he died in 1914.

Sidney Paget, illustrator of Sherlock Holmes stories, starting with *The Adventures*, who, according to Conan Doyle, used his brother Walter, also an artist, as the model for the great detective; Conan Doyle referred to him as 'poor Sidney Paget', presumably because he was only forty-eight when he died in 1908. Frederic Dorr Steele is generally considered the best of the American illustrators of the Holmes stories.

Incidentally, it was the artist Leslie Ward who from 1871 until 1908 painted the full-page cartoons for the English *Vanity Fair* magazine, using the brush-name of Spy.

Miranda, Ernesto

In 1963, this twenty-three-year-old delinquent, a user and peddler of drugs, was convicted of kidnapping and raping a teenage girl of Phoenix, Arizona; also of committing an armed robbery, the proceeds of which amounted to eight dollars. He was sentenced to between forty and fifty-five years in prison.

In 1966, the Supreme Court of the United States of America overturned Miranda's conviction for rape, having decided by a five-to-four majority that his confession had been illegally obtained because the police had not advised him of his rights. Ever since that ruling, American policemen have known that if they do not recite the Miranda Warning[1] to arrested persons, or recite it imperfectly, those persons are likely to go free, no matter if there is iron-clad evidence against them.[2]

Miranda was tried again on the charge of rape, and, although the jury heard not a word about or from his confession, he was again found guilty. After his parole in 1972, he did quite nicely out of a sideline business of selling autographed Miranda cards, printed with the warning, to policemen and souvenir-hunters. In 1974, he was sentenced to jail for the parole violation of having amphetamines and a firearm in his possession—but, would you believe it, a few months later it was decided that as the arresting officers had not stuck to the strict letter of the law when searching for the incriminating objects, Miranda's parole should be reinstated.

He did not have long to savour and brag about his second triumph. On the last day of January 1976, he was stabbed to death in a sleazy bar in Phoenix, following a quarrel over a three-dollar poker bet. One hopes that when the police tracked down an illegal immigrant named Eseziquiel Moreno Perez, whom (I must be careful what I say) they suspected of being Miranda's assailant, they remembered to recite the Miranda Warning and made sure they got it right.

1 'You are under arrest. Before we ask you any questions, you must understand what your rights are.

'You have the right to remain silent.

'You are not required to say anything to us at any time or to answer any questions. Anything you say can be used against you in court.

'You have the right to talk to a lawyer for advice before we question you and to have him with you during questioning.

'If you cannot afford a lawyer and want one, a lawyer will be provided for you.

'If you want to answer questions now without a lawyer

present, you will still have the right to stop answering at any time. You also have the right to stop answering at any time until you talk to a lawyer.'

2 In June 1984, the Supreme Court ruled by a vote of 6–3 that suspects do not have to be advised of their constitutional rights 'in situations posing a threat to the public safety'. The ruling arose from the case of *New York* v. *Quarles, 82–1213*. Following the report of a rape, two policemen chased Benjamin Quarles into a store and apprehended him. Finding that he was wearing an empty shoulder-holster, they asked him where the weapon was, and he replied, 'It is over there,' pointing to a box. Not until the weapon, a loaded .38 revolver, had been retrieved was Quarles read his Miranda rights. He was first charged with rape, but later the charge was changed to criminal possession of a weapon.

Moses, Alfred and George

The sons of a Polish-born Jew with the emphatically holy name of Moses Moses, who traded in secondhand clothes in the vicinity of his slum dwelling in the East End of London, they forsook the surname of Moses for that of Moss, and gathered none of the latter when they embarked on a joint career in the retail gents'-rag trade. Mainly due to the energy and acumen of Alfred, they made headway: so much so that in 1898 they were able to open a shop on the corner of King Street and Bedford Street, running down to the Strand; shortly afterwards, they opened another shop, in King Street, and then acquired the premises between the two shops so as to create a large store, which is still the headquarters of the firm of Moss Brothers, colloquially known as Mossbross, famous through civilised but impecunious society for its hiring of costumes for formal occasions (though this accounts for less than one-third of the company's business).

The hire trade began fortuitously, and was egged on by two happenings in which neither of the brothers had a say. Around about 1910, Alfred started to attend smoking concerts, and it was through this that he became acquainted with Charles Pond, a stockbroker who, away from the Exchange, was something of a card, frequently invited to house-parties in the Home Counties because he could be relied upon to be the heart and soul of such affairs, ready to entertain the other guests in the drawing room should the weather turn inclement. But then some of Charles's stockbroking ventures went awry, and he went broke. Never mind, said respective country hosts and hostesses: he was such good fun that it would be a shame to exclude him from their swell-elegant gatherings: he could, as it were, sing for his supper. This kept Charles well-nourished; but before long his formal clothes showed signs of wear. Visiting Alfred Moss, he diffidently asked whether he might borrow a tail-coat from the brothers' stock. Of course, Alfred said, and arranged for the loan. Twenty diffident requests later, Alfred suggested that if Charles could see his way to paying half-a-crown per loan, he, Alfred, would ensure that the tails were always immaculately pressed when required, and that if and when they lost fashionableness, they would be superseded. Charles agreed that this was a fair arrangement; and he told cronies, as financially straitened as he was, about it. As word got round, an increasing number of Micawber-like[1] gentlemen turned up at the Moss Brothers' emporium, asking for a discreet word with Mr Alfred. So the hire business was born.

It received a fillip following the First World War, when young ex-officers, who recalled seeing a still-diminutive FORMAL-GARMENTS-FOR-HIRE sign when they had patronised the brothers' military-tailoring department, came, as borrowers, in droves. And another in 1924, following the formation of the first Labour government: King George V, fearful that the new rulers would appear at state and royal occasions wearing cloth caps, mufflers and clogs, instructed his private secretary Lord Stamfordham to send a letter to all Labour members of parliament, apprising them of the facilities offered—yes, even to people like themselves—by Messrs. Moss Brothers.

1 Mr Micawber, a character in *David Copperfield*, written by Charles Dickens in 1849–50; played by W. C. Fields (◊ William Claude Dukinfield) in the Hollywood film based on the novel, made in 1934.

In the twelfth chapter of the book, Mr Micawber expounds his monetary philosophy: 'Annual income twenty pounds, annual expenditure nineteen nineteen six, result happiness. Annual income twenty pounds, annual expenditure twenty pounds nought and six, result misery'.

Mozee, Phoebe Anne Oakley

Born to Quaker parents in Darke County, Ohio, in 1860, she was only just into her teens when she began shooting small game on behalf of restaurateurs in nearby Cincinnati. Though a moppet—full-grown she was no more than five feet tall, a mite higher than the length of her musket—she possessed a prodigious eye, and soon developed into a deadly markswoman. At the age of fifteen she entered a contest against a travelling sharpshooter, Frank Butler, and beat him hollow, so impressing him that he proposed marriage, a notion that appealed both to her and to her parents, who had seven other children to support. The newly wed couple straightway became a peripatetic show-business partnership under the title of Butler & (as the female quarter of the act had been known as Little Annie Oakley for some time) Oakley. For ten years, they showed off their skills on fairgrounds, in circuses, and at theatres, amazing audiences but never catching the attention of a leading impresario. But in 1885 they joined Buffalo Bill's Wild West Show (◊ Edward Zane Carroll Judson). Annie, billed as 'Little Sure Shot', became a solitary star, her husband relegated to a supernumerary job as holder and hurler of things for her to shoot at; eventually, he dropped out of sight and became Annie's manager. Her prowess was quite extraordinary: she could slice a playing card held up edgewise by an assistant standing thirty paces away; by looking into a mirror, she could fire over her shoulder and break a glass ball being whirled round on a piece of string. And she had great stamina and a high threshold of boredom: once, using 16-gauge shotguns that assistants kept reloading for her, she shattered 4,772 out of 5,000 balls that were thrown in the air during a snackless, napless period of nine hours.

She was probably the first non-actress to become a pin-up girl. One of her legion of male devotees wrote: 'Many a man now grey, who once perched on a hard wooden plank and watched her through a haze that was half powder-smoke and half boyish dreaming, will still confess that Annie was his first hopeless love.'

Her appeal was universal, unhampered by frontiers and social barriers. The Wild West Show was in London in the summer of 1897, the year of Queen Victoria's jubilee, and two royal command performances were given, the second attended by the Queen herself. There seems to be no truth in the suggestion that the Widow of Windsor's long-drawn-out mourning was broken by her enjoyment of the show (the story was probably first put about by one of Buffalo Bill's publicists), but certainly she was amused: most of all by Annie, whom she complimented as being 'a very, very clever little girl'. Kaiser Wilhelm II saw the show during its second engagement in Berlin, and was so captivated by the slip of a girl in fringed buckskin, and by her performance, that he insisted on getting in on the act, ordering her to shoot the ash off a cigar clenched between his teeth. Annie casually clipped the end of the Havana: the wrong end, she remarked in 1917, when the United States declared war on Germany; writing to the Kaiser, she suggested a repeat performance, adding that she would not guarantee the same result.

In October 1901, a train chartered for the Wild West Show was involved in a collision with a freight train at Charlotte, North Carolina. No humans were killed, but 100 horses were crushed to death in the stock cars. After Annie had been freed from a shattered stateroom by her husband, she was found to be suffering from internal injuries and a paralysis of her left side. Her hair turned white overnight. Frank Butler took her to their home at Nutley, New Jersey. Not until several weeks later was she able to hobble around with the aid of a brace and a walking-stick. But eventually she was considered, or considered herself, well enough to rejoin the show on a part-time basis. She continued to make guest appearances with Buffalo Bill until 1912, when she and her husband settled down at Pinehurst, a holiday resort not far from the scene of the train-crash; there, they became the shooting equivalent of golf professionals, tutoring, overseeing, and providing trigger-happiness to dude visitors to a clay-pigeon range attached to an hotel.

In 1946, the Butlers' fame was revived posthumously. It was in May of that year that *Annie Get Your Gun*, with music and lyrics by Irving Berlin (◊ Israel Baline) and book by Herbert and Dorothy Fields, opened at the Imperial Theatre on Broadway, where it would remain for three years. One of three modern musicals that are replete with great songs (another is Cole Porter's *Kiss Me, Kate*), it came to the London Coliseum in June 1947; the part of Annie, created by Ethel Merman (real surname, Zimmerman), was played by the unbelievably blond Dolores Gray, and that of Frank Butler by Bill Johnson. A truant from school on the day of the opening, I joined the waiting-line for the gallery before dawn; even so, I was among the last of the fortunate queuers. Nearly three years later, in May 1950—having meantime seen the show more than a dozen times—I was at the final performance. What a night that was! Bill Johnson, wearing his white costume, rode to the theatre on a white horse. When the last official curtain-call had been taken, the cast stayed behind and sang the songs the audience wanted them to sing: all reprises except for 'I'll Be Seeing You', movingly sung by Dolores Gray, sitting cross-legged near the footlights and at the side of the stage.

Annie Oakley has another theatrical reminder: in America, her name is applied to free passes to shows, perhaps because the holes punched in such passes resemble .22 bullet holes.

A diminishing few Americans say 'Annie Oakley' when they mean all right—a usage that is probably explained by the fact that the first syllable of the surname sounds like oke, short for OK (the derivation of which has been so variously ascribed—even on bottles of OK fruit sauce—that one cannot, pinless, choose one from among others).

Mudd, Dr Samuel Alexander

A general practitioner living near Bryantown, Maryland, who fixed a splint to John Wilkes Booth's leg, fractured near the ankle when the actor, after shooting Abraham Lincoln and then getting the spurs of his riding boots tangled in the Stars and Stripes festooning the President's box at Ford's Theatre, Washington (◊ Lord Dundreary) had landed heavily on the stage. Chiefly because Dr Mudd was slow in informing the authorities that he had had suspicious visitors, he was charged as a conspirator; found guilty, he was sentenced to life imprisonment, and served about three and a half years before being pardoned. In 1980, President Carter exonerated him of all guilt, but still 'his name is mud'—an expression coined before the American Civil War but given currency by the doctor's disgrace. It may be that the toast 'Here's mud in your eye' comes from the same source.

Negro, Lady

The woman allegedly referred to in Shakespeare's Sonnets 126–52 has come to be called the Dark Lady. The word *allegedly* is important, for some students believe that the Dark Lady wasn't a person but a mere figment of Shakespeare's imagination; others think that she is a composite figure, inspired by two or more sirens, and yet others gaily suggest, 'That was no Dark Lady; that was the man in Will's life.'

A few literal-minded literary scholars assert that the Dark Lady was a prominent courtesan, sometime abbess of Clerkenwell, who was known as Lady Negro. Well, she was certainly dark; but whether she deserved to be called a lady is open to question.

Predictably, Queen Elizabeth has been cited.

One theory has it that the sonnets were commissioned by Shakespeare's patron Henry Wriothesley, Earl of Southampton, as gifts to Elizabeth Vernon, who was his mistress before she became his wife. This fits neatly with the notion that Wriothesley, his initials transposed, was Mr W. H., the dedicatee of the sonnets (◊ William Hughes).

There is support—waning, it seems—for the candidature of Jane D'Avenant, whose husband John kept a tavern at Oxford where Shakespeare is said to have been a frequent overnight guest, breaking his journeys between London and Stratford. In 1606, Jane gave birth to a bastard son, named William, of whom Shakespeare may have been the father. According to an observer of the Oxford scene, 'Mrs D'Avenant was a very beautiful woman of a good wit and conversation, in which she was imitated by none of her children but by this William.' When grown up, William wrote and presented plays, and composed poems that pleased the Queen, who requested that he be made Laureate after the death of Ben Jonson; he was subsequently knighted. The diarist John Aubrey noted that 'Sir William would sometimes when he was pleasant over a glass of wine with his most intimate friends . . . say that it seemed to him that he writt with the very spirit that Shakespeare [did], and seemed contented enough to be thought his son.'

The current favourite for the title of Dark Lady is Mary Fitton, a native of Cheshire, where she was born in or about 1578, the daughter of a land-owner who had been knighted through the influence of a grandfather of William Herbert, 3rd Earl of Pembroke (a front-runner as Mr W. H. [◊]). Mary Fitton arrived in London when she was seventeen, and after staying for a few months with the Pembrokes—during which time William Herbert fell in love with her—became a maid-of-honour to the Queen. Sir William Knollys, comptroller of the royal household, professed to be taking a fatherly interest in her when he was in fact using her as his mistress. However, she discarded Sir William when, within a very short time, a host of younger courtiers began vying for her affection. William Herbert emerged as winner, and their goings-on became a public scandal. When she became pregnant in 1600, Herbert admitted responsibility but refused to marry her. This angered the Queen, and soon after Mary had given birth to a stillborn son, Herbert was sent to the Fleet Prison, subsequently to be banished to the Continent; he didn't dare return to England until after the Queen's death in 1603.

Mary took up with other men—including Sir Richard Leveson, vice-admiral of England, by whom she had two bastard children—before marrying, first, Captain William Polewhele, second, a Captain Lougher. Those who submit her as the Dark Lady remark that her marriages to commoners indicate that she would not have let social considerations stand in her way if she had felt like enjoying a liaison with Shakespeare: 'an ornament to the stage of which Pembroke was a generous patron, an actor who was also a famous playwright and poet.' Though there is no direct evidence that Shakespeare even flirted with Mary Fitton, let alone bedded her, those who nominate her as the Dark Lady point to the dedication of a play called *The Nine Days Wonder*, which was written in 1600 by Will Kempe, an actor in Shakespeare's company. The dedication reads, 'To Mistress Anne Fitton, Mayde of Honor to the Mayde Royal'—but since Mary Fitton, unlike her sister Anne, was a maid-of-honour, it seems probable that the play was intended for her.

As an aside, let me mention that in 1776 Elizabeth Chudleigh, for twenty-five years a maid-of-honour to the Princess of Wales, was tried for bigamy by the House of Lords, the charge being that she had married the Duke of Kingston while still the wife of the Earl of Bristol. Found guilty, she claimed the privilege of Peerage, and, after a long legal argument, was discharged. One of the several broadsheets on the case contained the verse:

> There was a maid—
> A Maid of Honour,
> And strange, 'tis said
> Of this strange maid,
> She was no maid,
> She had no honour.

Nissen, George

An American who in 1926 invented the trampoline, which, year for year, has caused almost as many spinal injuries as jogging has heart attacks; respectively vertical and horizontal in their urgings to exceed ability, they have contributed in no small measure towards that surgent medical phenomenon, the excessively healthy corpse.

Nissen, Peter Norman

The Canadian-born designer of the semi-cylindrical corrugated-iron hut bearing his name, the prototype of which was erected at Hesdin, France, in 1916, when Nissen was the officer commanding the 29th Company of the Royal Engineers. During the war, other types of hut were named after RE officers—Armstrong, Aylwin, Liddell, Tarrant, Weblee—but none seems to have survived as a brand.

O'Brien, Willis

The creator of, and moving force behind, the large gorilla who became over-enamoured of Fay Wray in the 1933 film *King Kong* (the posthumous brainchild of [Richard Horatio] Edgar Wallace). For sequences in which Kong was shown on the move, O'Brien manipulated an 18-inch model on miniature sets; for close-ups, he fashioned the separate components of a foot that stomped petulantly, a paw large enough to grip the screaming Miss Wray, and a massive head with glittering eyes . . .

. . . not quite as large as those on the billboard in the valley of ashes in F. Scott Fitzgerald's *The Great Gatsby* (◊ Max Gerlach):

> The eyes of Doctor T. J. Eckleburg are blue and gigantic—their retinas are one yard high. They look out of no face, but, instead, from a pair of enormous yellow spectacles which pass over a non-existent nose. Evidently some wild wag of an oculist set them there to fatten his practice in the borough of Queens, and then sank down himself into eternal blindness, or forgot them and moved away. But his eyes, dimmed a little by many paintless days, under sun and rain, brood on over a solemn dumping ground.

Oliver, Dr William

This Cornishman, far more astute at business than at physics, practised for a while at Plymouth, and then, round about 1725, when he was thirty, set up his shingle at Bath and soon became the most fashionable of that spa's extravagance of leeches. His endearing bathside manner helped; as did the confidence of his claims, copied from the advertising of an earlier, unrelated namesake, that wallowing in the warm waters on some occasions, drinking it on others, constituted a sure cure for, among other ailments:

The gout (from which he himself, abstaining from his own sure-fire antidote, suffered), palsies, convulsions, colic, consumption, jaundice, the itch, scurvy, scab, leprosy, scrofula (known, outside royal circles, as the King's Evil), gravel in the kidneys or bladder, coldness and pain in the head, most diseases of the eyes, deafness and noise in and running of the ears, palpitation of the heart, sharpness of urine, piles, and every single one of the special diseases of women, not excluding infertility and the Green Sickness, sometimes called Virgin Distemper. And, oh yes, the pox—often a side-effect of the hydrotherapeutics, picked up by male bathers from whores who frequented the baths (particularly the Cross Bath, which was 'more fam'd for Pleasure than cures'), and by bathing beauties from dandies with Cupid's Itch.

The good doctor prescribed a strict diet as consociate with the healing waters; and, as a profitable means of toning down belly-rumbles, created and sold a healthy biscuit: round, slim, white, and untainted by sweetening. The cookie came to be called a Bath Oliver. Just before Dr Oliver died in 1764, he confided the recipe to his coachman Atkins, and bequeathed him £100 and ten sacks of wheatflour so that he might start in business on his own. Atkins did so: to such effect that, years before the normal retiring age of men of his class, he was able to sell his shop in Green Street, Bath, having made near as large a fortune as had his benefactor.

Olmedo, José Joaquin de

Following his death in 1847, this Ecuadorian poet, least forgotten for a couple of nationalistic odes, was singularly misrepresented. Someone had the idea of erecting a statue of him in his home-town of Guayaquil, but a few enquiries indicated that the cost of commissioning such a work was prohibitive. So a second-hand statue of the Greeks- and Greece-loving English poet George Gordon, Lord Byron (1788–1824), acquired at a knock-down price, became a counterfeit presentment of the local hero.

Parker, Bonnie

The moll and helpmeet of Clyde Barrow, the diminutive, psychopathic, sexually indeterminate, saxophone-playing leader of the Barrow Gang of robbers who, adjunctive to their activities in the early 1930s, committed at least eighteen murders. On 23 May 1934, Bonnie and Clyde were killed in an ambush near Arcadia, Louisiana. The following lines were inscribed on the headstone above Bonnie Parker's grave:

> As the flowers are all made sweeter
> By the sunshine and the dew,
> So this old world is made brighter
> By the lives of folks like you.

Incidentally, an equally inapt epitaph was provided for Myra Belle Starr, *née* Shirley (died 1889), the American outlaw known as 'the petticoat of the plains' whose crimes included horse-theft, murder and torture for gain. The quatrain is said to have been composed by her illegitimate daughter Pearl:

> Shed not for her the bitter tear,
> Nor give the heart to vain regret;

'Tis but the casket that lies here,
The gem that fills it sparkles yet.

While on the subject of poetry for the dead, I must mention
that an *in memoriam* announcement printed in the *Liverpool Echo*
in the early 1950s contained these lines:

Moses blew a trumpet,
Jehovah beat a drum,
Peter opened the Pearly Gates,
And in walked Mum.

Parry, Richard Gordon

In the early evening of Monday, 19 January 1931, a man calling
himself R. M. Qualtrough telephoned the City Café, in the
centre of Liverpool, and asked to speak to William Herbert
Wallace, a fifty-two-year-old agent for the Prudential Insurance
Co. who was a member of a chess club that met at the café on
Mondays and Thursdays. As Wallace had not arrived, the call
was taken by the captain of the club. Qualtrough explained: 'I
have my girl's twenty-first birthday on, and I want to do
something for her in the way of Mr Wallace's business. I want to
see him particularly. Will you ask him to call round to my place
tomorrow evening at 7.30?' He then spelt his name, gave the
address of 25 Menlove Gardens East, and rang off. When Wallace
turned up, the message was passed on to him. He seemed
perplexed. He said that he knew no one named Qualtrough, and
had no idea of the location of Menlove Gardens East. A member
of the club told him that there were several cardinally pointed
Menlove Gardens off Menlove Avenue, a main road in the
Mossley Hill suburb of Liverpool.

The next evening, Wallace set out from his home, 29
Wolverton Street, near the Liverpool Football Club's ground at

Anfield; after three tram-rides, he reached Menlove Avenue and began asking around for the address he had been given. He found Menlove Gardens North, South and West; but no Menlove Gardens East. At last concluding his search for a man unborn, a house unbuilt, a street that did not exist, he returned home.

His wife Julia was lying dead in the tiny parlour, which was like an abattoir, garish with blood and brain-tissue that had sprayed from the many wounds to her head.

From the start of the Keystone-Kops-like[1] investigation, the police suspected Wallace of the murder: they believed that, the evening before, he had telephoned the City Café, posing as R. M. Qualtrough, so as to give himself an alibi of sorts—that he had slaughtered Julia (for a reason they couldn't explain; everyone believed that the Wallaces were a devoted couple) shortly before starting off on the wild-goose chase. Wallace was arrested, and after a four-day trial at St George's Hall, Liverpool, was found guilty and sentenced to death.

The case created three precedents. The costs of Wallace's defence were guaranteed by the Prudential Staff Union (previously, unions had only done this in cases relating to union matters). On the Sunday before the Appeal, special prayers, described as 'intercessions extraordinary', were offered at services at Liverpool Cathedral. And the three judges of the Court of Criminal Appeal quashed the verdict on the ground that 'the case against the appellant . . . was not proved with that certainty which is necessary in order to justify a verdict of guilty'.

Wallace returned to Liverpool—to 29 Wolverton Street—and tried to pick up the pieces of his life. But insurance clients refused to open the door to him; he was threatened when he walked the streets; poison-pen notes were stuffed into his letter-box.[2] He moved to a cottage in Cheshire. Having refused to seek treatment for a kidney disease (thereby, according to his housekeeper, 'committing slow suicide'), he died only two years after the murder of his wife, and was buried with her at Anfield Cemetery.

I became interested in the case while I was working at Liverpool Playhouse (home of the oldest repertory company in the world, established on 11 November 1911). Years later, following a depressing but profitable period as a television producer, I re-investigated the case. I was able to prove Wallace's innocence; also, I garnered evidence against, and eventually tracked down, the man who had masqueraded as R. M. Qualtrough.

His name was Richard Gordon Parry. Twenty-three when he killed Julia Wallace, he had recently been sacked from his job as an insurance collector for the Prudential because Wallace had discovered that he was embezzling company funds. His father became Assistant City Treasurer of Liverpool, his uncle was the City Librarian; and his father's secretary was a daughter of the head of the Liverpool CID, who took personal charge of the investigation into the murder—and who ignored evidence that Richard Gordon Parry was the culprit.

Parry was still alive in 1969, when I published *The Killing of Julia Wallace*: what I knew about him could only be hinted at; he had to be referred to as Mr X. That remained so when subsequent editions of the book appeared. I spoke of him when I read a paper on the case following a dinner of Our Society;[3] but the society has an invariable rule that anything said by a speaker, or raised during the subsequent discussion, is confidential to members and their guests.

On 20 January 1981, the fiftieth anniversary of the murder, I was the consultant for, and took part in, a marathon programme on the case broadcast by Radio City, the independent station for Merseyside. As Parry had died a year or so before—and had been a widower—I named him in public for the first time. The programme created a stir, one result of which was that Roger Wilkes, the producer, interviewed a man who had held incriminating evidence against Parry for half a century and was now willing to reveal it. In 1984, Roger Wilkes published *Wallace: The Final Verdict*, a book about the case, the research for the broadcast, and what the programme sparked off; included in the book are the notes made by Richard Whittington-Egan, who, as witness and bodyguard, accompanied me when I talked to Richard Gordon Parry for the first time, standing on the doorstep of a seedy house in South London one sunny evening while a candidate in a local-government election drove up and down the street, using a wonky megaphone to plead with the residents to vote for him.

1 In August 1912, an ex-bookmaker who called himself Mack Sennett (his real name was Michael Sinnott) founded the Keystone

Film Co., and before the end of the year put together a posse of apprentice comedians, under the leadership of Ford Sterling, who became known as the Keystone Kops: there were seven at first, but the numbers and membership continually altered during the four or five years of the Kops' existence.

2 There was extreme prejudice against Wallace even before his arrest; this inspired several pieces of doggerel—one of which was doubly-inspired, for it was a parody of the rhyme in Baroness Orczy's novel, published 1905, about the Scarlet Pimpernel (Sir Percy Blakeney):

> They seek him here, they seek him there;
> Is he alive, do you know?
> Either in Hell . . . or the Pruden-shell,
> That damned elusive Qualtrough.

3 Extract from the rules book:

> Our Society, commonly called the Crimes Club, was formed in 1903 as a result of a dinner at 1 Upper Woburn Place, the house of H. B. Irving [son of Henry Irving, ◊ Alice Grey], on 5th December, at which were present:- Arthur Lambton, Professor John Churton Collins, J. B. Atlay, Ingleby Oddie, H. Crosse, H. B. Irving.
>
> They decided that it would be a good thing to form a private dining club at which famous criminal cases could be discussed quite freely, and at which other interesting psychological, legal and criminological problems could be openly ventilated by the members.
>
> The club grew from the original six to the present number [limited to 100 men; in recent times, women have been allowed as guests].
>
> George R. Sims, one of our early members, summed up the thoughts of many members when he wrote: 'In memory of many delightful evenings, excellent dinners, atrocious crimes, good fellowship.'

His Honour Judge Henry Elam has been the secretary since 1952; the present patron is HRH The Duke of Edinburgh.

Paul Pry

When first espied by Sir Edwin Landseer, this black-and-white Newfoundland dog was carrying a basket of flowers in his mouth. Impressed by his beauty, Landseer posed him on a table for the painting *A Distinguished Member of the Humane Society* (1838), which was much admired; one person went so far as to say that Landseer had 'breathed Promethean fire' into the portrait. There was great demand for engravings of the picture, dedicated to the Royal Humane Society, and black-and-white Newfoundlands got to be called Landseers, a name that has stuck.

The original Paul Pry was a nosy-parker in a comedy of the same name, written by John Poole, which was first presented in London, at the Haymarket, in 1825, and revived a dozen times during the next half-century, once with an actress, Mrs Glover, playing the title-role. There seems no doubt that the first Paul Pry, the comedian John Liston, fitted the part most perfectly; successors tried to imitate his characteristics of voice and manner, and copied his make-up and costume. But, from all accounts, Liston was a hard act to follow at any time; the playwright and journalist James Boaden said of him, 'He must be seen to be comprehended. Other actors labour to be comic; I see nothing like labour in Liston.' (Boaden, by the way, was a keen Shakespearian: he took part in the correspondence on the forgeries by [◊]William Henry Ireland and in 1837 published a pamphlet on the Sonnets in which he nominated William Herbert, Earl of Pembroke, as 'Mr W.H.' [◊ William Hughes].)

Perske, Betty Joan

An ex-model who, under the name of Lauren Bacall, achieved stardom in her first film, the 1944 adaptation of Ernest Hemingway's novel *To Have and Have Not*, in which she played the part of Slim opposite Humphrey Bogart as Harry Morgan; Walter Brennan was Eddie 'the mummy'. Soon afterwards, she and Bogart were married, and they subsequently starred in the film based on Raymond Chandler's *The Big Sleep* (1946) and—with Edward G. Robinson (◊ Emanuel Goldenberg)—in the screen version of Maxwell Anderson's play *Key Largo* (1948). In the early 1970s, she starred on Broadway and in the West End in the musical *Applause!*, based on the 1950 film *All About Eve* (she played the part of Margo Channing, created by Bette Davis), and towards the end of that decade again appeared on Broadway, this time in *Woman of the Year*, the musical based on the 1942 film in which Katharine Hepburn and Spencer Tracy made the first of their nine appearances together.[1] (Incidentally, this film was produced by Joseph L. Mankiewicz, brother of Herman (◊ Gandhi), and it was he who wrote the script[2] of, and directed, *All About Eve*, and received Oscars for both contributions.)

1 The subsequent eight were in *Keeper of the Flame* (1942), *Without Love* (1945), *The Sea of Grass* (1947), *State of the Union* (1948), *Adam's Rib* (1949). *Pat and Mike* (1952), *The Desk Set* (1957), and *Guess Who's Coming to Dinner* (1967).

2 Which includes a definition of theatre. It is delivered by the director (played by Gary Merrill, who after the making of the film was for a while married to its star, Bette [really Ruth] Davis), trying to curb his temper in a scene with the aspiring actress Eve (Anne Baxter) whom the film is All About:

The theatuh . . . the theatuh—what book of rules says the
theatre exists only within some ugly buildings crowded into
one square mile of New York City? Or London, Paris, or
Vienna? Listen, junior. And learn. Want to know what the
theatre is? A flea circus. Also opera. Also rodeos, carnivals,
ballets, Indian tribal dances, Punch and Judy, a one-man
band: all theatre. Wherever there's magic and make-believe
and an audience—there's theatre. Donald Duck, Ibsen, and
the Lone Ranger. Sarah Bernhardt, Poodles Hanneford, Lunt
and Fontanne, Betty Grable . . . Rex the Wild Horse and
Eleanora Duse: you don't understand them all, you don't like
them all—why should you? The theatre's for everybody—
you included, but not exclusively, so don't approve or
disapprove. It may not be your theatre, but it's theatre for
somebody, somewhere.

Pierce, Oscar

Since its foundation in 1927, the Academy of Motion Picture
Arts and Sciences has each year awarded gold-plated statuettes
for 'outstanding performances in the various fields of the motion
picture industry'; but not until 1931, when Margaret Herrick,
then the librarian of the Academy, later its executive director,
saw one of the statuettes for the first time and remarked that it
reminded her of her uncle Oscar, have they had a name.
Actually, Oscar Pierce was Miss Herrick's second cousin.

The Oscar was designed by George Stanley, a Los Angeles
sculptor, from rough sketches made by Cedric Gibbons, art
director of the Goldwyn Pictures Corporation (◊ Samuel
Goldfish), later Metro-Goldwyn-Mayer, from 1916 until his
death in 1956.

Since 1975, the French Académie des Arts et Techniques du
Cinéma has awarded Césars: so called not because they were
designed by a sculptor of that name (and, he insists, that name
alone), but as a compliment to Marcel Pagnol, who wrote the

'Marseilles trilogy' of *Marius* (1931), *Fanny* (1932), and *César* (1936), adapting the first two from his extraordinarily successful stage-plays, and directing the third at studios he had built from the profits of the second. César, played by (Jules Muraire) Raimu, is one of the characters that crop up in all three films; so are Marius (Pierre Fresnay) and Fanny (Orane Demariz).

Returning to America, but turning to the stage, the major award on Broadway is the Tony, named after Antoinette Perry, who ran the American Theatre Wing during the Second World War.

The London theatre has similar awards. They are called SWETs, for the insufficient reason that they are presented by the Society of West End Theatre. Far better, it seems to me—few appellations could be worse than SWET—if they were known as Binkies, as a reminder of Hugh 'Binkie' Beaumont, who, as managing director of H.M. Tennant Ltd., was the most powerful theatrical producer in London from the 1940s until the mid-1960s.

Pratt, Honoretta

She achieved posthumous fame by being the first person to be officially cremated in Great Britain; that was in September 1769, when her body was burnt in an open grave at St George's burial ground, Hanover Square, London. Her monument recorded:

> This worthy woman believing that the vapours arising from graves in the church yards of populous cities must prove hurtful to the inhabitants and resolving to extend to future times as far as she was able that charity and benevolence which distinguished her through life ordered that her body should be burnt in the hope that others would follow her example, a thing too hastily censured by those who did not understand the motive.

Pulitzer, Joseph

The twig-thin son of a Jewish grain merchant and an Austrian
gentlewoman, who brought him up in Budapest, he travelled to
America during the Civil War as a recruit to the Union Army (it
is said that he jumped from the ship when it arrived in Boston
harbour and swam ashore to collect his own bounty), and stayed
on at the end of hostilities to found a newspaper empire, the
brightest jewel of which was, in his estimation, the New York
World: untainted by modesty, he claimed that that paper was the
most important teacher and moral agent in America. He died in
1911, leaving a will that, among other bequests, provided $2
million for the foundation of a school of journalism at Columbia
University; the income from half of the amount was applied to
'prizes or scholarships for the encouragement of public service,
public morals, American literature, and the advancement of
education'—the Pulitzer Prizes, which have attracted great publicity, not all favourable, and created a good deal of controversy
over the years. Leaving aside the several instances of newspaper
stories turning out to be works of fiction shortly after the
honouring and rewarding of the authors, the quaintness of some
decisions of the prize-givers has caused astonishment, anger, and
amusement. Take, for instance, what happened in 1935, the year
that saw the first productions on Broadway of Maxwell Anderson's *Valley Forge*, Lillian Hellman's *The Children's Hour* (◊ Dr
Charles Hill), Clifford Odets' *Awake and Sing*, and Robert E.
Sherwood's *The Petrified Forest*: the Pulitzer Prize for Drama
went to Zoe Akins's stage-adaptation of Edith Wharton's *The
Old Maid*.[1] The aberration so incensed the New York critics that
they started awards of their own, the New York Drama Critics
Circle Awards, honouring a play (or two) and a musical each
season, which still go strong. (◊ Oscar Pierce and Salvatore
Quasimodo.)

1 Unlikely to be confused with the comedy of the same title, adapted by Arthur Murphy from the French, which alternated, always successfully, between two London theatres, Drury Lane and Covent Garden, from 1761 until 1820.

2 As far as forecasting is concerned, the notion that the recipients of theatrical prizes should be chosen by a jury of peers is contradicted by the record of the Clarence Derwent Awards (named after the English-born actor and producer who divided his time between Broadway and the West End), which are presented annually by the American Actors' Equity Association to the actor and actress considered 'the most promising newcomers': of the 81 novitiates who received $1,000 and a crystal egg between 1945, the first year of the awards, and 1983, only nine have so far fulfilled their promise.

Pygmalion

A legendary king of Cyprus, who fashioned an ivory statue of a woman, then fell in love with it; Aphrodite gave it life, and the woman bore Pygmalion a daughter, Paphos. (◊ Beatrice Stella Tanner.)

Quasimodo, Salvatore

An upright Italian poet, he won the Nobel[1] Prize for Literature in 1959.

1 When Alfred Bernhard Nobel, the Swedish industrialist who invented dynamite, died in 1896, it was announced that he had bequeathed a fund for annual awards of medals and money to people 'who have . . . conferred the greatest benefits on mankind'. Odd choices, some of them: for instance, the prize for literature has gone to such persons as (let me make sure that I spell the names right) Spitteler, Laxness, and Sully Prudhomme; while nominated writers who have failed to impress the Swedish Academy include Anton Chekhov, Leo Tolstoy, Thomas Hardy, and Henry James.

Quiller-Couch, Sir Arthur Thomas

He called himself that—or most of it—when he wrote 'weighty' books (including the excellent *Shakespeare's Workmanship* of 1918) or compiled anthologies (he edited *The Oxford Book of English Verse*, first published in 1900), but used the slight pseudonym of Q for his short stories and novels, many of which were set in his native Cornwall.

Radomyslsky, Gregori

A Bolshevik who adopted the alias of Zinoviev so as to mislead the Tsar's security forces, and retained it when, in April 1917, at the age of thirty-four, he returned to Russia, together with Lenin (Vladimir Ilyich Ulyanov), from exile in Switzerland. Between 1920 and 1926 he was a leading light of the Communist International (Comintern for short), being its chairman for a time.

According to the London *Daily Mail* of 25 October 1924—four days before a general election caused by the fall of the first, short-lived, Russophile but Liberal-propped Labour government, led by (James) Ramsay MacDonald—Zinoviev's real name was not Radomyslsky: actually, he was a Jew called Apfelbaum. This genealogical amendment appeared in a shock-horror report headlined 'CIVIL WAR PLOT BY SOCIALISTS' MASTERS', the centre-piece of which was a copy of a letter said to have been sent to the headquarters of the British Communists. The letter, signed 'Zinoviev, President of the Presidium' and countersigned 'A. MacManus, Member of the Presidium' (Arthur MacManus was chairman of the Communist Party of Great Britain), explained how British Communists could control the Labour Party and thus start a revolution.

After noting a report that 'agitation and propaganda work in the Army is weak, in the Navy a little better,' the letter stressed the need to have Communist cells in all army units, military stores, and munitions factories: in the event of an imperialist war, the cells could get together with the transport workers to paralyse the military preparations of the bourgeoisie and cause civil war. The letter complained that the 'military section of the Communist Party suffers from a lack of specialists, the future directors of the British Red Army', and suggested the appointment of 'a directing operative head of the military section'.

There is still uncertainty whether the Zinoviev Letter was genuine (as the Foreign Office, which agreed to its publication, seems to have believed) or a Tory dirty trick (as all true-red Socialists, the chargé d'affaires at the Soviet Embassy, and Zinoviev himself insisted), but there is no doubt that it contributed to a landslide Conservative victory at the polls.

In 1926, Zinoviev fell out with Stalin (Josef Vissarionovich Djugashvili), who accused him of being a supporter of Leon Trotsky (Lev Davidovich Bronstein), and was divested of power. Nine years later, he was sentenced to life imprisonment for treason. In August 1936 he was brought from Lubyanka Gaol to be tried again, this time on a charge of plotting with enemies of the state; within hours of being found guilty, he was killed by a firing squad.

Ramée, Marie Louise de la

Her name notwithstanding, she was an English woman who, under the pseudonym of Ouida (a childish version of Louise), thrilled Victorian domestic servants and their betters with flamboyant romances of fashionable life.

Relph, Harry

The sixteenth child of a Kent farmer who was seventy-seven when Harry was born—he looked, relatives thought, so like the Tichborne Claimant (◊ Thomas Castro) that he was nicknamed Little Tich. He had six fingers on each hand.[1] When fully grown, his height was 4 foot 6 inches. He made his first stage appearance when he was twelve, singing and playing a tin whistle, and later did a black-faced comedy act at London music halls. After a visit to America, where he found that nigger minstrels were out of fashion, he became a white-faced impersonator of fairy queens, Spanish dancers, *et al*: very successfully, particularly in panto-mimes at Theatre Royal, Drury Lane. He usually concluded his act with a dance in which he balanced on the tips of his boots, which were as long as he was short. He died in 1928 at the age of sixty. By then, the word 'tich' had come to be applied to people of diminutive build.

1 Although Anne Boleyn, the second wife of Henry VIII and the mother of the future Queen Elizabeth, had an extra finger on only one of her hands, it may be thought that her possession of a third breast made her Little Tich's equal in terms of redundant appendages. If a contemporary description of her is anything to go by, she somehow managed a variation on the saying that two is company, three is none: 'Madame Anne is not one of the handsomest women in the world. She is of middling stature, swarthy complexion, long neck, wide mouth, *bosum not much raised*, and in fact has nothing but the king's great appetite, and her eyes, which are black and beautiful.' This listing excludes mention of her hair, which she wore long—excessively so, in the view of Thomas Cranmer, Archbishop of Canterbury, who observed that, during her coronation, she was 'sitting *in* her hair upon a horse litter'.

Ritz, César

Born in 1850, the thirteenth child of a Swiss peasant, he went into the catering business at an early age, and by the time he was twenty had teamed up with Auguste Escoffier, [1] the master chef, in running a restaurant in Paris, which was then under siege during the Franco-Prussian War; as food was in short supply, the pair of them raided the nearest zoo and subsequently made up the menu with exotic culinary treats composed of bits and pieces of an elephant. In the 1880s, after a spell in London as manager of the newly-opened Savoy Hotel,[2] Ritz returned to Paris to open the first hotel called after him. Over the years, his name became descriptive, adjectival with a 'y' on the end, at first meaning chic, and then ostentatiously smart. It has been borrowed by, among others: Harry, Al and Jim Joachim, components of the Ritz Brothers comedy act, which tried to be Marxian and on a few occasions got quite close; a manufacturer of salted crackers; Irving Berlin (◊ Israel Baline), who composed a song, 'Putting on the Ritz', which was featured in a 1929 film of the same title; the writer of a poor play, called *The Ritz*, in which Rita Moreno gave an award-winning performance on Broadway in 1974; and, of course, F. Scott Fitzgerald, who in 1922, when he was still happy, wrote a short story about 'The Diamond as Big as the Ritz'—referring to the Ritz-Carlton in Manhattan.

1 Was 'scoff' taken from his name to make the slang-verb meaning to eat indiscriminately or in an ungainly fashion? Perhaps. Most authorities believe that the verb started life as an Afrikaans noun, *schoft*: a quarter of a day, hence each of the four meals that many Victorians somehow managed to eat every day.

2 Adjunct to the Savoy Theatre, which was built by the impresario Richard D'Oyly Carte as the home of Gilbert and Sullivan light opera: the first public building in the world to be lighted by electricity, and the first theatre at which admission to the pit and gallery was obtainable by queuing.

Robinson, William

Calling himself Chung Ling Soo, wearing a costume that resembled but was rather more ornate than that of a Ming dynast, and with his eyes clenched into slits, this Yorkshireman did a conjuring act at music-halls throughout the country until, during the second house at Wood Green Empire, North London, on the night of Saturday 23 March 1918, he took his last bow. (Unlike that of Sherlock Holmes, it really was his last.)

One of his most spectacular tricks he called 'Catching the Bullets'. At Wood Green Empire, he presented it as the climax of his act. The routine went like this:

Two male members of the audience were invited on to the stage, first to examine a pair of muzzle-loading rifles, and then—after Soo had put a match to a pinch of gunpowder to demonstrate that it really was that and not something unexplosive such as gravy browning—to select a couple of lead balls from a box and examine them to make sure that they were unmarked. These were dropped in a cup proffered by a female assistant (Robinson's wife, though no one was supposed to know that), who then made her way across a gangway to the stalls, where two more members of the audience, one sitting on the right of the centre aisle, the other on the left, got into the act by scratching their initials on the balls. While the assistant was engaged on her errand, Soo explained in a sing-song voice that as soon as she returned with the marked balls they would be loaded into the rifles and fired at him—or, to be exact, at a plate (china, of course) that he would be clutching in front of his heart. All being well, he would then display the plate, unbroken and with the two balls rolling about on it. By the time he came to the end of his spiel, the female assistant was back on stage. He poured the gunpowder into the barrels, waited while the two men from the audience rammed home the charges and handed the rifles to two other assistants, took up a Kung-Fu-like stance, plate held like a shield, and nodded for the triggers to be pulled.

The last time he attempted the trick, the assistants fired and waited for the sound they had heard hundreds of time before: a double ping, supposedly the sound of the balls striking the plate. But on this occasion, what they heard instead was a cry that mingled pain with shock with surprise. Soo staggered back into the wings and fell dead. One of the balls had passed clean through his heart; it was subsequently found embedded in a piece of scenery. Although somewhat perplexed by the unorthodox way that Soo had made his exit, the capacity audience cheered and clapped. It would be nice to think that William Robinson heard the ovation as he died.

The police were called to the theatre, and in the course of their questioning of members, suddenly ex-members, of the Chung Ling Soo troupe, learnt that Mrs Robinson, the carrier of the balls to the stalls and back, had been estranged from her husband for some years. This made them suspicious.

But their suspicions were quelled the following day, after the famous gunsmith Robert Churchill (whose favourite piece of music was Tchaikovsky's 1812 Overture) had examined the props of the Catching-the-Bullets illusion. In his biography of *The Other Mr Churchill* (published 1963), Macdonald Hastings quotes what the gunsmith had to say:

> I found that they were 12-bore single-barrelled muzzle-loading rifles with a small ramrod tube laid under each barrel. All muzzle-loading rifles have rods, which are used to ram home the charge into the barrels. In the act, the ramrods were always put on one side as soon as the rifles had been loaded; and not returned, as one would normally have expected, to the tubes. I had remarked on this myself when I saw Chung Ling Soo's act, when I was also as bewildered as everybody else as to how he did it . . .
>
> In my examination, I soon discovered that the removal of the ramrods was in fact the key to the mystery. The ordinary percussion-fire muzzle-loader has a plug screwed into the barrel. The plug is fitted with a nipple. The hole in the nipple penetrates into the end of the barrel where the charge is seated. To fire the gun, a copper percussion cap is fitted to the nipple like a hat. The pull of the trigger releases the hammer, which hits the nipple and explodes the cap. The flash from the cap passes through the hole

into the chamber of the gun, where it ignites the powder charge which propels the bullet on its way. . . .

The difference between Chung Ling Soo's rifles and other rifles was that the hole which ordinarily leads from the nipple to the barrel was effectively sealed, and another hole was drilled from the nipple to the ramrod tubes underneath the barrel. So the operational barrels of the trick guns were not the proper barrels, loaded with powder and ball, but the ramrod tubes underneath which were loaded with a small and harmless charge of powder like a blank cartridge. After the act, all Chung Ling Soo had to do was to draw the charge in the barrel proper, and reload the ramrod tube with enough powder to made a harmless bang for the next performance.

The rest of the trick was relatively simple. The cup which the girl carried into the audience with two bullets in it had a false bottom. In the under-chamber were a pair of bullets marked by Chung Ling Soo himself, one with an X and the other with a few dots and scratches. He had counterparts of these which he slipped into his sleeve. After the shooting, he showed the two representatives of the audience on the stage his own marked bullets. They were satisfied because they had never seen the marks made by the people in the audience. When the girl went back into the stalls, she simply operated the trick bottom a second time and gave the people there the opportunity of establishing that the marks on them were the same, too. Actually, of course, their bullets had never left the cup.

Once the ingenious illusion is explained, it seems fool-proof. What went wrong on the night Chung Ling Soo was shot dead? Of course, he made a mistake. The mistake he made was that, after every performance, he unscrewed the breech plug in the base of the barrel to remove the bullet and powder. It was an unusual thing to do. The normal way of unloading a muzzle-loader is to draw the charge with the worm screw which is fitted inside a brass cap on the end of every ramrod. But, if he had done that, it would have scarred the marks on the carefully matched bullets which he used for performance after performance. So he went the long way round.

No muzzle-loading gun could stand up to that treatment for long. Normally, the breech-block would never be removed except by a skilled gunsmith, and then only occasionally for the purpose of lapping the inside of the barrel. The result was that in one rifle—the rifle that killed Soo—the thread had worn until the fitting was quite loose.

The final factor was the powder employed. It was a fine grain sort, milled into the consistency of dust. For safety, he should have used a powder of much coarser texture. It would have been quite adequate for his purpose. As it was, during constant loading the powdery powder had worked its way along the gaping thread in the screw of the breech plug until there was a train of it leading to the hole in the nipple. Inevitably, there came a time when the exploding cap ignited both the blank charge in the ramrod and the fatal charge in the barrel as well.

The tragedy of the affair was that Chung Ling Soo was in such terror of sharing his secret that he never sent his rifles for overhaul. Any skilled gunsmith would have noticed the fault, and could have rectified it before it became dangerous. Chung Ling Soo, by being too miserly with his secret, contrived his own end. Sooner or later, the accident was bound to happen.

Rorschach, Hermann

A Swiss psychiatrist who, shortly before his death at the age of thirty-eight in 1922, had the idea of using bilaterally symmetrical ink-blots in the study of personality; other psychiatrists, thrilled by the notion, blotted copybooks galore, displayed the pretty patterns to people who were silly enough to be their clients, asked them to say the first thing that came into their heads, and if the answers were nothing like their own, diagnosed battiness (◊ Sir Bertram Clough Williams-Ellis) and prescribed long, and, of course, expensive courses of treatment for the disorder.

Rule, Thomas

In 1798, having sown wild oats for far longer than his family considered desirable, he settled down to running an oyster bar in Maiden Lane, a dingy thoroughfare running parallel with the Strand. The enterprise prospered: exceedingly when Thomas, needing a speciality attraction for months without an *r*,[1] introduced a steak and kidney pie that was unusual for its abundance of the latter filling. The restaurant, being close to the Covent Garden and Drury Lane theatres, soon became a popular haunt of stage people: more so when the Adelphi, the rear of which was across the road from Rules, opened in 1806, and when the Lyceum was completed two and a half years later. Writers, too, favoured the place: Charles Dickens (who, so it is said, had as a boy left the blacking factory where he worked and made jaunts to Covent Garden, specifically to savour the aromas wafting up from Rules' kitchen), William Makepeace Thackeray, William Hazlitt; subsequently, and continuing well past the middle of this century, until businessmen with expense-accounts took up so many of the tables, literati (such as John Galsworthy, H[erbert] G[eorge] Wells,[2] Graham Greene, and John Betjeman) tended to treat Rules as a sort of club.

The Prince of Wales (later Edward VII) became such a regular customer—insisting on a table by the window on the first floor, at which a frequent companion was the actress Lillie Langtry (real name, Emilie Charlotte Le Breton; nicknamed the Jersey Lily)—that a special door was put in so that he could enter and leave without creating a stir. The 'royal door' was still there in the 1920s, but it was never used by another Prince of Wales (he who for a while was Edward VIII) who often popped into the downstairs bar for drinks and snacks with friends.

In 1897, close to the time when Rules acquired an extra door, the Adelphi Theatre, opposite, had two stage doors, one of which was used solely by William Terris, the most adored of the matinee idols, who was appearing at the theatre,[3] as he had done, always to a packed house, for some years. At about seven o'clock on the night of 16 December, Richard Arthur Prince—who was called, behind his back, Mad Archie—skulked in the main doorway to Rules. Prince was a supernumerary actor; he had once appeared as an extra in a Terris production at the Adelphi, but he had not worked for many months. He had got it into his crazed head that his lack of success was due to Terris: the star, so Prince thought, was intent on 'keeping him down', fearing that if he were given half a chance, he would outshine all the stars in the West End. As Terris approached the private stage-door, chatting with a friend, Prince darted across the road; as Terris inserted a key in the lock, Prince plunged a filleting knife between his ribs, mortally wounding him. By a horrifying irony, the one-and-ninepence that Prince had paid for the knife had come from a sovereign that Terris had given him, as a hand-out, a day or so before. He made no attempt to escape. Next day, at Bow Street Magistrates' Court, and months later, when he was tried at the Old Bailey, he thoroughly enjoyed being the star of the show. He was sent to Broadmoor Criminal Lunatic Asylum, where, deserting the stage for the concert platform, he became the conductor of the inmates' orchestra.

Although the present-day management of Rules prefer to gloss over the fact, the restaurant has two other criminous associations. Dr Thomas Neill Cream,[4] who in the autumn of 1891 and the spring of the following year used strychnine to deplete the number of prostitutes in the area of Waterloo Road, frequently ate at Rules. And so did Dr Hawley Harvey Crippen (◊ Marie Manning); he became so friendly with Harry Davis, who was then the manager, that more than once he had him as a dinner-guest at his home, 39 Hilldrop Crescent.

Having survived several threats from city planners and property developers, Rules—a place of mahogany splendour, its walls patched with mirrors, framed photographs, and playbills—remains the second oldest eating-house in London.[5]

---

1 A saying quoted in Harrison's *Description of England*, Book 3, published 1577: 'Oysters are not good in a month that hath not an 'r' in it.'

At one time certain oysterphiles excused their indulgence during August by spelling that month 'Orgust'.

2 Whose mistress for several years, during which she bore him an illegitimate son, was the ardently feminist author who wrote under the pseudonym of Rebecca West (the name of the heroine of Ibsen's play *Rosmersholm*). Born Cecily Maxwell Fairfield in 1892, she married a man'named Andrews after her affair with Wells; in 1959, she became a Dame Commander of the British Empire.

3 As Captain Thorn in a revival of *Secret Service*, the melo-drama by William Gillette (who later wrote and starred in the play *Sherlock Holmes*). Reviewing the original London production of *Secret Service*, George Bernard Shaw pointed to a number of incredible plot contrivances, noting in particular 'that before half an hour has elapsed, the heroine quite forgets an act of fratricide on the part of the hero'. Another play in which Terris starred at the Adelphi was *One of the Best*, written by Seymour Hicks, who later became his son-in-law; Shaw headed his review of the production, 'One of the Worst'.

4 He is among the many persons nominated as Jack the Ripper (◊ Peter J. Harpick)—regardless of the fact that he was listed as an inmate of Joliet Prison, Illinois, serving a life sentence for murder, when the prostitutes were being killed in Whitechapel.

5 The Cheshire Cheese pub and chop-house has been in Wine Office Court, next to·the *Daily Telegraph* offices in Fleet Street, since 1667. The name may have been chosen because land thereabouts had once belonged to the Abbey of Vale Royal, Cheshire.

Schwarz, Bernard

The real name of the film-actor Tony Curtis, whose hair-do in the 1950s was so often copied that the style acquired his adopted name. More than thirty years before, the sultry actress Theda Bara (a perhaps unintentional anagram of 'death arab'; her real name was Theodosia Goodman) had popularised and given *her* adopted name to a hairstyle, and in the '40s there was the Veronica Lake 'peek-a-boo bang'. Other stars are remembered as much for their coiffures as for their performances; and two, Yul Brynner and Telly Savalas, have profited from having no hair at all.

Selcraig, Alexander

Born in 1676, the seventh son of a shoemaker at Largo, Fifeshire, he was encouraged by his mother to amend his name to Selkirk. When he was nineteen, he ran away to sea (perhaps to evade a charge of indecent conduct in church), and in 1703 was considered experienced enough to be appointed sailing master on the *Cinque Ports*, one of the vessels engaged in Captain William Dampier's privateering expedition to the South Seas. In September of the following year, the ship put into Juan Fernandez, one of the objects of the visit being to recover two men who had accidentally been left on the island some months before. A quarrel with the captain, Thomas Stradling, led Selkirk to say that he would rather stay on the uninhabited island than be a member of Stradling's crew. Taking him seriously, Stradling left him behind when the *Cinque Ports* sailed away. More than four years passed before Selkirk was rescued by another of Dampier's ships. Towards the end of 1711, when he eventually got back to England, others' accounts of his adventures on the island made him a celebrity. Not enjoying this, he returned to Largo, where for a while he lived reclusively in a sort of cave that he had dug in his father's garden.

In 1719, Daniel Defoe, the writer,[1] businessman, and perhaps occasional secret agent, published *The Life and Strange Surprizing Adventures of Robinson Crusoe of York, Mariner*, based on Selkirk's time on the island. (There seems to be no truth in the story that the book was actually written by Lord Oxford in the Tower of London.) It was a great success: a second volume appeared within a few months, and in 1720 Defoe published a sequel, *Serious Reflections during the life . . . of Robinson Crusoe*. Via Defoe, Selkirk's adventures influenced Jonathan Swift in the writing of *Gulliver's Travels*. Sad to say, one or two present-day liberal librarians want to ban the books on the ground that the portrayal of Man Friday is a hindrance to racial equality.

'Robinson Crusoe' as rhyming slang for 'do so' seems to have died out. The usage was derived from a song in a pantomime of the late nineteenth century:

> Mr Robinson Crusoe—
> You dirty old man to do so. . . .

Many films—American, Danish, French, Mexican, Russian—have been based on Defoe's novel. Based? Well, more or less. A 1927 Hollywood version managed to include 'a slight love interest', and in 1964 the insularity of the story was blown more than sky-high for *Robinson Crusoe on Mars*.

1 According to some literary scholars, Defoe's 'A True Relation of the Apparition of one Mrs Veal' (1706) is the original ghost-story.

Selima

Horace Walpole's usually pensive cat—'demurest of the tabby kind'—who drowned in a river, inspiring Thomas Gray to write 'Ode on the Death of a Favourite Cat, Drowned in a Tub of Gold Fishes' (1748):

> . . . one false step is ne'er retriev'd . . .
> Not all that tempts your wand'ring eyes
> And heedless hearts is lawful prize;
> Nor all that glisters, gold.

This is not the source of the 'fool's gold' saying. 'Non teneas aurum totum quod splendet ut aurum' appears in the *Parabolae* of Alanus de Insulis (1294), and in the following century Chaucer wrote (in *House of Fame*), 'Hit is not al gold that glareth', and in *The Canon's Yeoman's Tale*:

> But al thing, which that shyneth as the gold
> Nis nat gold, as that I have herd it told.

Sexton Blake

This creation of Hal Meredith (the pen-name of Harry Blyth, who died in 1898) is now little more than rhyming slang for cake,[1] but for a few years at the end of the last century and some sixty years at the start of this one he was a poor man's Sherlock Holmes:[2] a great detective who, with assistance from a young man called Tinker and an amazingly bright bloodhound named Pedro, solved a case a week in the Sexton Blake Library series. He also appeared in several series of B (some might say C) pictures, and in 1962 suffered a sex-change in the film *Mix Me a Person*, which was based on one of his adventures but had Anne Baxter, who wasn't even lean and ascetic, playing him.

1 And for fake: this rhyme apparently having been spotted and coined by Tom Keating, the faker and forger of paintings, whose artistic illicitry was made public, then condemned in a court of law (though, as he was ill, he escaped punishment), a few years before his death in 1984.

2 The di-di/dum scansion of his name is echoed in the names of a surprisingly large posse of fictional detectives: Sexton Blake is one, of course, and among others are Bertha Cool, Colonel March, Harley Quin, Samuel Spade, and the great immovable Nero Wolfe of West 35th Street.

Shaw, Captain Joseph Thompson

To whom Raymond Chandler dedicated *Five Murderers*, a paperback volume published in 1944 which contained stories[1] that he had written for *Black Mask*[2] magazine from 1933 to 1936. The dedication was given

> with affection and respect, and in memory of the time when we were trying to get murder away from the upper classes, the week-end house party and the vicar's rose garden, and back to the people who are really good at it.

Black Mask, the best of the American pulp magazines that specialised in the so-called hard-boiled school of detective fiction, was founded in 1920 by H(enry) L(ouis) Mencken and George Jean Nathan to give financial support to their 'intellectual' magazine *Smart Set*. By 1927, when 'Cap' Shaw[3] was appointed editor, *Black Mask* had been sold to the Warner Publishing Co. (later, during Shaw's editorship, the magazine became part of a string of pulp magazines collectively called Popular Publications).

Shaw, who had won national championships as a fencer but had never made the grade as a writer, and who continued to call himself 'Captain' after serving in the army during the war, got the job with *Black Mask*—a magazine he had never seen or heard of before—through the intercession of a friend. Dashiell Hammett[4] and Erle Stanley Gardner[5] were among the writers already contributing to the magazine.

There is no doubt that Shaw was a good editor, though he seems to have been less expert at spotting talent than at developing it. (After looking at the first script that Chandler sent him—which was meticulously typed so that the right-hand margin was justified, giving an appearance of linotype—Shaw opined that the author was either a genius or crazy.) Shaw was publicly modest about his importance in the history of the detective tale: 'I never "discovered" an author,' he wrote; 'he discovered himself. I never "made" an author. He made himself.' But Chandler, in a letter he wrote to Erle Stanley Gardner in 1946, commented: 'I have always received from Shaw the definite impression . . . that he invented the hardboiled dick story with a ready assist from Hammett.'

1 'Blackmailers Don't Shoot' (Chandler's first published detective tale), 'Spanish Blood', 'Guns at Cyrano's', 'Goldfish', 'Nevada Gas'. According to Jacques Barzun and Wendell Hertig Taylor, the authors of *A Catalogue of Crime* (published 1971): 'The best and worst of Chandler are here found side by side . . . The last two [stories] give signs of the later characteristic style.'

2 A title previously used by E(rnest) W(illiam) Hornung (Arthur Conan Doyle's brother-in-law) for a group of stories, published 1901, about the amateur cracksman Raffles, told by his friend and accomplice Bunny.

It is likely that the printed-fictional use of the name Raffles stems from tales, told as though true, about Sir Thomas Stamford Bingley Raffles, of the British East India Company, who in 1819, during his traipsings around the Far East, happened upon a swampy settlement off the tip of the Malay Peninsula and, liking the look of the harbour, straightway purchased the place from the man who claimed to own it, a Temenggong of Johore. Legend had it that, many centuries before, a prince of the Sri Vijaya empire had landed there, caught a glimpse of a leonine animal that was new to him, and on that slender basis altered the settlement's name from Temasek (Sea Town) to Singa Pura (Lion City). The coalescence of those words and then the amendment of the new word's ending resulted in Singapore.

Raffles Hotel, 'the Savoy of Singapore', was built in 1886 by Armenian brothers who were partial to the French Renaissance style of architecture; to make space, a tiffin house run by a Captain Dare and his wife was pulled down. Colonial administrators found the reception rooms handy, specially as the Singapore Cricket Club, just along the road, did not encourage guests of the female sex, and in the years from the start of this century until the Second World War, Raffles was the hotel for wealthy visitors to the island: writers among them, including Rudyard Kipling (◊ James Brown), Noël Coward (who in 1929, taking in Singapore during a round-the-world cruise, came across an English theatrical touring company called The Quaints and agreed to appear with them in *Journey' End*, thus forming a friendship with John Mills), and (William) Somerset Maugham, who believed, so he said, that Raffles Hotel 'stands for all the fables of the exotic East'.

Prior to finding and buying Singapore, Stamford Raffles spent years in and around Java, and while there noticed and took notes of a stemless, leafless parasitical plant that bore enormous flowers; in 1822, it was given the name of Rafflesia.

Early in 1891, acting on a commission from the newspaper tycoon Alfred Harmsworth (later Viscount Northcliffe), Arthur Conan Doyle wrote a rather bad book called *The Doings of Raffles Haw*; the story was about a chemist who, having discovered the secret of boundless wealth, was exploited by men of whom he had thought well. The book appeared just before the earliest Sherlock Holmes short stories (*The Adventures*), and so, although deservedly unsuccessful, may have been identified by E.W. Hornung with Conan Doyle's 'period of compensation'.

Hornung dedicated the first Raffles book (*The Amateur Cracksman*, published 1898) to 'A.C.D., this form of flattery', and that leaves no doubt in the mind of the literary historian Owen Dudley Edwards that 'he modelled the Raffles stories on the Sherlock Holmes stories and that the name itself came from the forgotten *Raffles Haw* story'.

The association of cricket with the Raffles tales may be connected with the fact that Conan Doyle and Hornung both played in a team representing Jerome K. Jerome's (◊ Carl Hentschel) *Idler* magazine and later in an eleven put together by Conan Doyle himself. Indeed, cricket may have brought the two together, thus leading to Hornung's marriage to Conan Doyle's sister Constance.

3 An earlier Captain Shaw will be recalled by music-loving pyrophobics. The Irish-born Captain Eyre Massey Shaw, chief of the London Metropolitan Fire Brigade for thirty years from 1861, attended the first performance of Gilbert and Sullivan's *Iolanthe, or the Peer and the Peri*, on 25 November 1882, and heard the Fairy Queen, a buxom contralto, sing:

> . . . Oh Captain Shaw,
> Could thy Brigade
> With cold cascade
> Quench my great love?
> I wonder!

4 Most of Hammett's short stories were first published in *Black Mask*, which also serialised many of his novels, including *The Maltese Falcon*. Chandler, who admired and was to some extent influenced by Hammett, said that he 'took murder out of the Venetian vase and dropped it in the alley'. (◊ Clyde Wynant.)

5 Pseudonyms: A.A. Fair, Charles M. Green, Carleton Kendrake, Charles J. Kenny.

Spooner, the Reverend William Archibald

An albino cleric who was Warden of New College, Oxford, from 1903 until 1924, six years before his death. *The Dictionary of National Biography* says that 'his sermons, good in substance, suffered from his difficulty in reading'—a drawback that must also have had something to do with his unintended transposition of letters: spoonerisms. 'The Lord is a shoving leopard,' he said on one occasion; 'Kinkering kongs their titles take,' on another.

The columnist Bernard Levin is a master of the deliberate spoonerism. For instance, during the period when Sir Reginald Manningham-Buller (later Lord Dilhorne) was attorney-general (1954–62), Levin twisted his surnames into Bullying-Manner; and Miss Mandy Rice-Davis, one of the female leads in the Profumo Scandal that ran during 1963, was Levinised as Randy Mice-Davis.

Some theatre people enjoy devising spoonerisms. Samuel Beckett's one-character play *Krapp's Last Tape* has the first and last words of the title transposed, and the apostrophe transferred;

but only by people who might blaspheme in church or nibble bacon-butties in a synagogue. A play called *Home is the Hero* was presented for the first time—and, it is safe to say, the last—at Liverpool Playhouse in the early 1950s; but in the train of quite untrue rumours about the author, it was referred to by members of the repertory company as Here is the Homo.[1]

Many years ago, I was the stage director for a private-eye[2] play. Just prior to the opening performance, the actor cast as the detective was incommoded by dysentery, so I was forced to take over the part. With the aid of crib-sheets scattered strategically about the office-set, I managed to speak most of the lines written by the author—apart from those at the end of a duologue between the detective and a crime-reporter, played in this production by a young actor recently freed from a drama school. Speaking of a mysterious death, he was supposed to exclaim: 'Shot in the head?—my Aunt Fanny!' Instead, probably because he was unnerved by the sudden replacement of the actor he had rehearsed with, he cried out: 'Shot in the fanny?—my Aunt Edna!' The false cue upset me, and, departing from the script, I told him to leave. After a long pause (◊ William Charles Macready), during which he partially recovered from acute shock, he whispered a reminder that we were only halfway through the scene; but when I repeated the order, he slunk offstage, muttering confusedly, while I tried to find the crib-sheet for the post-lacuna dialogue between the investigator and his next visitor. (Months later, the young actor and I were conjoined as a single part, and I had reason to be thankful that he was not overtly stricken by any ailment at all like that which had been the root cause of our first encounter on stage. In a pantomime, he played the front legs of a horse, I the back—for me, a theatrical ambition youthfully fulfilled that, during the fulfilment, I yearned to look back upon, with dread at having to go through again.)

---

1 To illustrate the importance of the title to the success of a play: in 1959 a comedy I had written, called *Chopsticks in Waltztime*, was presented at the Group Theatre, Belfast; a run of three weeks was intended, but this period was doubled when the box-office was besieged by music-lovers who had noticed an advertisement in which the title of the play had become Chopin in Warsaw.

2 A term that probably owes its origin to the advertising symbol and slogan—a large open eye with the motto We Never Sleep—of the Pinkerton Detective Agency, founded in Chicago in 1850 by Allan Pinkerton, an emigrant from Glasgow who had been the first detective officer in the Chicago police force.

Tanner, Beatrice Stella

The maiden name of Mrs Patrick Campbell, the English actress who was noted for her beauty, caustic wit, and occasional indiscipline. (It is said that, bored with a scene in *Antony and Cleopatra* in which she had few lines, she flicked paper pellets at the sky-backcloth.) She created the part of Eliza Doolittle in Shaw's *Pygmalion*, playing opposite Sir Herbert Beerbohm Tree as Higgins; the first night was on 11 April 1914 at His Majesty's Theatre. Mrs Campbell wrote in her autobiography: 'Surely no first night has ever gone with more success, and with such joyousness. The 'bloody' almost ruined the play; people laughed too much.' But in a letter to Shaw, written six days after the opening, she said: 'Come soon—or you'll not recognise your play. I hope you make £40 ordinary nights and £80 Wed and Sat—then perhaps you can accept the mushy show with some sort of tolerance. . . . [P.S.] Tree takes five minutes between each word and each bite of the apple in Act 4. I have facial paralysis from trying to express some sort of intelligent feeling so now I hide my face until it is well again.' Her correspondence with Shaw (she was 'Stella', he 'Joey') began in 1899, when she was thirty-four and he forty-two, and continued until 1939, a few months before her death. Her most quoted comment is:

It doesn't matter what you do in the bedroom as long as you don't do it in the street and frighten the horses.

Toklas, Alice Babette

The Autobiography of Alice B. Toklas (published 1933) was written, not by the San Francisco-born Miss Toklas, but by Gertrude Stein, the writer from Allegheny, Pennsylvania, with whom she lived from 1906, acting as amanuensis and general helpmate, in a painting-filled apartment owned by Miss Stein and her brother Leo at 27 rue de Fleurus, Paris. Alice, a shy, thin woman with an extravagant nose, who almost invariably wore black or grey, was, physically speaking, a near-antithesis of Gertrude, who was dumpy, garish, and quite recognisable as the subject of the portrait Picasso painted of her; F. Scott Fitzgerald, whom she encouraged, said that she looked like 'the Great Stone Face' and once commented, 'What an old covered-wagon she is!' Alice was an excellent cook: or rather, an ingenious one—artists and writers who flocked to 27 rue de Fleurus were partial to her speciality confection, hashish-flavoured brownies.

On Saturday 27 July 1946, when Gertrude came out of the anaesthetic after an unsuccessful operation, she enquired of Alice and others at her bedside: 'What is the answer?' As no one replied, she murmured: 'In that case, what is the question?' Those words—like her writing, opaque yet transparent—were the last she spoke.

Her grave in the cemetery of Père-Lachaise is marked by a massive rectangular headstone designed by Francis Rose, the last artist she patronised. Since 1967, she has shared the plot with Alice B. Toklas.

Van Meegeren, Hans

If this Dutchman's own account of the why and how of his life of crime is to be believed, it was an art expert who caused him to try his hand at art forgery. That was soon after the First World War, when Van Meegeren was a promising but virtually unknown painter. A critic offered to publicise his work. At a price. Either because Van Meegeren was poor—finding it hard enough to afford paints and brushes, let alone give a bribe—or because he was then unswervingly moral, he turned down the offer. The next thing he knew, his work was being savagely attacked by the critic.

Partly to buttress his self-esteem, partly as an act of revenge (and, whatever Van Meegeren afterwards said, partly because he was short of cash), he used the very skills that the critic pooh-poohed to fabricate paintings by Old Dutch Masters. The fakes, which Van Meegeren arranged to be 'discovered', fetched high prices as soon as the experts had examined them and, having noted the 'distinctive brush-strokes' and 'characteristic tonal patterns', pronounced them genuine. They graced art galleries throughout the world, became centre-pieces in the collections of millionaires.

While things were going well for the Nazis during the

Second World War, Field-Marshal Hermann Goering plundered a beautiful painting here, a great statue there, and arranged for the treasures to be shipped to his mansion at Berchtesgaden. When the building became so crowded with works of art that the stout, medal-bedecked Goering began to feel cramped, further loot was deposited, for safety's sake, in a salt mine.

With the collapse of the Nazi regime, Goering lost his art collection shortly before he lost his life. The items were catalogued; the rightful owners sought. Of the 1,200 paintings , one was distinguished by the fact that it had been purchased rather than plundered. An agent acting for Goering had bought it from someone in Amsterdam. Goering had provided cash for the painting: a large amount, the equivalent of £150,000, because the canvas carried the signature of Jan Vermeer of Delft, one of the most esteemed Dutch Masters.

The search for the seller led the Amsterdam police to a night club owned by Hans Van Meegeren, who admitted that he had raised part of the capital by selling half a dozen Vermeers. He claimed that he had bought the paintings from an Italian family; a perfectly legitimate deal. And just as legitimate, he said, was his sale of the paintings. Five were now in Dutch museums. True enough, the sixth had been sold to an individual, but he had had no idea that the man was acting on behalf of Goering.

Still suspicious, the police arrested Van Meegeren. They interrogated him; threatened him with execution for collaborating with the Nazis. And after three weeks, he told the truth: the paintings were fakes—all his own work.

No one believed him. Certainly not the experts, the men who had verified the authenticity of the works. Desperately wanting to be branded a faker, Van Meegeren gave details of some of his other artistic deceptions. The experts riposted that he was simply adding to the height of his already tall story. So he offered to produce a Vermeer to order. The title chosen was 'Young Christ Teaching in the Temple'.

He started work—in a studio that was locked and barred, ensuring that he could not have a real Vermeer smuggled in. But he never finished the painting. As soon as the experts saw what was taking shape, they admitted that they had been hoodwinked.

In the summer of 1947, in a courtroom whose walls were almost hidden by Van Meegeren's 'proxy paintings', he was found guilty of forging *signatures*, and was sentenced to a year's imprisonment. That penalty was not exacted, however, for he suffered a fatal heart attack shortly after the trial.

It turned out that the great deceiver had been deceived (in the same way as was [◊] Elyesa Bazna). The money used by Hermann Goering to buy the counterfeit Vermeer was itself counterfeit.

Von Losch, Marie Magdelene

The real name of the German-born film actress and cabaret entertainer Marlene Dietrich. In 1930, some eight years after her first screen appearance, she played the fatal Lola-Lola in *Der Blaue Engel* (*The Blue Angel*), directed by Josef von Sternberg, and was immediately signed up by the Paramount Pictures Corporation; the first six films she made in Hollywood were directed by Von Sternberg, and included *Shanghai Express* (1932), in which, as a coaster or *traviata* (◊ Marie Duplessis), she explained, 'It took more than one man to change my name to Shanghai Lily.' Her best subsequent part was that of Frenchy in *Destry Rides Again* (1939), in which she sang 'The Boys in the Back Room'.

Von Sacher-Masoch, Leopold

For reasons that I don't need to go into, during the late 1880s and early '90s, the last years of his life, this son of an Austrian policeman became an object of fascination to the German psychiatrist Richard von Krafft-Ebing, who coined the word masochism from his name.

On the other side of the word-coinage, Donatien Alphonse de Sade, generally known as the Marquis de Sade (1740–1814), was a Frenchman, only five feet two inches tall, whose sexual enjoyment from inflicting pain or humiliation on others, and whose listing of 600 variations on the sexual act, caused his name to become a noun: sadism.

There is a useful aide-mémoire for knowing which word is which:

Thrash me,' said the masochist.

'Certainly not,' the sadist replied.

Walter Plinge

A theatrical alias, printed in cast-lists against one—usually the
smaller—of two parts played by the same actor. Probably
because most plays have more parts for actors than for actresses,
there is no feminine equivalent. The name of George Spelvin is
used in America—where, as a legacy from the early days of
vaudeville, when members of the orchestra sometimes left the pit
to play small parts or be supernumeraries in non-musical acts on
stage, an actor playing two roles is said to be 'doubling in brass'.

Weare, William

Thomas De Quincey's essay 'On Murder Considered as One of
the Fine Arts' makes a convenient starting point for any discussion of how writers, fascinated by criminal cases, or aspects of

them, have created literary art from nature. It is no more than convenient; for accounts of cases, and fictional transmutations of them, have a far longer history. One thinks, perhaps straightway, of the fourth chapter of the Book of Genesis, with its hearsay report on the case of Cain and Abel. And in Elizabethan times, the anonymous play *Arden of Feversham*—once attributed to Shakespeare—took its plot from a murder recorded in Holinshed's *Chronicles of England, Scotland and Ireland*, which was one of the story-sources of the murder plays that Shakespeare undoubtedly wrote (◊ Macbeth).

The decade or so around 1827, when De Quincey's essay appeared in *Blackwood's Magazine*,[1] was special in the sense that a number of things came together to give impetus to literary murder. With the foundation of the popular press—relatively cheap newspapers vying with catchpenny broadsheets reporting particular events—the details of murders became common knowledge, public property. And, as it happened, the period had more than its fair share of picturesque cases. Murders were no long parochial affairs, and people in the south were able to tut-tut delightedly at the pioneering entrepreneurship of Messrs (◊) Burke & Hare in Edinburgh, while in that same year of 1828, residents of Auld Reekie (old smoky = Edinburgh) could savour the rural nuances of the murder of Maria Marten, the molecatcher's daughter, in the Red Barn at Polstead, down in East Anglia.

Often, it was the embroidery on a case, asides from the criminal act, that pricked the fancy of contemporary writers: men like Thomas Carlyle, Walter Scott, and Charles Lamb (who, poor fellow, was not only for a short time suspected of being an accessory to a fatal mugging, but had the perhaps unique distinction among English writers of living with a murderess—his sister Mary, who had stabbed their mother to death during one of her bouts of madness). Also, there were George Borrow and William Hazlitt, both of whom had met John Thurtell when he was known simply as a low-life sportsman, not yet as the murderer—ham-handedly abetted by two flash acquaintances, Joseph Hunt, a bankrupt publican, and William Probert, a bankrupt spirits-merchant—of William Weare, a card-sharper and billiards-hustler who had cheated Thurtell of several hundreds of pounds.

Thurtell appears, scantily disguised as Tom Turtle, in

Hazlitt's essay 'The Fight'. But for a complete portrait, one turns to *Lavengro*, in which Borrow described Thurtell as

> . . . a man somewhat under thirty, and nearly six feet in height. He was dressed in a blue coat, white corduroy breeches, fastened below the knee with small golden buttons; on his legs he wore white lamb's-wool stockings, and on his feet shoes reaching to the ankles; round his neck was a handkerchief of the blue and bird's eye pattern; he wore neither whiskers nor moustaches, and appeared not to delight in hair, that of his head, which was of a light brown, being closely cropped; the forehead was rather high, but somewhat narrow; the face neither broad nor sharp, perhaps rather sharp than broad; the nose was almost delicate; the eyes were grey, with an expression in which there was sternness blended with something approaching to feline; his complexion was exceedingly pale, relieved, however, by certain pock-marks, which here and there studded his countenance; his form was athletic, but lean; his arms long. In the whole appearance of the man there was a blending of the bluff and the sharp. You might have supposed him a bruiser; his dress was that of one in all its minutiae; something was wanting, however, in his manner—the quietness of the professional man; he rather looked like one performing the part—well—very well—but still performing a part.

Thurtell crops up again in Borrow's *The Romany Rye*, though here one suspects that truth suffers in aid of an anecdote. A jockey recalls that he had asked the sportsman how he could repay him a debt:

> He bade me come and see him hanged when his time was come. . . . I arrived at Hertford just in the nick of time. There was the ugly jail—the scaffold—and there upon it stood the only friend I ever had in the world. Driving my Punch, which was all in a foam, into the midst of the crowd, which made way for me as if it knew what I come for, I stood up in my gig, took off my hat, and shouted, 'God Almighty bless you, Jack.' The dying man turned his pale grim face towards me—for his face was always somewhat grim, do you see—nodded and said, or I thought I heard him say, 'All right, old chap.'

The gig referred to by the jockey was not the famous one in the case. That belonged to Thurtell's victim, William Weare.

According to Thomas Carlyle, there was an exchange between counsel and a witness at the trial:

Question: What do you mean by 'respectable'?

Answer: He [Mr Weare] always kept a gig.

The idea of associating a gig with respectability so enchanted Carlyle that he coined the term *gigmanity* for bourgeois social pretension.

Though Walter Scott took the trouble to visit the scenes of the crime, it appears that he was in two minds about the case, uncertain whether it displayed sufficient panache to warrant all the fuss. The same applies to De Quincey, who, after allowing his Connoisseurs of Murder[2] their first fine careless rapture—'Well, will *this* do?' 'Is *this* the right thing?' 'Are you satisfied at last?'—concluded that when the enthusiasm had subsided, 'most judicious critics agree that there was something *falsetto* in the style of Thurtell'.

It was not the illustrious writers who ensured remembrance of the case, but a broadsheet balladeer, 'reputed to have been one William Webb, otherwise known as "Flare Up" (a brand of cheap gin) or "Hoppy", a former acrobat in a perambulating circus who had fallen to the low estate of linkman before being transported for stealing the jewels of a prima donna as she left the opera house'.[3] He cobbled together the quatrain:

> His throat they cut from ear to ear,
> His brains they punchèd in;
> His name was Mr William Weare,
> Wot lived in Lyon's Inn.

This verse was a favourite of Robert Browning's. He leanrt it as a child, and still recited it with relish when he was old, by which time he himself had made several contributions to murderous literature—most lengthily, inspired by an actual case, with *The Ring and the Book* (◊ Count Guido Franceschini).

It seems to me that the murder of Mr William Weare was the gig that gave crime literary respectability. Throughout the Victorian age—thought by George Orwell (◊ Eric Arthur Blair) to be 'our great period in murder, our Elizabethan period, so to speak'—writers, among them Wilkie Collins[4] and Charles Dickens (◊ Marie Manning), found inspiration in criminous reality.

1 Founded in 1817 by an Edinburgh publisher William Blackwood, who edited it until his death in 1834, when his son John took over. The last issue of what was familiarly called 'Maga' appeared in 1980.

2 A society of that name, founded by Thomas M. McDade, is the American equivalent of Our Society (◊ Richard Gordon Parry).

3 The quotation is from Richard D. Altick's *Victorian Studies in Scarlet* (published 1970).

4 I suppose *The Moonstone* (published 1868) is the most noted example of a Victorian novel partly based on actual crimes. Certainly, the episode in which Godfrey Ablewhite is lured to a house in Northumberland Street, London, and there attacked is a rephrasing of the so-called Northumberland Street Sensation of 1861, and one can be just as sure that Collins borrowed incidents and characters from the Road House Mystery of 1860, the murder of four-year-old Savill Kent, probably by his half-sister Constance.

Mary Hayley Bell's play *Angel*, first produced in 1947, is based on the Road House Mystery; and Francis King has woven salient details of the case into his novel *Act of Darkness* (published 1983).

Weller, Charles

An American who has not received the credit due to him for having concocted the sentence that, despite the fact that the quick brown fox jumped over the lazy dog, has been typed more often than any other:

Now is the time for all good men to come to the aid of the party.

West, Mae

A past-mistress of the *double entente* who, when performing publicly, on stage and in films, made fun of sex. Her most-quoted line, 'Come up and see me some time', was, so she says in her memoirs (published 1960), a frequently extended offstage/screen invitation, accepted on one occasion by a prodigy referred to only as Ted, who engaged her in love-making for fifteen hours on the trot. Her best line, inspired by the pre-prandial skinning activities of her pet-monkey Boogie, was uttered in the film *I'm No Angel* (1933), an order to a black maid: 'Hey, Beulah, peel me a grape.' During the Second World War, when she learnt that British airmen had given her name to a pneumatic life-jacket, she commented: 'I've been in *Who's Who* and I know what's what, but this is the first time I ever made the dictionary.'

Wightman, Hazel

An American tennis player (*née* Hotchkiss—but, as far as I can tell, not related to Benjamin Berkeley Hotchkiss, the American inventor of many dangerous things, including the revolving cannon bearing his name), she instituted the Wightman Cup annual challenge match between the United States and Great Britain in 1923.

Williams-Ellis, Sir Bertram Clough

An architect who, long before his death at the age of ninety-five in 1978, turned an impossible dream into reality by creating what he considered an 'ideal village', called Portmeirion, fanning from his home on the northern hem of Cardigan Bay, Wales: a motley collection of buildings (some transported from other sites) and masonried bric-à-brac, each item of which appealed to him in some way, and contributed or was thought to be an appropriate addendum to his grand, eccentric design.

The eccentricity of the place made it an ideal location for a television series called *The Prisoner*, a batty[1] brain-child of the actor Patrick McGoohan, who played the leading part of a balloon-fearing, flashback-minded, open-imprisoned person known as Number 6 (other characters—their lines recited by actors who were clearly unclear as to whether they were playing custodians, fellow-prisoners, or what—were similarly numerically identified). Franz Kafka (◊) might have approved of the idea, whatever it was, while criticising the flaccid construction of most of the episodes, happenings, spasms, or whatever the individual programmes were called. The last of these got high viewing figures when the series was first shown in 1967: people assumed that all would be explained. That assumption proved false (after all, how can the inexplicable be explained?)—though, to be fair to Mr McGoohan and his accomplices, someone said something that some viewers construed as being a statement about Vietnam or Clapham Junction or somewhere. Proving a component of Abraham Lincoln's most quoted comment, the bit about fooling some of the people all of the time, *The Prisoner* became a minor cult, students in Canada took degree courses on what it signified (◊ Macbeth: 'it is a tale/Told by an idiot, full of sound and fury, / Signifying nothing'; ◊ Harvey's note 1: in 1955, after sitting through the opening night of *Waiting for Godot* at the Arts Theatre, Milton Shulman, drama critic of the London *Evening Standard*, said that the play was 'another of those . . . that tries to lift superficiality to significance through obscurity'), and, for a time, Portmeirion was a place of pilgrimage as well as a spot for a nice day out.

1 Said to be derived from Fitzherbert Batty, a lunatic lawyer of Spanish Town, Jamaica, whose incarceration in an asylum in 1839 caused little wonder among the locals but was played up by the faraway London press.

Wisden, John

Cricket, the English national game, mystifies most Englishmen. It is the mystifications that make it appealing: having read in a newspaper report on a game between counties that a batsman (or 'wielder of the white willow' in cricket journalese) was 'caught Fiddling', one eventually fathoms the fact that a fielder named Fiddling caught the ball (or 'crimson rambler') before it hit the ground (or 'verdured turf')—but, reading on, one learns that Fiddling was positioned at silly mid-off when the crimson rambler rambled his way, which means that one then has to try to work out where he was standing in relation to the wicket: easier said than done, because if a batsman is sinistral, silly mid-off becomes silly mid-on. Each summer, as soon as it starts raining, there is at least one series of test matches (there we are again: why *test*?) between an England eleven and a side representing a foreign country; thousands of people pay for admission, either to watch the play or to take their clothes off and streak across the pitch at the van of uniformed policemen; millions watch the play and the streakers on television, or listen to radio commentaries on what is or is not happening; and during the series, even when the visiting side is not staunchly supported by immigrants from the same country, more than 20 million telephone calls are made to the British Telecom recorded-score service, chiefly by people who are supposed to be working in offices.

And cricket has its bible: *Wisden*—or to give it its present full title, *Wisden Cricketers' Almanack*—which has been published annually, without a break, since 1864, the year that over-arm bowling was legalised. It was started by John Wisden, a recently-retired professional cricketer who in his heyday was known as the Little Wonder, less on account of his batting, which was deemed 'solid', than because his bowling was 'very fast and ripping'. Although he was born on the south coast, in Brighton, in 1826, his association with the Leamington ground, Warwickshire, which he co-rented, qualified him to play for the North—most memorably at Lord's, the home of the Marylebone Cricket Club (MCC), in 1850, when he clean bowled all ten wickets in the second innings of the South. Five years after that feat, he and another cricketer, Fred Lillywhite (who also hailed from Brighton; or rather, from that town's posh[1] adjunct of Hove), teamed up to open a 'cricket, sporting and cigar depot' in Coventry Street, just off Leicester Square, in the West End of London. There, they continued publication of the annual *Young Cricketer's Guide*, which Lillywhite had founded in 1849. The business was successful, but Wisden and Lillywhite didn't see eye to eye about how it should be run, and in 1858 the latter stormed out, and soon afterwards partnered his elder brother James in starting a bat-making firm. Wisden stayed on in Coventry Street, though in the following year he employed a manager while he and another ageing professional took a United England side on the first major overseas tour, to the United States and Canada.

Wisden did not get the idea for *The Cricketer's Almanack* from Fred Lillywhite's *Guide* (which did not have the field to itself: there was also a *Chronicle*, an *Annual*, and a *Companion*, the last two published respectively by James Lillywhite and another Lillywhite brother, John[2]), but presumably he went ahead with the project because of his knowledge of the *Guide*'s profits. The first *Almanack* was a paltry thing, its 112 pages padded out with items which should have, but didn't, give rise to the saying, 'that's not cricket': before the score-cards of the previous summer's matches and the Laws of the Game, there were pages of

topical information and of anniversaries (the first line of the first
Wisden reminded readers, 'January 1st: British Museum closed',
and the entry for the next day read, 'British Museum re-opens';
among the anniversaries was Wisden's own birthday); spaces on
subsequent pages were filled with a potted history of China, a list
of horses that had won the Derby,[3] and the dates of battles of the
Wars of the Roses (considered sort of appropriate, perhaps,
because of the cricketing battles—Roses matches—at Old Traf-
ford and Headingley between Lancashire and Yorkshire). Still,
the first *Wisden* sold well; and the second—22 of its 160 pages
devoted to 'The Doings of the Twelve in Australia'—did even
better. Year by year, it grew in size (now it has more than 1,300
pages) and gathered fresh features: accounts of matches, for
instance (the 1878 edition carried a report on a match between
two Gloucestershire village sides, in which the opening batsman
Dr E.M. Grace made 200 runs, and Dr A. Grace, the last man in,
was 28 not out—entitling the reporter to muse: 'A doctor at the
beginning, and a doctor at the end. Such is life.')

1 A word that, until recently, was generally believed to be
derived from '*p*ort *o*ut, *s*tarboard *h*ome,' the cabin-sides, least
sunburnt, that were ordered by upper-class voyagers between
Great Britain and India in the days of the Raj. But, doubt having
been thrown on this notion, an etymological investigation is under
way.

2 The brothers really deserve an entry to themselves. In 1863,
they opened a sports shop in the Haymarket, and two decades
later, having bought a similar shop owned by a cousin, another
James Lillywhite, claimed that their business was the largest of its
kind in the world; the present main shop, in Piccadilly Circus, was
opened in 1925. As well as designing sports gear and helping to
popularise foreign sports in Great Britain, the firm has assisted
non-sporting endeavours: for instance, they created the Lillysport
Aviation Suit for ladies, worn by Miss Amy Johnson on her solo
flight to Australia in 1930, and in 1940 supplied equipment to the
ski corps drawn from the 5th Battalion of the Scots Guards to
assist the Finns in border patrols against Russia; two directors of
Lillywhites Ltd. accompanied the ski corps as technical experts,
and on the basis of information they brought back, the first string
vests were made.
As for the Lillywhite brothers' cricket books, in 1867 the

Guide was incorporated in the *Companion*, and this, in turn, was absorbed into the *Annual*, known as 'the red Lillywhite', in 1886; the *Annual* ceased publication in 1900, leaving the yellow-liveried *Wisden* unrivalled.

3 Legend has it that the name of the race, first run in 1780 and now started at three o'clock on the first Wednesday of each June, was decided by the toss of a coin between Edward Stanley, twelfth Earl of Derby, who suggested the event, and Sir John Hawkewood, who arranged it. The Kentucky Derby, held annually at Churchill Downs, Louisville, has become quite as renowned a fixture as the race on Epsom Downs, Surrey, and the word derby is now indiscriminately applied to sporting contests between animals or persons or both in concert. The Earl of Derby who, so it is said, correctly called heads also gave his name to a variation on the round felt hat called a bowler (after a London hatter or, more likely, because of its shape) and to a specially strong kind of boot that, as far as I can tell, is no longer made.

Wooldridge, Charles Thomas

Oscar Wilde's poem 'The Ballad of Reading Gaol' has the following dedication:
>*In memoriam* C.T.W.,
>sometime Trooper of the Royal Horse Guards,
>*obit* H.M. prison, Reading, Berkshire, July 7, 1896.

C.T.W. were the initials of Charles Thomas Wooldridge, who, believing his wife Ellen to be unfaithful, travelled from his barracks in Regent's Park, London, to the cottage in Arthur Road, Windsor, where Ellen was living under her maiden name, and when she tried to run away, murdered her by cutting her throat; he then gave himself up to a constable, saying, 'Take me. I have killed my wife.' The trial judge, Mr Justice Hawkins, ignored defence counsel's argument that a *crime passionel* could be treated as manslaughter rather than murder, and summed up strongly against Wooldridge. After an absence of just a couple of minutes, the jury returned a verdict of 'guilty', but asked the judge to recommend mercy. Hawkins[1] simply pronounced the death sentence, and Wooldridge was taken to Reading Gaol, where, in the three weeks before his execution, he was seen by Oscar Wilde (prisoner C3.3):

> A cricket cap was on his head,
>   And his step seemed light and gay;
> But I never saw a man who looked
>   So wistfully at the day.

1 Sir Henry Hawkins (later Baron Brampton) was on the Bench, often accompanied by his pet-dog, from 1876 until 1901, during which time he became known as The Hanging Judge. That title passed to Horace Edmund Avory, who was also known as the Acid-Drop during his judgeship, which lasted exactly a quarter of a century from 1910. Rayner Goddard, a judge of the King's Bench from 1932, and Lord Chief Justice of England from 1946 until 1958 (referred to as Lord Goddamn by Winston Churchill), was the last of the so-called Hanging Judges. None of the three deserved the title as much as did Isaac Parker, who is reckoned to have sentenced 79 men to be hanged in the course of dispensing justice in the Arkansas-Oklahoma territory during the final quarter of the last century.

Wright, Willard Huntingdon

An American aesthete and critic who, after writing a series of articles that picked holes in the eleventh edition of the *Encyclopaedia Britannica*, and soon afterwards publishing them as a book entitled *Misinforming a Nation*, which caused quite a stir, suffered a nervous breakdown. That was in 1923, when he was thirty-five. He remained poorly for two years, during which his doctor forbade him to read anything more stimulating than detective novels. Having got through a couple of thousand of them, he thought to himself: 'Why, if other writers, with far less experience and training than I have had, can achieve success at this kind of fiction, can't I? I have studied the detective novel, and I understand its rules and techniques. I know its needs, and have learned its pitfalls.' So he wrote thirty-thousand-word synopses of three books and showed them to Maxwell Perkins, the famous editor for Charles Scribner's Sons, discoverer and encourager of, among others, F. Scott Fitzgerald, Ernest Hemingway and Thomas Wolfe. Perkins's response was immediate. He told Wright: 'The books are just what we want—and I believe you can do them. We'll take all three.'

The first edition of the first of the books, *The Benson Murder Case*, published under the pseudonym of S.S. Van Dine in 1926, sold out within a week. The story was based on a real case: the unsolved murder of Joseph Bowne Elwell, the leading authority on the game of bridge, at his home on West 70th Street, Manhattan, on 11 June 1920—the closest that reality has come to the fictional locked-room mystery.[1]

The second book, *The Canary Murder Case*, published the following year, sold in greater numbers than any earlier book of its genre. Like the first, though less obviously, it was based on fact: the murder of the good-time girl Anna Marie Keenan, better known as Dot King, whose body was found in her apartment on West 57th Street, Manhattan, on the morning of 15 March 1923.

The first two books are still readable; the seven and a half that followed (all with titles ending 'Murder Case') are not. I should explain that the half-a-book is *The Winter Murder Case*, a thirty-thousand-word synopsis that was published after Wright's death in 1939.

The star of all the books is a master-detective named Philo Vance: partly a representation of the author, partly a representation of the sort of person Wright would like to have been or actually believed himself to be. Vance—who, in the opinion of Ogden Nash, deserved 'a kick in the pance'—lived in an art-filled apartment with his Boswell, S.S. Van Dine, smoked Regie cigarettes, rarely pronounced the g of words ending ing . . . and was easily burlesqued: by Christopher Ward, for instance, who published a parody in *The Saturday Review of Literature* of 2 November 1929 which reads, in part:

> Pants had been for several days immersed in a Coptic translation of Schizzenheimer's 'Nuovi Studi de la Physiologie des Heisshundes'. He could not read Coptic, but was trying to decide which was the right side up of the fascinating volume, when Barker came in.
> 'A new murder for you, Pants,' said Barker gloomily.
> 'Oh, I say, don't you know, eh what?' drawled Pants. 'How dashed amusin'. Most intriguin' and all that sort of thing. I could bear to hear about the bally homicide, old bean, don't y' know.'

A caricature of the original? Well, no. Here is an excerpt from one of the books:

> 'Kyle has been murdered,' the newcomer blurted, leaning against the library table and staring at Vance with gaping eyes.
> 'Really, now! That's very distressin'.' Vance held out his cigarette-case. 'Do have one of my Regies. . . . And you'll find that chair beside you most comfortable. A Charles chair: I picked it up in London. . . . Beastly mess, people getting murdered, what? But it really can't be helped, don't y' know. The human race is so deuced blood-thirsty.'

Between 1929 and 1947, thirty-odd Philo Vance films were released; the least unwatchable of them are the four that starred William Powell—*Canary* and *Greene* (1929), *Benson* (1930), and *Kennel* (1933). Among other spin-offs from the books, there was a Canary ice-cream sundae[2] and a Philo Vance cocktail.[3]

And the success of *The Benson Murder Case*, not the book itself, inspired two young New York advertising men, Frederick Dannay and Manfred Bennington Lee, to write, under the joint pseudonym of Ellery Queen, a detective novel called *The Roman Hat Mystery* (published 1929), which was the first of a stream of books they produced, most ascribed to Ellery Queen but some to Barnaby Ross, Daniel Nathan, or Ellery Queen Junior.

1 There *is* a solution to the mystery; but I intend to write a book about the case, and it would be foolish of me to reveal all—or, indeed, anything—beforehand.

2 There may be other ice-cream concoctions named after fictional characters, but I don't know of any. The most-often-offered person-honouring sundae is the Peach Melba, which consists of sliced peaches, ice-cream, whipped cream, and ('Melba') raspberry sauce. The first adult to put these ingredients together was the master-chef Auguste Escoffier, who committed the act as a treat for the operatic soprano Dame Nellie Melba—who was born Helen Porter Mitchell in a small town near Melbourne, from which she derived her stage-surname, in 1861. Bread cut thin browns and curls in a hot oven, thus becoming Melba toast, which is sometimes served in place of biscuits with Peach Melba. Dame Nellie's repeated farewell appearances gave rise to the Australian expression 'doing a Melba'.

3 There may be other cocktails named after fictional characters, but I don't know of any. However, ◊ Harvey for persons who, not always wittingly or willingly, have lent their names to mongrel drinks.

X, Mr

Ewen Montagu tells me:

He was known to Hitler,[1] to the German High Command and Intelligence Services, to many Spanish Ministers and officials, as well as to many others, including visitors to his grave at Huelva in Spain, as Major William Martin, Royal Marines—but that wasn't his real name. Since then, he has become known as The Man Who Never Was to many millions around the world—for nearly three million copies of the book of that name have been sold in thirteen languages, his story has been in many anthologies, and for nearly thirty years the film also called by his 'name' has been shown in cinemas and is still being shown on television. But that, of course, is not his real name either. He, in fact, died quietly in London of pneumonia under his real name, which I have promised never to reveal.

It happened in this way. It was obvious to any competent strategist that, after we had conquered North Africa, we would have to eliminate the airfields, troops and harbours in Sicily before we could make any landing across the Mediterranean. How *could* we persuade the Germans that we were going to risk anything else?

Our Inter-Service group, then responsible for deception,

decided to supply the Germans with a *very* high-level letter—in fact from the Vice-Chief of the Imperial General Staff to General Alexander, who commanded our troops in French North Africa, indicating that we intended first to attack Sardinia and Greece, hoping to catch the Germans by surprise. But how could we get the letter to the Germans? We decided to have it carried (notionally) by an officer on his way to North Africa in an aircraft which crashed into the sea off the coast of Spain—as we had no doubt that the Spaniards would show any documents that he carried to the Germans after his body had been washed ashore.

We found our body and built him up as a real person through the letters and so on that he had in his pockets—but he had to have a name. We chose Capt., Temporary Major, William Martin, Royal Marines, because there was a little group of Martins of about the right seniority in the current Navy List, and, if his 'name' became known, we hoped that the initials in any publication would be regarded as a misprint. It worked. After the book was published, I heard from the then Capt., Temp. Major, William H.N. Martin, Royal Marines, that when people were surprised to see him still alive, he had, quite believing it, said just that.

How did he get his second false name?

I had never imagined that the story could ever be published, even though it was a 'one-off' operation which could not give anything else away. Then Duff Cooper published his brilliant novel *Operation Heartbreak*, in which the dead body of an officer, carrying deceiving documents and, among other personal papers, a letter from his fiancée, is washed up on a neutral shore. It is almost certain that Duff Cooper, when a Cabinet Minister, had heard the gist of our operation from Winston Churchill. Someone on the outskirts of our operation leaked to the Press that Duff Cooper had based his book on a real operation that I had run. I was badgered day and night and had to prevaricate. When an official banning-notice had been put on the story, I was finally asked by the Beaverbrook Press to give them first refusal if the ban was ever removed . . . and, to get them off my back, I agreed—not believing that it could ever happen.

Then Rommel's diaries were hawked round Fleet Street. Journalists spotted that Liddell Hart, the military historian, had put as a footnote to Rommel's being appointed to command the

German resistance to our invasion of Greece (which never occurred) words to the effect, 'readers of Duff Cooper's *Operation Heartbreak* will realise the reason for this'—and some bright journalists shot off to Spain. One of them gathered from various sources some wholly garbled information—false information that could have had serious repercussions. Our government asked me to publish the *true* story, as the lesser of two evils, and to do it fast enough to kill the other one.

I immediately went to the editor of the *Sunday Express*, part of the Beaverbrook Press. He said that they *might* publish it, but only if they had at least the backbone of the story on Monday, when they were making up their programme of serials. This was on Friday morning! So I went to the country and, with a lot of black coffee and literally no sleep, produced 95 per cent of the story by Monday morning—with the possibility of rewriting it later. They accepted the story, then called by the title of our operation, 'Operation MINCEMEAT', and suggested that I should discuss possible alterations with Jack Garbett, one of their staff.

In the event, virtually no alterations were made; but, at one of our discussions, Jack showed me a proposed poster—the cap and uniformed shoulders of a Royal Marine Major, with, where his face should have been, the title 'The Man Who Never Was'—and asked me what I thought of it. I replied 'Brilliant,' and so the pseudo William Martin got the name by which he is known to millions.

Ewen E.S. Montagu
1st February 1984

1 During the war, some British and American journalists (Quentin Reynolds foremost among the latter) referred to him as Schicklgruber. That was the name of his paternal grandmother, who was a spinster, employed as a domestic servant by a Jew in Graz, Austria, when she bore a son whom she called Alois; it appears that the father was either the Jew or one of two brothers with the surname of Hiedler or Hüttler. Five years, later, Maria Anna Schicklgruber married one of the brothers. In 1877, long after her death and that of her husband, the surviving Hiedler/Hüttler brother arranged for her son, who was by then nearly forty, to be 'legitimised' as Alois Hitler; not all the legitimising formalities were adhered to. Alois married a cousin, an unedu-

cated Bavarian girl called Klara Pölz who had been his mistress while she was working at his house; three of the couple's children died in infancy, but Adolf, born in 1889, lived to the age of fifty-six—or longer, according to some legendists.

Yousoupoff, Prince Felix

Some interpreters of the Russian Revolution refer to him as Yusupov, but he himself (who was also entitled to the title of Count Sumarokov-Elston) wrote the name as Yousoupoff, and it seems only polite to give him the benefit of the doubt. Born in 1887, he married Princess Irina, daughter of the Grand Duke Alexander Mikhailovich and Tsar Nicholas II's sister, the Grand Duchess Xenia. In 1916, he, with others, murdered Rasputin (whose full surname was Rasputin-Novy or -Novykh); just what his motive was—whether political, patriotic, or superstitious—is argued over by people who believe that motives are tidy things, capable of being described in one or at most two words.

Lady Lucy Wingfield was the fascinatingly beautiful wife of the diplomat Sir Charles, who from 1915 until 1919 was attached to the British Embassy at Tokyo. From there, on 28 November 1917, she wrote to Lady Fane, in England:

Darling Mother . . .
This is the true story of the killing of Rasputin as told by Yousoupoff himself. It is particularly horrid and mediaeval but interesting. I remember first seeing him at the tourney when

Lady Curzon was Queen of Beauty. *He* was so beautiful I asked who he was.

Rasputin, besides being vicious, was given to drink and was quite illiterate. He had a fine presence, great physical strength and a highly developed magnetic power which enabled him to cure by the laying on of hands. Though he had relations with most of the ladies of the Court and society, he was never really more to the Empress and young Archduchesses than arch prophet and *hypnotiser*. . . .

Yousoupoff, who is young and handsome and of the intensely 'Russian' party, got news at the beginning of November that a separate peace was to be declared by the Court party. He could think of no way to prevent this but by the removal of Rasputin and set to work to devise means to remove him. This was extremely difficult as Rasputin was always shadowed by his secret police and, suspecting Yousoupoff's clique, always refused to meet the young man. Finally Yousoupoff went to one of the court ladies, who had had an affair with Rasputin, and told her he, Yousoupoff, was tuberculous—which he looks—and that having heard of Rasputin's strange powers he prayed her to implore Rasputin's assistance. Finally Rasputin consented, stipulating the interview must be at Rasputin's house.

Yousoupoff went on the day appointed, and was told to undress and lie on a sofa while Rasputin proceeded to make passes over him. Yousoupoff said that he felt as though streams of fire were running through him and he melted like wax except for one square patch of resistance in the middle of his chest. These visits and treatments continued daily for some time, the square of resistance each time increasing till finally Yousoupoff said he felt himself entirely proof against Rasputin's power. During these weeks he laid himself out in every way to fascinate Rasputin who ended by becoming quite infatuated with him and, being very musical, used to spend hours listening to Yousoupoff's singing and playing—but never forgot himself sufficiently to visit Yousoupoff at his own house or even to accept invitations to Yousoupoff's friends. By this time they were on Christian-name terms and extremely intimate.

The days were passing and Yousoupoff was in despair as he knew Rasputin was leaving for the Crimea at the beginning of December and he wouldn't get another chance in time to avert the disaster of a separate peace. He made a last appeal to Rasputin, saying he would take offence if he didn't pay him one visit to see his curios, etc. before his departure. To his amazement and joy Rasputin consented but only on condition that Yousoupoff's servants were sent away for the night—that no one knew of the visit, that they were entirely alone. . . . Overjoyed, Yousoupoff agreed to everything and dashed off to the Grand Duke Dimitri . . . who was his great friend and fellow conspirator. They finally added two more members to the plot—a doctor to prepare the poison (as they had settled that as the easiest way to do the deed) and a member of the Duma—of the right—as a witness.

The evening arrived—the servants were dismissed. Yousoupoff went off in his little two-seater car to collect Rasputin. He found him gorgeously dressed in a silk soutane with a jewelled cross on his chest. He helped him into a big fur coat and motored him to his house where he ushered him into the luxurious sitting room. This room was on the ground floor, filled with objects of art and had 6 doors to it. In the middle stood a table with poisoned fruit, cakes and wine at one end while opposite was corresponding refreshments *not* poisoned. This poison, prepared by the doctor, was supposed to work instantaneously. They sat down and pouring out some of the poisoned wine Yousoupoff handed it to his guest, saying, 'Drink, Gregory, to our next happy meeting.' To his horror Rasputin refused. He also refused to eat. This was the first time Yousoupoff had known him to refuse a drink and naturally concluded the plot was discovered. It wasn't till ages afterwards that he found out that Rasputin belonged to a strange sect which would not eat or drink the first time they crossed the threshold of a house.

Rasputin said, 'Fetch your guitar and play and sing to me as I cannot remain long.' Yousoupoff played and sang and Rasputin got more and more fascinated till suddenly he held out his glass to be filled. Still singing, Yousoupoff filled it and watched him gulp it down. Again and again he tossed down glassfuls of the poisoned wine and then began eating the poisoned cakes and fruit. Yousoupoff watched anxiously for the expected result and— nothing happened! The hours passed, Rasputin drank and Yousoupoff sang, thinking desperately what could be done, knowing this night was his last chance. The poison had no effect beyond making Rasputin rather drunk.

Suddenly Yousoupoff thought of a plan and leaning forward he said, 'You remember, Gregory, I told you of the fine crucifix I picked up last week and which you haven't seen yet. I simply must show it to you before you leave—just wait a minute while I get it.' He ran upstairs to his bedroom where the three other conspirators were anxiously waiting and wondering why things took so long. He hurriedly told them what had happened, seized the crucifix and his revolver and rushed back to find Rasputin leaning in an armchair half asleep. Handing Rasputin the crucifix, he said, 'Take it to the light, Gregory, it is a very fine one.' Rasputin rose and holding the crucifix in both hands up to the lamp was just saying, 'Yes, the expression is . . .' when Yousoupoff shot him through the shoulders from behind and Rasputin fell with a crash. The three other men came down, hearing the shot, and the doctor said that Rasputin was in his death agony and could only last a few minutes. Thereupon they left him lying on the floor and all four went up to the bedroom, shutting the door. All at once they heard a noise and there was Rasputin covered in blood and foam—on all fours—having crawled up the stairs. He seemed to have super-human strength. He wrenched the handle of the door and seeing Yousoupoff he gathered himself together for a spring when the deputy drew his revolver and shot him twice. Yousoupoff then seems to have broken down completely and, throwing himself on the corpse, tore it and mauled it like a dog.

By this time the secret police were hammering on the door. They sent the Grand Duke down to parley with them. The police asked what the shots were and Dimitri carelessly answered, 'Absolutely nothing—Yousoupoff's dog turned savage and flew at me so I shot him.' Seeing who it was, the police made no more enquiries and departed. They then dressed Rasputin in his fur coat, put the body on a sledge, drove it to the Neva, broke a hole in the ice and bundled him in—but, in so doing, one of Rasputin's fur boots fell off. This the police found next day and so recovered the body.

The Empress, on hearing of her favourite's murder, went nearly mad and swore that, when caught, the murderers should be hanged without trial. But Yousoupoff and Dimitri went to the Czar and confessed, and he didn't dare to touch them beyond banishing them. The Empress and her Lady-in-Waiting visited the hut on the Neva where Rasputin's body lay and wrapped it in rich silk. The Lady-in-Waiting's name was something like Vourouba.

This account of the macabre incident is from Lady Muriel Paget who has it direct from Yousoupoff himself. She arrived here on her way from Russia via Siberia with a troop of nurses and governesses. . . .

Love,
Lucy

Zelle, Margaretha Gertrude

Born in Holland in 1876, she married an army officer who was considerably older than herself, and lived with him in Java until 1904, when she left him and returned to Europe, where, making the most of an attractive belly, she earned her living as an oriental dancer under the name of Mata Hari, which is Malay for 'eye of the day'—the sun. After the outbreak of war in 1914, she continued to travel from country to country: a fact that interested the Germans, who engaged her as a spy. Then—for a fee of a million francs, it is said—she began spying for the French as well. En route to Belgium, she was arrested by the British, who had confused her with a German-born spy named Clara Bendix. In explaining who she really was, she mentioned her French connection; but when the British sought verification that she was employed by an ally, the Deuxième Bureau, suspecting that Albion was being perfidious, denied any knowledge of Mata Hari. Puzzled, the British decided that the best thing to do was to send her to neutral Spain. Almost certainly, before releasing her they signed her up as a spy. Once she got to Spain, she did away with her eastern trappings and posed as a Scottish dancer called Lady Macleod; her extra-professional duties as a triple-agent can have left her scant time for perfecting a Scots brogue. For some reason or other, she travelled to France; and there she was arrested as a spy, a German one. The Deuxième Bureau stayed silent as she was tried, convicted, and sentenced to death. Her execution, by firing squad, was carried out in Paris on 15 October 1917.

Zimmermann, Arthur

Thomas Woodrow Wilson, who had been the first non-clerical president of Princeton University, was, as a result of a split in opposing Republican ranks, elected twenty-eighth President of the United States in 1912, and was re-elected four years later on the campaign slogan 'he kept us out of war'. Two things above others caused him to go before Congress on the evening of 2 April 1917 to ask for a declaration of war against Germany, a request that he knew would be granted.

One was the sinking by a German submarine of the British liner *Laconia*, causing the death of, among many passengers, three Americans, two of whom were women, Mrs Albert H. Hoy and her daughter Elizabeth.

The other was the Zimmermann telegram.

On 19 January 1917, only a couple of months after his appointment as secretary of state for foreign affairs in the German government, Arthur Zimmermann sent an encoded message to the German minister in Mexico City, telling him that if war broke out between Germany and the United States, he was to propose an alliance with Mexico along several lines, including the following:

> That we shall make war together and together make peace. We shall give generous financial support, and it is understood that Mexico is to reconquer the lost territory in New Mexico, Texas, and Arizona.

The quotation is part of the translation of the telegram after it had been intercepted and decoded by the British, who are as ingenious in time of war at learning the secrets of their foes as they are ingenuous at other times with their own secrets. Of course, the British didn't keep the message to themselves (though, before broadcasting it to the Americans, they had to concoct a devious way of doing so without revealing that the German codes were as simple as ABC to Admiral Sir William Reginald Hall's band of cipher-crackers), and on 1 March it was reported and commented on in newspapers from coast to coast: the PRUSSIAN INVASION PLOT meant, said the Cleveland *Plain Dealer*, that there was 'neither virtue nor dignity' in turning the other cheek; it had, said the Oshkosh (Wisconsin) *Northwestern*, turned pacifists, critics and carpers into patriots overnight: Zimmermann had, in the words of a subsequent commentator, 'shot an arrow in the air and brought down neutrality like a dead duck'.

The insanity of Zimmermann's idea, of the way he broached it, and of his belief that honour barred him from lying when the uproar began, is merely illustrative of the fact that, nine times out of ten, wars break out, and thousands, millions even, die, in the wake of small acts of madness. Nuclear disarmers might employ Zimmermann as a sort of nonpatron saint of their cause: exemplar of the simplicity that might one day, or in a far shorter time, lead to Armageddon . . .

. . . which is, perhaps an appropriate place-name to end on. The symbolical battlefield of the Apocalypse, setting of the final struggle between good and evil, may have got its name from the battlefield of Megiddo, in the valley of Jezreel, now part of Israel.

Index

Names that appear in the book as entry headings are printed in **bold type**